DEPORTED COLONEL

a.k.a.

GRINGO CABRÓN

Laura Jeannette Gau Stone

2014

AMAZON EDITION

ISBN 978-1512-08-309-5

Deported Colonel   a.k.a.   Gringo Cabrón

Book Cover: Kevin Reimer, Koncept Studio
Panamá, Republic of Panamá

T172 Laura Jeannette Gau Stone

Dedicated to Panama's Civil Crusade
and the memory of
Monseñor Laureano Crestar Durán

DEPORTED COLONEL a.k.a. Gringo Cabrón

Before the dictatorship in Panama ended in 1989, torture and death besieged those citizens who opposed the military regime. Colonel Charles B. Stone (US Army Ret), his wife and family give testimony to their devastating ordeal living under Panama's dictatorship. At that time, cellphones and Internet were a dream of the future for this tropical country. The world never saw the horrendous atrocities committed by the Panama Defense Force. The lack of social media obscured the suffering of Panamanian people. The Stone family's testimony exposes a small segment of cruelty endured by them and thousands of families during tyranny years. To this day families victimized during the twenty-one years of military dictatorship dare not write their accounts. Perhaps that will change when justice arrives in this small nation. Each new democratically elected government reinstates the criminals of the past in some branch of public service.

Written like a novel, all events herein are true; certain names have been changed to protect the innocent and some dates shifted.

1

DOBERMAN TAKE MY DAUGHTERS

Fed up with military repression, the Panamanian people dressed in white and set out to march in protest of tyranny. Caught in the rapture of their patriotism, my daughters and I joined the Civil Crusade Movement demonstration on July 10, 1987. Waving white flags, our symbol of peace, we chanted, "Out with tyranny! Leave Panama! GO NOW!" One quarter of Panama's population sang off-tune. Naïve to the extreme, none of us suspected the brutal attack the dictator had mobilized to launch against us.

Chanting along with us, my daughter's classmates from Maria Inmaculada High School flaunted confidence. They were convinced regime soldiers would not dare attack such a huge crowd. History records our march as Black Friday, the darkest of them all, proven by atrocities perpetrated upon Crusaders by regime elite police, the Doberman.

Within minutes of our march towards El Carmen Church, the roar of rotor blades halted marchers. Above us helicopters hovered, their downdraft slashed at giant palm fronds bordering the avenue. Shots rang. The crowd burst into hysteria and shouted: "They'll kill us! Run!"

Confused and panicked, Crusaders crashed into each other and some fell. In the chaos we three managed to hide in an apartment on Via Argentina along with a dozen Crusaders crowded into a small living room. From there, we heard screams coming from marchers trapped in the avenue below. Doberman, the Panama Defense Force police, beat Crusaders with weighted rubber hoses then dragged unarmed citizens to their pickup *chota* and drove them to Cárcel Modelo Prison to torture them.

That night, before the regime cut telephone communications, my daughter Sofia's friends called incessantly. Sobbing, they described Doberman abuse of Crusaders. Later, lines cut, Sofia worried about her friend's fate. Aware of the risk involved, she and her younger sister insisted on going out the next day, twenty-four hours after Black Friday.

Sofia relates what happened

The first weird sign I noticed driving down Via Brazil was the orderliness. Everything looked so clean, like someone washed away all the blood and brutality we saw yesterday. You were there, Mom, you witnessed the disaster. Burned cars, smoke, and streets full of debris. Another phenomena: the silence. Weird. Missing was the usual deafening music blaring from cars. Salsa. It didn't feel right. I worried Trinity would detect my fear so I turned on music, our favorite. Ruben Blades. We sang along with his song, "*Sorpresas,*" until we stopped for the red light. You know the intersection, *Casa de la Carne* market. I glanced in the rearview mirror and froze.

Out of nowhere Noriega's troops in their pickup *chota* pulled up behind us. I dreaded the worst but didn't want to frighten Trinity. How ironic, yesterday we left her home 'cause the march was dangerous, and now I brought her here. The same soldiers who attacked our march had us trapped. She knew everything: the phone calls last night giving details of Doberman brutality to Crusaders at Cárcel Modelo Prison.

She saw the pickup, *chota,* and panicked. The *chota* full of Doberman backed up. I thought: "Great, they're leaving, we're safe. What luck." No such thing. They swerved around to my left and stopped smack next to my window, blocking on-coming traffic. From the *chota* window a soldier hollered.

"Don't move that car!"

I pretended not to hear. Surely, he wasn't talking to me. The light changed. The soldier yelled again.

"Don't move that vehicle!"

Cars behind honked and drove past. Soldier yelled again. I thought of poor Crusaders they took to Cárcel Modelo. If I drove off, they'd shoot us. The guy barked, nearly in my ear. I saw his rifle and painted on their pickup door was the face of a Doberman pinscher, their mascot, teeth bared and snarling, ferocious. Dog looked like the Panama Defense Force soldier barking at me.

Trinity threw a fit. She tore at my sleeve.

"Get us out of here! Hurry! They'll take us!"

Doberman soldier growled.

"Get out of the car!"

Six Doberman in black combat uniforms jumped from the *chota.* 'Armed to the teeth,' like Dad would say.

Cars behind crawled around us and paused to look, then roared past leaving us suffocating with their fumes. Trinity gagged.

Doberman grabbed my car door yelling, "Get out of the car!"

I answered, "What did I do wrong? Want to see my license?"

Doberman ignored my question. Cars stopped to look closer. Doberman used his rifle to wave them on. They sped away. Six Doberman surrounded the Volvo aiming rifles at us. I reached for Trinity to apologize for bringing her. Never got the chance. Two Doberman yanked my door open.

"I told you to get out! Now!"

Like hell was I getting out of the Volvo! I started shaking. Tremors ran down my body to my foot and it stabbed the accelerator. The engine roared and choked. I clutched the steering wheel. More Doberman came running to help the first soldier drag me out. Then I saw them go after Trinity. That's when I jumped out, caught them off guard. I wasn't gonna let those SOB's touch me. Trinity ran around the car and grabbed my hand. I felt her panic and she felt mine. Poor thing; only sixteen.

People gathered on the sidewalk to watch; others on their balconies. They knew what was happening to us. Knew we needed their help. What'd they do? Ducked into their apartments and slammed doors and windows.

That really hurt. You have no idea how much it hurt, Mom.

There we stood, a spectacle in the middle of Via Brazil. Six Doberman aiming rifles at us. Red traffic light dangling over our heads like a guillotine. I saw no way to escape, like we did yesterday. They had us surrounded. For some reason they wanted to punish us.

"Move," yelled a Doberman pointing at the supermarket. One of them drove the *chota* onto the sidewalk.

I walked slowly. Glancing back at the Volvo, I saw a Doberman reach into the back seat and pull something out. Hooked to the tip of his rifle hung a white cloth he dragged out the window. A white handkerchief? The kind we took to the Crusader march yesterday? The Doberman waved it from his rifle, parading it like a trophy.

Where did the white flag come from? We didn't drive the Volvo to the march. Did Trinity put it there? She must have. Before we left home. Doberman waved the white handkerchief at the other soldiers, acting ridiculous. Another soldier swat it down to the ground. He stomped on it like a cockroach. They laughed like maniacs. Then a soldier shoved me hard. Nearly knocked me down.

"Move!" he growled.

I asked where they were taking us.

"You're arrested."

I asked why I was being arrested? Why?

"For waving a white flag."

Arrested for that? I nearly barfed the cheese I ate for breakfast. Doberman saw my disgust and aimed the gun butt at my face. I panicked, stepped aside to avoid the blow and saw a rifle nudge Trinity. She screamed. I decided to obey and walk to the market.

Women shoppers coming out of the market took one look and ran. Each step took us closer to the hated *chota*. I knew we needed to escape. Quick. I stopped. Doberman got mad. Raised his rifle.

"Get in the truck!"

"Why? Where are you taking us? We've done nothing wrong."

At that moment a woman screamed.

"Stop! Don't do that! Leave those girls alone!"

All of us, including our attackers, turned to see who yelled. A chubby Old Woman wobbled toward us. Flab pulled her left and right, but she kept coming and shouting.

"Those girls are innocent. Leave them alone! Don't touch them!"

The Old Woman approached a soldier, stood in front of him.

"Release those girls!"

Doberman ignored her. She insisted so much the soldiers formed a barrier to separate her from us. She tried to squeeze through a gap between them. She missed and crashed into a soldier. He lost balance and his brusqueness knocked the Old Woman down. From the pavement she yelled.

"Stop it! Don't touch those girls! Leave them alone!"

Doberman looked down, aimed the gun butt at the Old Woman's face and snarled, "You want to go to jail too?"

She ignored him, crawled to her knees and while still down scolded him. "Respect me. Do you understand? I could be your grandmother."

Her ferocity stunned the Doberman. He lowered his rifle and stepped aside.

The leader Doberman threw a rage seeing the Old Woman tame his dog. He walked over and whacked the Doberman on the ear.

"You imbeciles! Get those women in that *chota*."

The Old Woman got up. She poked the soldiers' backs. Cars slowed to watch the spectacle. Here's this Old Woman trying to rescue us by fighting six, armed Doberman. Not one motorist stopped to help. Nobody else risked themselves to help us. And we don't know who she is. A wonderful woman. I think she was an angel, Mom.

When she saw them dragging us away, she went berserk.

"Tell me your phone number! I'll call your mother!"

I yelled the number, but she kept insulting Doberman. How could she hear me?

I screamed, "*Señora*! Listen! Please. 6-0-0-6-5-4!"

A bunch of hands lifted me by the elbows and shoved me into the *chota*. Trinity scrambled in next to me. Doberman jumped in after us, shattering our last hope of escape. I lamented to myself. Are these devils taking us to Cárcel Modelo Prison? Because of a white flag?

Desperate, I prayed the Old Woman wouldn't forget our phone number. She was our only hope.

Trinity seemed weird, too calm. She must have been in shock. Poor kid, so young for so much terror. She rubbed her nose, probably itching from Doberman's stinky fatigues. Too many of us packed into this cage. Doberman uniforms smelled rancid. Dad's fatigues never smell. Trinity opened her mouth and it scared me. I shook my head hard fearing she'd say something nasty about the stench. She caught on and hushed. Poor thing. She needed to believe in miracles a little longer and forget the terrible things my classmates said on the phone last night—how Doberman tortured Crusaders in Cárcel Modelo Prison.

Trinity broke out coughing, choking.

I thought of the Old Woman; determined to save us. A stranger willing to die for us. God sent her. Those Doberman are cowards without their guns. The Old Woman is the brave one. I wonder who she is? Don't even know her name.

Back home

Sofia and Trinity had been gone an hour. I had no idea they'd been kidnapped and going through hell. Alone. I lingered in the front yard pruning shrubs, anxious for their return and feeling more tense by the minute. Every car turning the corner made my heart jump hoping it was the Volvo. Then disappointment.

Our phone had been dead for twelve hours. Ever since the blood-curdling calls last night telling the horrors of Crusaders dragged to Cárcel Modelo.

Ringing, something rang, a dull ring. It couldn't be our phone. It was dead. The ringing started again. It was our phone! I charged into the house, grabbed the phone so hard it nearly pulled off the wall. A woman's voice cracked, inaudible.

I asked her to speak louder.

"They took your daughters!"

She must be mistaken. "What? It can't be my girls. They went to visit a friend."

"Doberman! Six Doberman dragged your daughters away!"

"What are you talking about?"

"Two pretty girls. One taller. In a Volvo station wagon. Brick-colored."

My head spun. The woman knew what she was saying.

"Doberman also took the car."

I collapsed onto the stool.

"Please, lady, who are you?"

"Isidora Marichal."

"How do you know this?"

"I was there. On Via Porras. I tried to stop them but there were too many Doberman. I asked the girls for your phone number. Hurry! Get them back. Before they hurt them."

She hung up. Gone, the last person to see our girls. And I failed to get her number. I gripped the black phone fearing to cut the connection to my daughters. Clutching the instrument of pain, I stared at the black holes in the receiver. Damned holes. Marks that scar a face. Noriega's face: the cause of my pain. My girls . . .

A voice inside me screamed: "Quick! Hurry! Get their father!" I ran to the red telephone on his desk in our bedroom—the hot line connected to the US Embassy. It was urgent I call my daughter's father; tell him what happened. But it was Saturday. He had no reason to be there. In my desperation I forgot that possibility. I planned to tell the marine guard who answered to relay the message to him.

My thoughts flew to Cárcel Modelo Prison. Did they take the girls there? I dialed; the red phone rang. My ears recorded the ring. To this day when I recall the incident, I feel the vibration in my ears. Same as then.

"Yes, Ma'am?" the Marine guard's voice.

"It's urgent I speak to Colonel Stone."

"Yes ma'am, soon as he comes in, I'll give him the message."

His courtesy offered no relief.

I called the golf course. Someone said he wasn't there. Two p.m. Saturday. Where was he? His daughters were in danger! I could not sit, had to do something to help the girls. I ran to the terrace where one can see the entire city. I focused in the direction of Cárcel Modelo Prison. Straining, my eyes invented strange visions. An object crawled up the side of a tall building in Golf Heights—the blob resembled King Kong. Monster gorilla. Same as the inhuman gorillas who took over our city. My girls! I squeezed my eyes shut and delayed to open. Opening again, the gorilla had begun to shrink, taking on the shape of a palm tree.

A familiar sound came from out front; a car door slammed. I rushed out. It was their father. Still running, I hollered.

"Those damned Doberman!"

He looked my way, surprised; I tried to explain.

"The Doberman took Sofia and Trinity!"

His expression quizzical, nothing I said made sense to him. As I spoke, he proceeded towards the trunk of the car. Yesterday he angered when we marched with the Civil Crusade to show opposition to the regime. My argument that every Panamanian had a moral obligation to march failed to convince him. In fact it was our two oldest daughters who dragged me to the march.

Reaching him, I yanked his arm.

"Don't you understand? They arrested our girls! Maybe took them to Cárcel Modelo Prison!"

"What? Who?"

"The Doberman!"

"How do you know this?"

"A woman called. Her name is Isidora Marichal. She saw Doberman take them!"

He walked into the house in silence. I followed, watched him stack Panama beer into the refrigerator.

"Hurry. Isidora said Doberman might hurt them."

With me on his heels he walked to our bedroom. He unbuttoned his blue shirt. Slow fingers seemed to massage the buttons. He folded the shirt—laid it in the dirty-clothes bin and pulled a white shirt off the hanger. White. Why now? I wanted to accuse him of being too late for Crusader white. He, a former US Army Psychological Warfare Commander, acted cool during life's crucial moments, calculating the enemy's next move. I reacted with pain and passion. He analyzed the problem, used military strategy to make his move. Did he know these soldiers were being trained to maim civilians and kidnap girls? The very men he worked with these past five years; his "chosen." And now they reveal their true criminal antics by following their dictator's orders. Those same criminals held our daughters.

This was no time to fight. He was not the enemy. His daughters needed him.

He left in silence, without inviting me. Nor did it occur to me to go with him. My place was here, to see if they called. Anxiety craved I tear something apart; shred it, as my heart shattered. In the washtub I found filthy car-cleaning rags and latched on, scrubbed them by hand until I felt punishment in my spine. My husband should reject his criminal colleagues. Despicable. So many times I asked, practically on my knees, that he reject that damned job. Only a fool chooses to be Pentagon Liaison to a murdering dictator.

Where are my girls?

I recalled the words our parish priest, Laureano Crestar Durán, repeated often: "When bad things happen, despair overpowers us. Prayer evades us during crisis. Anxiety takes over our emotions and weakens our faith. The key is to pray before crisis strikes. Daily prayer strengthens our spirit, assures us of God's love. When tragedy strikes, our resilience is there, in our soul—the place where God lives. And He sustains us".

But my soul, bursting with pain, did nothing but scream. "Where did they take my girls?"

2

NOSTALGIA

How did my family get sucked into this terror? It all started back in 1980 when my beloved husband, drink in hand, predicted I would be instrumental in promoting the collapse of Panama's tyranny.

Back then we lived in North Carolina. I longed to go home to Panama, but had failed to convince my husband to take steps to retire. Homesick, I hoped that if I went back home with our three girls, he would follow.

The moment of decision came one night at a military gathering. I rushed, the rat-tat-tat of my spike heels hurrying me into a reception at the Fort Bragg Officer's Club. How long had I chased my husband, Colonel Charles Stone and his demanding US Army Infantry career? Twenty years. Longevity gave me confidence, the notion that I knew him perfectly. A surprise awaited me, the revelation that certain men are experts at concealing secrets and hiding their thoughts, especially dangerous ones.

But could Wild Turkey Bourbon prompt a man to tell a stranger something criminal and alarming about his wife?

We approached the reception hall. My mate grunted, tugging at his stiff white collar. He disliked wearing the short white jacket with gold epaulets on the shoulders. He preferred jungle fatigues. Knowing this and anxious to relieve his discomfort, I flattered him.

"Dear, someday I'll make you a centurion uniform so I can admire your great physique."

For me the reception offered a great opportunity to flaunt my country's Mola Art made by Kuna Indians. Bright colored hand-stitched ducks, exquisite Molas, adorned the border of my long skirt. We shook the commanding officer's hand and his wife's and I noticed her poor taste. Her low-cut gown revealed long, wrinkled breasts. We edged away, and I promised myself never to dress that way in my old age.

I squeezed my centurion's hand just as a young lieutenant approached. Sporting a natural tan he smiled and glanced at our nametags. We did likewise.

Lieutenant William Coy said, "I see you were stationed in Panama, Colonel Stone."

Before he could answer Lieutenant Coy flattered the Mola ducks sewn to my skirt.

"Mrs. Stone, those are gorgeous Molas."

I asked if he was Panamanian. He nodded enthusiastically. "I have dual citizenship," and resumed talking about home and Molas.

Accustomed to being the center of attention, my soldier gulped another Wild Turkey Bourbon, eyed the lieutenant, and sulked. I needed to steer the conversation back to him.

"My husband's grandmother was Mexican. She nicknamed him Chico."

The lieutenant missed the cue, anxious to reminisce about the homeland.

"Colonel Stone, when were you in Panama?"

"Jenny's Panamanian. We married there."

"Have you been home lately, Mrs. Stone? Things are very different."

Chico interrupted.

"Jenny's going soon. To kill Omar Torrijos."

Was he crazy? How could he put me in such grave danger? To say such an atrocity was a death sentence. My accuser shook his glass, banging the ice with the same vehemence as his punishing words. General Omar Torrijos, the dictator, wielded power capable of making people disappear. The lieutenant's natural suntan faded, he cleared his throat and stared at me, opened his mouth as if to plead—deny the lie, woman. My tongue went mute. Never had I heard a death sentence directed at me and my tongue died in anticipation.

The lieutenant reached in his pocket and jiggled loose change. Chico's steely blue eyes stared at the nuisance-pocket to admonish its noise. The lieutenant pulled out a white handkerchief and dried his forehead.

Sweaty, my hand dropped the evening bag. We three stared at the floor. But I no longer saw my purse, instead, a black lump representing the thousands of body bags of cadavers flown back from Vietnam.

Chico bent over, retrieved my purse and brushed hard against the ducks on my skirt. I felt the ducks recoil. The face handing me the bag was a stranger's whose bed I shared 5,000 nights. In all that time how did I fail to assess his soul and see what hid there?

The lieutenant, nervous, stammered on.

"As I was saying, big changes are taking place in Panama. Did you know Torrijos founded a new political party? PRD. My Mom's a member and has been appointed to work at the Consulate in Atlanta."

PRD. The Democratic Revolutionary Party was established to comply with US treaty demands forcing Panama's dictator to someday hold democratic elections. Torrijos included chosen civilians in his dictatorship to legitimize his deeds. In the process, they both became rich.

A waiter offered a tray of drinks. Both men declined. My accuser, now mute, thought silence divorced him from complicity. The lieutenant excused himself and left. We did the same. In the car I choked in the fear that Omar Torrijos awaited me. No Panamanian of sane mind dared mention his name except to praise him. We pulled up to our duplex; the radial tires crunched gravel. I jumped out, intending to run, but my high heels sunk in the pebbles. Behind me Chico's shoes grated gravel.

"You drunk," I yelled, "I'm gonna tell the girls."

"Big mouth," he answered.

He calls me a big mouth? I reached the door first and jammed in the key. Just as I jumped over the threshold I felt a tug behind me, a pull on the bow of my halter-top. His hand pulled my tie loose and the front of my halter dangled open. Something fell out and lay at my feet on the floor. Two, white balled-up socks lay there teasing and winking at me. My secret! Vanity had prompted me to improve my appearance and enlarge my breasts with those white puffy socks rolled up and stuck inside my halter. All this effort to inflate my chest and look like Chico. Chesty. There on the floor lay my two little white lies—defiant.

Tempted to kick them, I saw the futility. Behind me, he roared.

Playing the role of victim, next day I dared buy tickets to go home to Panama for our three daughters and me.

On departure day their suitcase keys were missing. They went to Dad. As expected, he had stashed them. Holding the tiny keys, he beckoned them to stay and talk.

They sat down at his feet, cross-legged. The reading light behind him cast a shadow similar to the abyss during the empty years when lengthy war separations left empty pages in their lives. The first year he went to Vietnam, Daniella, our oldest, then a preschooler, developed a stutter that lasted years. On his second tour, Sofia, by then a third grader; drew pictures of a man dying on the cross, each new drawing in bolder color. Trinity cried at the sight of his photographs and I hid them. The girls still had unanswered questions of those lost years and yet now we four women were leaving him by our own choice and tearing the renewed bond.

"Are you gonna' tell us about Vietnam?" Daniella asked.

As always, he joked about it, avoiding the subject. His daughters, resigned to his unanswered questions about war, traipsed off to lock their luggage.

On our way to the airport, I observed changes in the girls. When we left Panama, Daniella and Sofia were preteens and delicate. Sweetness they retained but cunning they acquired from Taekwondo. Circumstances of our surroundings toughened them. Exposure to pot, the F word and a stabbing occurring in Daniella's high school had hardened them. I counted on my tropical paradise to renew my girls' sweet femininity.

Frayed, the hems on the girl's blue jeans dragged, sweeping dust as they walked. Clasped to their heads was Walkman, instrumental in the phenomenon about to take place—a cultural metamorphosis. At the snap of their seatbelts they would leave behind the English language and all it had represented for us. Sofia closed her eyes singing to Ruben Blades' *Ella Era una Chica Plástica*—a song targeting snobbish women.

Hearing my older girls sing in Spanish loosened the knots in my stomach. Trinity sat writing to her father, pleading he'd join us soon.

Time flew and landing gear screeched; our airplane tires hit tarmac. Omar Torrijos' name crowned the terminal in sulfurous-colored lights. Too late to go back; my foot was in the ground. We stood in line. Behind the customs booth a uniformed guard blinked sleepily. Handing our passports to the customs inspector, I dared not glance at the uniformed guard. He moved, lifting something from behind. A rifle! Swinging it to his front he planted it between his feet. If he arrested me, I'd say Chico was a drunken big mouth.

BANG!

I flinched. At the adjacent counter an inspector slammed a rubber stamp on travelers' passports. Throughout the shuffling of our documents, the inspector never looked at my face. I was no threat to anyone. Daniella and Sofia charged out the terminal door with an attitude of ownership.

Outside in the dark, headlights illuminated us. The sudden focus on us rekindled my fear. Instinctively I wished the girls had dark skin and blended in. Where was my mother?

"Abuelita!" The three girls squealed running to their grandmother in her Panama hat. They hugged her small frame. The smell of swamp and cow manure embraced us. A shrill cry pierced the dark sky. Did night birds screech to warn us of something on our return?

My mother's pick-up truck zipped through the dark to Arraijan. In 1980 her beloved town still awaited running water while Abuelita's home gushed with the precious liquid from a deep well dug by her father a century earlier. Abundant water made my mother the town envy.

Along with her reputation as eccentric, Abuelita enjoyed teasing the local men. Whenever a neighbor, relative or drifter came asking for a handout or seeking chores for a certain fee, she responded to the macho ego calling them "*chacarón,*" which disarmed them. The term she used on men, "big balls," may have seemed flattering, but their facial expression questioned—how can she tell? For Panamanian women who knew their men and the uncommon term, it meant 'you're lazy'.

As a child in Arraijan, I ran barefoot near the neighbor's pigpens. Boils developed in my feet, *niguas*. Painful, oozing worms wriggled out of the skin on my feet. Pigs were not indicative of squalor. On the contrary, they were the good feature of the town with few amenities and plenty of bars. My father disliked Arraijan, and refused to visit calling it the dump.

Yet, I took our daughters to the dump, my childhood playground where they could swim in Abuelita's pool whooping and hollering with joy. Until one day riding runt horses disaster struck. Trinity's horse slid on a muddy slope, fell on her and fractured her hand.

With music Abuelita intended to distract Trinity from her misery. She played her Steinway piano with a repertoire ranging from waltz to salsa. It failed to cheer up Trinity. Abuelita grew impatient and turning her back on the keys she warned Trinity.

"You're lucky. If the horse breaks a leg, we shoot him."

Frightened, Trinity avoided Abuelita and clung to Sofia. I made excuses for my mother, blaming her strange ways on my brother's death at twenty-one. She made my girls and I the center of her screwed-up neediness. She'd say, "You're my only kids left in this world." So, I brought my girls to my mother hoping Chico would be transferred here soon. Where he met me.

Trinity's cast curtailed roughneck activities. Bored, the girls asked to explore downtown. In Abuelita's Toyota we drove past charred hills where once dense jungles teemed with iguanas, a delicacy we ate all summer. Fraught by the ugly sight of slash and burn barren hills, we sat in silence as the car rolled on. Reaching the gleaming turquoise Pacific Ocean and its Bridge of the Americas spanning the Panama Canal, I recited the history of its construction.

"The US Corps of Engineer's outdid themselves digging this marvel. It's a shame thousands of men died of malaria and yellow fever on the job."

Trinity interrupted. "Oh Mom, I've heard that story a hundred times."

We descended the bridge into Chorrillo town, a ghetto bordering the canal. Barefoot boys chased a soccer ball past termite-riddled residences. From a rickety balcony a boy peed on our car. Perched on high-tension wires, buzzards gawked lovingly at piles of trash.

Cárcel Modelo Prison loomed on the left attracting Daniella.

"Look, what are those strange things hanging from between iron bars?"

"Human arms dear. Arms of the prisoners held inside."

She shrunk away from the window and turned to peer out the other side. An imposing bastion with barbed wire coiled along the top of its wall filled our view. Past its large entrance soldiers marched inside the compound.

"Look at those soldiers, Abuelita! They goose-step like Nazis!"

"That's dictator headquarters. People call it Hellquarters. That's why they march that way. "

Abuelita drove faster. At Stanziola's Pawnshop we purchased gold necklaces and departed traipsing past pedestrians, the girls wearing their gold. Suddenly, Sofia yelled from the rear.

"Watch out, Daniella! A loud WHOMP followed! Then a scream.

"Great karate chop, Dani! You're the best Black Belt!"

Daniella, rubbing her neck, glared down at the shirtless urchin she floored. He picked himself off the street where she'd knocked him and dashed away. She walked past me still pawing the pink welt on her neck caused by the thief's pull. Sofia skipped alongside happily patting her sister's back.

"Our instructor would'a loved seeing you kick-ass!"

"That idiot tried to rip off my chain. I'd like to kick him again." Her bruised confidence improved with each step. A shark's tooth dangled from her pawnshop purchase. She rubbed her gold chain proudly.

In vain I searched for a policeman. Abuelita took umbrage to deride the military.

"Don't waste your energy on these cops. They only rescue their superiors."

On the drive home to Arraijan we crested the bridge over Chorrillo town and Hellquarters. I began to question my choice. Could I tolerate living under a dictatorship after the orderliness seen in the US and Fort Bragg? Sacrifice all that security to please my mother?

I scrutinized Chorrillo residents' living conditions. They lived a daily hell. Their dilapidated buildings surrounded Hellquarters. These people's houses bordered the famous canal that produced so much wealth. Neither entity contributed to improve the people's welfare. The beauty in it was the people's attitude; poverty failed to drown their cheer. They were the essence of a unique happiness that demands nothing. I felt the opposite. Anger stung me all night.

Summer flew, and our enjoyment of the warm weather kindled our desire to remain in the tropics. We four Stone women concluded life in Panama was better than Bragg. I called Chico often and begged he get transferred to a US Army base here, of which there were plenty. He conceded slowly.

By the time he arrived, our girls were enrolled in Maria Inmaculada High School and twirling batons in the school band. They sashayed to the sound of the school's marimba band of xylophones, cymbals and drums.

Eager to live far from a US military base, I agreed to buy the house of his choice, an unaffordable residence on a hill in Bethania. We cashed-in his life insurance policies and I landed a translating job. Home at last, where I met my mate, in paradise, where people dance for every celebration. Country folk, sweet as Panama's pineapples, make up songs covering every day occurrences.

3

BLESS OUR HOME

Padre Laureano Crestar Durán blessed our new home. Originally from Spain, he was Director of CARITAS *Nacional,* an equivalent to the US Catholic Relief Service. Delighted our daughters had enrolled in a Catholic school, Maria Inmaculada, he doused each of us with an extra splash of holy water. His blessings became a habit; but too soon those same blessings turned urgent.

House number fifty-six, our new residence, needed retainer walls for the precipice that was our yard plus iron gates for security and tons of grass. One morning I stood spraying new sod covering the front yard when Chico walked past leaving for work. He squeezed my elbow.

"You should pluck weeds, Jenny. While grass is still wet."

I squatted to dig, and while weeding a neighbor walked over, a woman I yearned to meet. Our houses shared a breezeway. For days I'd been eavesdropping on her, listening through my bathroom window when she chatted in her living room. Her melodic voice held the timbre of crystal chimes, so I had dubbed her Crystal Voice.

"Welcome," she said. "Did you know this neighborhood is called millionaire's hill?" She noticed I had no idea what to respond and she continued.

"Tell me, is that handsome man in uniform who leaves daily your hubby?"

Her effusive sincerity caught me off guard and my mouth spoke before my brain engaged. My response, curt and jealous, appalled me.

"Well. He's not so sweet on the inside."

"Where does he work, this stone-hearted man of yours?"

She caught on fast. I liked her style and explained he was director of the US foreign assistance program, information that visibly pleased her.

"Does your stone-hearted husband have to deal with General Torrijos?"

"No way!" I said, still on my haunches and about to topple over.

Had Lieutenant Coy spread Chico's drunken lie?

Crystal Voice fiddled with her hair, as if nothing bigger rested on her mind.

"Torrijos is inaccessible."

She quickly lost interest in my digging, turning to leave.

"Come see me sometime. We'll have a cup of wine."

No other neighbor had visited since we moved in, so I decided to invite them for tea and inform them I had no interest in politics. Fifteen women came. Their effervescent chatter over cold mango juice with lemon charmed me. I returned to digging weeds with gusto until Crystal Voice appeared again inviting me to a meeting on Liberation Theology.

Sitting in her cream-colored Chevrolet, I asked: "What's Liberation Theology?"

She shrugged her shoulders, indicating not knowing. We sped through green traffic lights until arriving at a Catholic school. In a classroom two Panamanian priests chatted with laity. The older priest, Padre Fernando Guardia, S.J, invited us to sit. He announced that Panamanian clergy was unarmed and had no intentions of taking up arms for any reason. He went on to outline a plan to alleviate the misery that oppresses the poor. We left exhilarated and driving home, Crystal Voice told of a priest's murder that occurred while we lived in the US. The victim was Padre Hector Gallegos, a hero to the poor who practiced Economic Liberation with subsistence farmers.

The young Colombian priest worked shoulder to shoulder with poor farmers, *campesinos*, and taught them how to organize and manage the sale of their produce. Padre Gallegos led his community of *campesinos* to establish their own co-op. At the peak of the community's prosperity, 1971, dictator emissaries assassinated Padre Gallegos. The investigation prosecuted no one.

Padre Gallegos freed farmers from manipulation and control by big landowners, associates of General Omar Torrijos. The dictator's public displays of devotion for the poor *campesino* were fraudulent.

During the same time frame of the priest's assassination, Torrijos expelled the US Peace Corps from Panama, another entity dedicated to working with subsistence farmers. Paradox surrounded Torrijos. Serious thinkers of his time were perplexed by his chameleon antics. His convincing displays of love for the less affluent and his capacity to promise them great things and then turn around and do the opposite confused analysis.

Yet, many of his victims loved Torrijos long after his death.

4

MEET THE MAN

Everybody loves a parade until it turns into a charade. Precisely that special parade I awaited, with its cymbals, trumpets and drums charging the air with melodious static. In a huge field manicured for the event, I sat on a folding chair smack in the center of Howard Air Force Base, Panama. Aromatherapy wafted from fresh-cut grass emitting a mint scent. It added to my bliss for having bought our new home. Hard work on the new house showed in my split fingernails, destroyed from digging to transform a precipice into a yard with garden. The parade delayed starting. Waiting permitted daydreaming. I pretended the nearby purr of airplane engines were doves cooing and beginning today great things marched my way. The dream ignored the intriguing figure approaching.

A young soldier handed me a program. A dozen other soldiers, all clones in khaki uniforms, hustled past in robot motion. Cut from the same mold and wearing his US Army olive-drab-dress-green uniform, my own soldier stood chatting with other officers.

The parade honored a US four-star general in the pompous act of relinquishing his command to another four-star. General Omar Torrijos, one of the honored guests, was guaranteed to be absent. So popular was the dictator that he reigned from his beachside hammock to the sensuous rhythm of the waves—unfettered by government planning. Sixty-five miles from the capital, the same breeze that cooled me fanned him. At that magic moment in his career he governed dressed in civvies.

Revered, the handsome strongman's facial portraits in public offices showed him wearing his trademark cowboy hat, also in olive drab. Notorious idolatry did not stop there.

His dark hand holding a Havana cigar hung in local museums. Female photographers and politicians were not the only ones bewitched by his personal charm of a virile and handsome man. Graham Green wrote a book about the general.

Campesinos, country folk, poor as the dirt they tilled, adored Omar Torrijos. His helicopter would descend unexpectedly into the midst of their remote village, scattering chickens and frightening babies. Mothers hid in huts. A smiling Torrijos removed his fatigue jacket to sit and chat. Whatever anguish his misguided decisions cast on their livelihood, including Padre Gallegos death, people faulted his subordinates. Primarily, his Hatchet MAN, Manual Antonio Noriega, took the blame and the populace preferred it that way.

"My husband retires soon," I wanted to shout, bragging to the men Chico spoke to.

He pointed and the three men followed his finger towards a mountain at the end of the airfield. Repeated burnings for slash and burn agriculture had scalped the once tree-lined mountain, Cerro Cabra, situated at the end of the airfield. Torrential rains gouged it deeper causing erosion. But my soldier's story had nothing to do with the mountain's condition. It entailed parachuting, or so I surmised by the sweep of his arm.

"I made my fiftieth free-fall over there."

All four men wore flying-saucer hats in olive drab. The hat's beak gleamed with heavy brocade, the gold-braid insignia called scrambled eggs, which makes a great target and never ventures on the battlefield. The hat marks the distinction of a field-grade-officer and is the crowning feature of the uniform.

Before my eyes could see, my suspicious nature detected an unsettling change in the happy gathering. A figure drew closer. Protocol attendants made no fuss over a certain individual strolling towards them. Why should they know anything about the intelligence officer, G-2 in military talk, who headed straight at them? Foreigners knew zero about his reputation. Years would pass before international press labeled Manuel Antonio Noriega the cruelest dictator of recent times. But in Panama mentioning his name at social up-scale gatherings made the room temperature rise five degrees. Panamanians referred to him as MAN, not only for his initials—he was Torrijos' Hatchet MAN.

And precisely he approached.

Chico kept chatting while Noriega, unfazed by a cold shoulder from the protocol officer, picked his way along the edges of the grassy plain. He delighted moving in obscurity. His profession dictated it. He ambled, uninterested in the exuberance of the Gringo's festive parade atmosphere. In his path Chico still held his small groups' attention. Noriega had to walk past them and seeing they failed to recognize him, he gave them a subliminal sign of disrespect. He lifted his index finger and flicked his hat as one would flick-off a bothersome fly.

The finger-flick bothered me, disrespectful. Chico outranked him and he, together with the other three officers acted indifferent, unaware of Noriega's slight. They threw their shoulders back, clicked their heels and rendered a formal salute in a spiffy choreography, same as they would to any officer. Then they relaxed, turned their backs on Noriega and resumed chatting.

A US soldier-usher paused, read Noriega's chest nameplate and not recognizing he was Panama's number one spy, unceremoniously pointed to a seat for him and walked away. Noriega's photograph seldom appeared anywhere back then, but his critics and enemies knew him well. They called him *Cara de Piña,* Pineapple Face, for the scars on his face left by childhood pox.

As G-2, he lurked in Torrijos' shadow and took the blame for citizens' disappearance, torture, and rape during that era.

"Lies," Chico said, "he's a bright intelligence officer."

Could be. But, as far away as Panama's remote rain forest, the peasants, upon hearing his name, made the sign of the cross. They whispered when using the Noriega name. That same individual headed my way.

Wearing sunglasses, Noriega slid through the narrow lane of folding chairs. His go-to-hell hat, originally identical to Chico's flying saucer version, was smashed down on the sides. Its stiff crown bent, changed its dapper halo appearance. Both sides curled down like a woman's bonnet; the rims nearly touched his ears. Below the hat and sunglasses rippled deeply scarred cheeks. His enemies swore his skin carried the mark of every person he ruined or killed. Others said his type skin would never wrinkle and with age the pits deepened as though medals for his accomplishments.

Noriega plopped down next to me. His nametag confirmed his identity. His nearness was synonymous with being struck by lightning. Unlike Noriega, I wore no nametag. Even if he was a brilliant intelligence officer, I was incognito. My head said, "Get up and go." I tried but my feet turned to lead, perhaps from the spell he cast over me.

For a while I held my breath. Not that he smelled. I dreaded he'd notice I was alive, breathing, and then he would introduce himself. I'd have to say my name to him, the one who held absolute power. Chico, a full colonel, outranked him, but was small fish compared to my whale of a seating companion who made no effort to say Hi. He snubbed me and as moments dragged, I became grateful.

My vision blurred. I thought of lucky Chico, on escort duty to a South American General visiting for the parade. Seeing so poorly, the parade and precision-perfect marching troops turned into a diffused streak of caramel. I barely heard John Philip Sousa's, "Stars and Stripes Forever," played by the 79th Army Band with base drums, tuba horn and crashing cymbals. Cannons fired a salute. If it roared and shook the ground, I missed the jolt. My mind ruminated all gossip about Noriega. He would someday be world-famous, but not for his kindness or his looks. He took pride in his profession of being a *sapo*, the deprecating term in Latin countries for a spy; yet the title gave him pride. His office displayed a gallery of frogs cast in silver, ceramic, crystal, wood and straw. As *sapo*, he was paid by the US CIA to spy on Castro. In cahoots with his boss, General Omar Torrijos, they beat the US boycott of Cuba by smuggling US goods and technology through the Panama Free Zone into Cuba. Not satisfied, they reversed the smuggling and pushed Cuban goods into the US through Panama's same Free Zone.

Cannonball smoke wafted our way all afternoon. Sniffing sulfur I learned Noriega was an expert connoisseur of silence. Had a blonde beauty sat next to him, he might cross one leg over his knee in the restricted space, bump into her, smile, and say *"Perdón."* But stuck with me he probably concluded, "I won't waste my time with this skinny bitch. She probably belongs to one of those gringo soldiers in the ridiculous flying saucer hat."

The program ended with the band playing "God Bless America." Before troops marched off the parade field, I mustered the courage to peek behind Noriega's sunglasses. His eyes were closed. The country's top spy snubbed me, reduced me to small fry not deserving of a glance.

Soon as US troops marched off the field, Noriega left. Had he faked sleeping? Why wonder? Not once did his head flop. The crowd swept me to the center of its happy melee.

My own soldier husband walked up; his smooth skin gleamed with pleasure while I babbled on about my seating companion.

"Did you know spies don't croak? I mean snore."

"What are you talking about? What spy?"

"Noriega sat practically in my lap for two hours and never spoke."

"Oh, really? Where is he? Where did he go?"

"Wait a minute, do you know him? I mean, personally?"

He shook his head; his face filled with interest and excitement. He looked around behind. Searching for Noriega? Anxious to meet him? Didn't he understand I was panicked from having sat next to my country's most feared spy? Instead of concern for my fears he was looking for top spy. I pretended not to notice. Back then I understood little about military mentality. What I remembered at that moment, something my grandmother from Arraijan once said.

"That's what you get for marrying a soldier!"

5

THE JOB

Agua! Agua! The clamor for "Water! Water!" makes dancers wiggle and shout during carnival time, heralding *La Vida Loca.* Life is *fiesta.* Embedded in a Panamanian's DNA is the need to sing and dance for carnival to the tune of drums and accordions. Young and old dancers sing and gyrate in the streets under a hot equatorial sun. Non-stop. Four days of reveling at carnival time causes sunburns, soothed best by the Anaconda-sized water hose spraying cool *Agua* at wriggling bodies.

We packed our car to join the hundreds of thousands leaving the city for the hinterlands, the *Interior*—the remote and poor sector of Panama. Four dancing days of *La Vida Loca* fall prior to Lent, ending the party on Ash Wednesday.

A favorite destination: Las Tablas, in Azuero Peninsula, a small community that venerates the tranquil life 361 days of the year and explodes during four days of carnival. Those who survive the *fiesta,* will then bury the symbolic sardine singing a somber *Pescao!* To a dead fish. Grieving not the dead fish, dancers mourn a different reality: sorrow for the end of the best party of the year.

Months after the *fiesta* to bury the sardine, the biggest fish on dry land perished in a small airplane. In 1981 General Omar Torrijos died when his plane crashed in a rainstorm. His untimely death eventually led to a power struggle that affected everyone. Had he survived, our family and the country may have been spared terrible events. But while Torrijos' followers mourned him, I rejoiced. My spouses' retirement approached.

Other citizens suffered a complicated grief brought on by two phenomena: slash and burn deforestation and heavy rainstorms that bring floods and erosion.

Our tropical paradise makes life difficult if not dangerous for people whose homes perch on muddy hillsides. Padre Durán, our parish priest, invited us to visit this slide zone. We trekked uphill to observe people living under tarps. "Roofless," the priest called them. As we scooted back downhill, I imagined the hazard during rains—slippery as soap. These people received no assistance from the military regime. When they did seek help, the regime sent them to Padre Durán, who always found ways to ease their misery.

Once we had returned home from visiting the "Roofless," I asked Chico what he planned to do for them. He claimed civic action was not his job but increasing our donations to Padre Durán was preferable. His lame response conflicted with civics courses our daughters took at Maria Inmaculada High. Nuns taught social sensitivity and indoctrinated students with community spirit and a desire for social justice, a concept that originates in sacred scripture. The lessons, so different from the individualist approach back in the States, made the girls focus beyond teenage vanity. The nuns' teaching eventually led them to follow a doctrine made perilous when living under a dictator.

The saplings in our yard grew keeping pace with Chico's approaching retirement. My dream to grow pesticide-free vegetables with him made me impatient for the memorable event: his last day as a soldier. Until one evening he came home and sauntered straight through to his favorite spot on the terrace. No hello, nor request for a cold beer. Curious, I joined him to watch the suns' last, hot rays painting the town pink. I touched his arm, but he kept looking afar. He rebuffed me and continued staring at a mysterious world. Something was amiss. He was tense. Facing away, he finally spoke.

"I have a new job." He bristled at his own words.

"Job? We came back here to retire. Remember?"

"At the US embassy. I'll be Military Group Commander." Still looking away, he blurted as if the words burned his tongue. "Working with Noriega."

What? Struck mute by his announcement, I searched his profile. His air of nonchalance failed. I resisted vertigo.

"No you won't! He's a criminal. Every Panamanian says so."

"I'll change that. Wait and see how I work wonders with the Panama Defense Force. And him . . . "

He gripped the iron rail still staring straight ahead, avoiding me. I called the idea dangerous; he disagreed; I pursued until finally realizing I butted into a wall.

"Don't you know Noriega's background? Nobody changes the PDF."

His profile hardened. Who was this stranger and where was the man I knew? When did he become arrogant? Believe he could change people. Was it that last job at Fort Bragg? Commander of a US Psychological Operations Battalion. Psychological? Damned secrets. Our daughters questioned his job often but he explained nothing, only that he ran a radio station and printing plant. He never invited us to visit the premises. Tonight, if he'd said, "Our marriage is over, I love another." No problem! I could handle that like any woman reared in Arraijan. If their man steps out of line, the women cut off a testicle or set fire to his pajama crotch while he sleeps. But for him to choose a job with Noriega! Formidable. Such power—greater than any female rival—impossible for me to compete in such an arena.

Out front of our house, the iron gate slammed announcing Daniella was home from baton practice. Her books crashed to the floor and she hollered.

"Sofia. Are you still sick?"

Sofia came out of her room blowing her nose. Daniella went on.

"Sorry kiddo. But wait'll you hear!" She pulled her sister toward the kitchen.

"I got the formula."

"My homework assignments?" Sofia's voice nasal.

"Yeah. Got 'em. I'm starved. Come on."

They headed for the kitchen, not noticing their parents on the dark terrace. Pots clanged and Daniella carried a dish to the table and explained.

"Sis, you know why our friends never bother to study on weekends? They're party animals. Cheat on exams. You've seen their stapled answers under the hems of their skirts."

Without looking our way, Daniella hollered.

"Delicious plantain, Mom."

All along she knew we were out there. Sofia snorted into tissue and cleared her throat to expound upon the subject at hand.

"I rather flunk than cheat. Why bother to go to school?"

"From now on, we go to parties uninvited. We just drop in. We parachute."

"Wow, I miss one day of school and you lose your head."

I left Chico to go caution the girls on the risks of parachuting. Daniella laughed.

"Mom, it's an expression. It doesn't mean we'll jump out of an airplane. If we don't get invited to a party, we go anyway, drop in like *paracaidistas.*"

I caught on. Everybody was doing their thing. But for me, the sky was falling.

Daniella's major achievement when she graduated from Maria Inmaculada, besides perfecting her Spanish language, was her mastering the aerial sport of social persuasion, 'parachuting' into parties. I dove back into my job of weeding grass with a vengeance, extricating my pent-up anger.

One morning Crystal-Voice came by while I dug. I expected her usual, "Your husband's a lucky man." Instead, she threw me a curve, "You enjoy punishment don't you, Jenny?"

I took a closer look at her, same nice hairdo, same syrupy caramel skin. Well, I knew how to fix her, knock her down to my level. I'd dump some dirt on her, not the cemetery kind, the dirty deceit my husband dumped on me.

"Chico accepted a job with Noriega and the PDF." Then I kept silent, awaiting her shock.

She dallied choosing her words, and finally with an air of disdain she delivered.

"Bad choice. Working with MAN is dangerous. For men and women. Sooner or later you get kicked in the ass."

Her foot moved as if kicking something before she continued.

"But your husband is probably accustomed to snake pits. Isn't that what the US does best? Train snakes?" She laughed hard, shaking, until her long black hair slapped her face. "Don't look so worried, Jenny. Chico has the perfect face for the job."

"Oh? What kind of face does he have?"

"*Cara de yo no fui.* Innocent. A face that hides all evil."

She left me speechless. On a roll, she asked how old I was when I married. Without waiting for an answer she concluded.

"Second marriages are the best. I proved it," and laughed again.

Long after she'd walked away, her laugh resonated with each weed I pulled.

6

OCÚ FAIR

Men and guns enjoy an affiliation unparalleled by love of family. Chico proved it by choosing to work with Noriega's Panama Defense Force, the PDF, an institution with a sullied reputation. His choice brought me shame. How could anyone believe they could change Noriega and the PDF? Unless they believe themselves omnipotent.

Daniella enrolled in Panama's National University. With our family submerged in the moral confusion of her father choosing to pledge allegiance to undesirables, she may have lost her bearings. Daniella embarked on a secret adventure with an older man, a suitor unwilling to come visit her home and meet Mama.

Sofia's graduation night was nearly as catastrophic. In bed with flu but determined to participate, she wobbled onto school grounds, handed Trinity her mortarboard, and ducked behind a shrub to throw up. Band music concealed her retching sound. She climbed auditorium bleachers to the top and joined classmates. Within seconds, her head drooped, her mortarboard tumbled off and her knees buckled. Sofia had passed out. Girls on either side grabbed her arms and held tight. She recovered, endured the speeches, walked up for her scroll, and went home to collapse.

Sofia also chose a new route. When she left for Rollins College in Orlando, Florida, Trinity and I lost our bearings, two wheels minus the main axle. Sofia had been her younger sister's idol. Trinity's baton twirling in the Marimba band failed to fill the loss. So she focused attention on Daniella, who ignored her. Peeved by the cold shoulder, Trinity snooped on her sister and came to a conclusion.

"Daniella's up to no good."

I made excuses for Daniella even though Trinity's classmates had seen Daniella at the snobbish, *Club Union*, "Drinking, smoking, and smooching with this oldie." I eavesdropped on Daniella. She curled around the telephone, her voice seductive. My conscience balked, scolding me: Moms should respect their college daughter's choices. I backed off knowing Trinity and her classmates intended to delve deeper. And they did.

"He's a banker named Osvaldo. Has a bad reputation with girls and likes sorcery."

The witchcraft detail thrilled my mother who decided to invite him to Arraijan. With Daniella.

Chico's new job brought social engagements I preferred to avoid. My hobby of planting trees provided an excuse to by-pass commitments. Nighttime I worked on tree seedlings and days I planted trees on friends' properties. Owning no land for this enterprise, friends welcomed my reforestation efforts. The good life prevailed, until Noriega invited us to the Ocú Fair.

"Will his wife be there?" I inquired.

"I don't know." His answer meant, "Trash your convictions and go."

I did, anticipated earth-shaking revelations and received an overdose. We invited Daniella. Her blunt "No" bothered Trinity. She decided to pressure her to go, no matter what. I kept my distance until one day I saw her following sis to the bathroom, like a forlorn pup. She found the door locked and begged: "Please, Daniella, come with us to the fair," and wiggled the knob.

Daniella barreled out intending to escape, heading for the exit. Trinity chased after, bumping into her heel and knocking her off balance. Daniella spewed anger.

"Cut it out!"

Sobered by her near crash, she came to me, humbled.

"Mom, I can't go 'cause I have rehearsal for the Miss Panama Beauty Pageant." Having said that, she resumed her race to the iron gate. Trinity followed, nearly breathing on Daniella's hair. They resembled two fillies, nose to the gate, bristling with brawn, and reacting harshly to loves' pull in opposite directions.

Saved by Sofia. She arrived from Rollins College for semester break and agreed to go to the fair. The car packed tight with oranges, cashews and anything eaten with one hand, we drove to Ocú in a new Toyota Cressida issued to Chico as Pentagon liaison. Its newness smelled of kerosene-based floor wax, courtesy of the PDF and Manuel Antonio Noriega, MAN. He lived up to his initials by promoting himself to general while the country slept proving his power over everything both living and petrified.

Sofia and Trinity drowned the car with laughter as they compared Rollins College to Maria Inmaculada. Their joy soothed my apprehension until we rolled into Ocú alongside two oxen yoked to a wood cart. Its loud crack-crack prompted Trinity to fawn over the cart. We assessed the town and its houses. Upon learning that wattle and dung were used to construct the quaint residences surrounding the town square, she grimaced, "Primitive."

Her father interjected, "Cow dung makes excellent plaster for house walls. These people are very resourceful. I consider them the country elite. We could all learn from them."

The country elite showed good taste. Their porch stools, chunks of petrified tree stumps, would fit well in our rock garden at home. I asked Chico to buy me two. He talked me out of it.

"They'll ruin the PDF car's shock absorbers. It's not our vehicle."

Chicken soup aroma wafted heavily in the air as we ambled into fairgrounds, sniffing in search of the delicious *Sancocho*, a hearty national dish made with chicken and vegetables like yucca. Steam rose from the pot set on three rocks. We ate the savory brew while watching skydivers, the US contribution to the fair.

Bored, our girls left to find younger fare and missed the highlight of the fair: *Manitos*, hill people dancing on a wood stage. Two shuffles forward and one step backwards, stomping to a monotone drum—similar to a Texas stroll. The women wore fragile lace ensembles, the same attire brought here by Spain's Conquistadors centuries ago. Many descendants inherited green eyes. Farming in the bright sun darkened their skin and turned it leathery.

An ugly, loud slap jolted our enjoyment. People nearby uttered painful groans and pointing at a woman, they whispered, "The slapper is a PRD legislator's wife."

The aggressor continued scolding the policeman she had just slapped. He shook his head with an expression of embarrassment and rubbed his cheek. The woman's husband pulled her away.

We went searching for Sofia and Trinity and found them nearby with a group their own age dancing salsa. We had to drag them off to seek our lodging. In the car Trinity had questions.

"Dad, how'd these country people get so rich? Two girls we were talking to just returned yesterday from Europe on a Concord flight."

"Rich? I don't know how. But historically, Ocú breeds doctors and lawyers. Maybe their fathers work with Noriega."

He realized immediately what that meant and eclipsed the comment to lecture us on geography. He insisted we look for the Señales sign, the road to petroglyphs carved on river rock a millennium ago by Ngobe Indians. He described the carvers as descendants of a Maya group in the area. Nobody showed interest. Many dusty miles ahead the villa appeared and we slept by the rippling Señales River of the carved stones.

Early in the morning Trinity jumped out of bed saying, "I smell fried liver!"

Within minutes she went tripping across a plain decorated with bougainvillea. I followed her to a huge thatch hut on the edge of the Señales River, the stream with the ancient etchings. Dozens of multicolor hammocks hung under the thatch hut cooled by the river. Laughter from the same girl and boy dancers from the previous afternoon rocked the hut and woke Sofia. I stood filling my dish with breakfast and met one of the villa owners. She was the policeman slapper!

Untouchable, she belonged to the pyramid of power. I sidled away and flopped into a hammock to hide. Maids clinked dishes at the far end of the hut. Dish clatter and human chatter stopped, making way for another sound. Gravel crunched under footsteps, many human feet headed our way. I sat up. An entourage of men approached, all wearing baseball caps. Voices from hammocks hollered.

"*Hola Mi General*!"

Almost immediately came a distinct "*Oye Chico*! How are you?" followed by loud patting on each other's back. I witnessed the power group conquering my husband.

Noriega stood in the hut beaming while guests paid him homage. Days earlier an editorial in La Prensa called them, "Sycophants. Parasites. The new oligarchy that cripple the economy to enrich themselves." I showed it to Chico and his response to the article was: "Don't believe everything you read."

Trinity left the power group and flopped into the hammock next to mine. I asked her if Noriega's wife came. "Nope," she said, swinging the hammock with her eyes fixated on the tortilla she munched. Sofia stood in the crowd of elegant civilians shaking hands with the general.

Her regal height forced her to bend noticeably. She remained in the adulator's circle. Voices droned on, monotone words that seemed to rise from the depth of a clay urn; soothing voices lulled me to sleep. I missed the military intrigue aimed at Sofia.

CLOMP. CLOMP. Pounding hooves wakened me. Vision blurred, I sat up and wiped saliva from my chin. Through sun's haze and dust, a giant horse pranced in our direction. CLOMP. CLOMP came closer, hammering louder. The horse's mahogany mane waved to one side.

"Who is Sofia?" asked the man in the saddle.

"*Yo.*" She replied sleepily.

I shot straight out of the sleep-trap hammock snaring my foot in the rag-bound contraption that tangled and threw me to the floor. Who wanted my Sofia? From the floor I studied faces of people asleep in hammocks. Mouths open, flies buzzing over them, none bore bad skin. Where was Noriega?

"Which one is Sofia?" The horseman demanded again.

Sofia sat up and faced the insisting horseman. She stared in silence at the horse. Once before a strange man tried to claim her. Four years earlier a cameraman from a local TV station spotted her marching and twirling her baton on November 3rd, Panama's Independence Day. Wearing her blue plaid Maria Inmaculada uniform among dozens of classmates waving their batons in the same blue attire, the pretty girls sashayed to the music of their school band. The photographer zoomed in on Sofia, attracted by her elegance and height. We watched from home, awed, while our girl momentarily starred on TV as they marched past the presidential palace. Tossing the baton high, she caught it, pranced, circled and wriggled to the rhythm of the marimba band. Her raven hair and winsome blue eyes had captivated the photographer. Perhaps she reminded him of a conquistador's daughter, men who conquered Panama.

While I thought of the devil invader, the horseman announced, "Sofia, General Noriega invites you to fly in his helicopter."

"Chico! Get up!" I yelled.

Ready to fight, I needed support from my Gringo Colonel.

"Did you see Noriega leave?" I barked. Chico wore a goofy, sleepy look.

"Hey Mom, you're not much of a watchdog."

Trinity giggled, delighted this terrible thing was happening—to me—to Sofia—to us! She was unaware the danger local newspapers had been reporting. PDF troops had not yet revealed to the world their criminal tendencies. And her father supported them.

Sofia yawned and lay back in the hammock, ignoring the horsy messenger. I feared the rider would climb down and take her so I grabbed her arm. Thrilled, Trinity stated her desire to ride the helicopter. I wanted to drag her too but she wasn't the object of desire. Metal braces over her teeth protected her.

"Come Sofia. Help me pack," I said. "We're leaving right now!"

In the hustle to get out I forgot my new red shoes. Once inside the car, my anger found its target. Chico.

"Never again will that lecher see Sofia."

He gripped the steering wheel, his knuckles turning white. Anything he said would make me angrier.

"I wish he'd invited me," Trinity lamented, "Wonder how it feels to fly a chopper?"

He ignored her; his fight with me had not ended.

"Jenny, you overreacted. Nothing happened."

"What? You need to see blood to see danger?"

My own husband? Noriega's lackey? I glared at the gray road ahead, a long tape to nowhere. Undaunted by the incident, the girls sang along with Ruben Blades. *"El Padre*

Antonio y su monagrillo Andres," his famous song about a priest and his acolyte.

Sofia snapped her fingers to the music. Trinity asked, "Is that the song where they murder a priest or is it the acolyte? Please, gimme one of your earphones. Pretty Pleeezz . . ."

Chico drove faster, angry with me, the wrong person. He slowed at narrow bridges, creeks dried to bedrock. Once a rain forest covered the entire province, rivers overflowed. We approached a cluster of houses with a police checkpoint. A policeman stopped Chico and asked for his license. Whether he was speeding was irrelevant; without reason he demanded to see it.

I enjoyed it, opened my window to gloat over Chico's guaranteed ticket if he didn't pay a bribe to the cop. Outside spread a brutal patch of ruined earth, the result of a millennium of Indian slash and burn agriculture. Heartbreaking sight. I turned back to see the policeman smirking, a toothpick dangling from his teeth. He chewed with delight until Chico handed over his license instead of the expected bribe. The license was odd, different. The policeman examined the booklet. His toothpick dropped. He clicked his heels and saluted like a soldier. At the booklet! Then he shoved it through the window as though too hot to handle. Chico retrieved his powerhouse license and pulled away.

"Wow! What did you show him, Dad? Your license?" Both girls leaned forward.

Chico handed it to me. Scrawled inside the booklet was Noriega's signature.

"You're getting one too, Jenny," his enthusiasm revolting.

Like hell, I thought, Noriega isn't including me in his empire. Our car slowed and I opened the window to ask the wind, "Why do people compromise their souls?"

Trinity reached over and rubbed my shoulder, consoling me.

"Watch me. See how I change the PDF," Chico said. "Including Noriega."

"Mom, Dad can do anything," said Trinity. "He made you love a Gringo."

Trinity had never called her father a Gringo. The three roared. Not me. Chico was theirs; he pledged himself to Noriega, the PDF and PRD. Was I willing to do the same to remain in Panama?

Time would tell. If only I'd read the signs back then, foreboding indicators.

Behind me, the girl's soft snore filled the car until we reached home. Glad to be back, I helped unload our Ocú treasures—three stools made of petrified trees. Chico had conceded to bringing them to appease my anger. Heavy as the centuries it took to convert wood to stone, the prehistoric relics came at a high price. Sofia was nearly pawned for the pile of rocks.

7

WEDDING

Caveman stools from Ocú took honored places in the vestibule. Ancient treasures erased disagreeable memories, namely dangerous overtures to Sofia from the country's top villain. Upon our arrival Daniella's sugary, "Hello," came as stark contrast to our last encounter. Why the change? Trinity brushed hard against me going through the vestibule carrying a suitcase. She stopped in front of Daniella to inquire.

"Did you miss us?"

"Nice stones," Daniella said smiling too much. "Are they petrified trees?"

"I can't stand it," Trinity stomped off, "You people are all weird. All you care about are rocks."

Suppressing thirst and sleepiness I walked over to sit on the sofa and study Daniella. Sofia joined me, watching her older sister twirl past us in a freaky pirouette. Humming, she lifted an arm, extended her opposite foot and raised it in a gawky ballet pose. Trinity came back to watch her sister's quirky antics. Her father stood stupefied and I applauded her performance. Her sisters, in a sleepy trance, hid their curiosity; we craved asking her if Mr. Sneaky still hung around.

"You missed a great party," Sofia said.

"Yeah," Trinity added, "Sofi was nearly kidnapped. By helicopter."

Daniella's curiosity piqued; the three huddled on the sofa, yakking about our trip. I showered, went to bed and nudged Chico while he read.

"Daniella's boyfriend is nine years her senior."

He kept reading. I pushed on.

"Honest men show their face."

He lowered the book, "You dislike a man without meeting him," and soon snored.

I changed tactics. Could Chico be right? Perhaps influenced by events in Ocú where wild men usurp power and try to abduct daughters, I launched a new approach to Daniella's suitor. I placed little faith in any chance of Daniella's romance dying easily; so next day I called the bank where Osvaldo worked and addressed him courteously and with sincerity.

"Please. Give Daniella a chance to finish college. Court her after she finishes studying."

His charming response, *"Si, Si,"* misled me to believe he agreed to leave her alone.

Finals for the Miss Panama Beauty Pageant included Ruben Blades singing to the array of beauties. Daniella finished third. I had encouraged the activity hoping she'd win, be swept into a whirlwind year of appearances and forget Osvaldo.

Sofia left for her final semester at Rollins College in Florida. Several days later the phone rang while I was in the kitchen. Trinity answered.

"Hola Abuelita." I went to the living room to hear what her grandmother said.

"No Abuelita." Her voice dropped. "Re-a-l-l-y?" Then her pitch rose. "No kidding!" She stood up. "No. No." She rolled her eyes at me. "I promise I won't tell Mom. No, you don't have to pay me." Trinity hung up, her face a patina of pain. She walked over and collapsed on the sofa next to me.

"Abuelita says Osvaldo sleeps in Arraijan with Daniella."

"That snob goes to Arraijan? That dump? And he won't stoop to come here?"

"Yes, Mom, the hypocrite. Abuelita says he walks around town wearing slippers and making friends with all the bums."

"Why didn't my mother tell me? How long has this been going on?"

"She told me not to tell you anything."

"Oh, Trinity. Your grandmother is sick."

"Sickening is more like it. Evil too, like I've always said."

Next morning, Daniella rose early, hummed her way into the kitchen and announced, "Osvaldo's gonna start coming over. And Trinity, don't tell him he smells bad like you do with Sofi's admirers. Understand?"

Twenty-four hours later Mr. Sneak-behind-my-back-to-court-my-daughter arrived. Our cowbell doorbell clanged, or better described, it exploded. Daniella flew. Running to the entrance, Trinity and I collided and made lady-like recoveries to stand sedately observing Daniella unlock the gate. Mr. Admirer flinched when the iron door closed hard behind him, banging on the iron doorjamb. Trinity's classmate said he was ugly. False. His chiseled nose was smaller than Daniella's.

Trinity elbowed me and nearly caused me to lose balance. She whispered: "Don't be fooled by his business dress-up. Bank uniform. He wears rags in Arraijan. Abuelita said so."

He walked up the vestibule, could have passed for the prince of hides with his pristine white shirt and necktie slim as a dagger. He smiled, nice teeth.

"*Hola, Suegra*. Hi, Mother-in-law."

He planted a kiss on my cheek. Daniella clutched his arm and pulled him into the house. Trinity elbowed me again, her bone sharp as a knife. Mouth to my ear she hissed.

"He dared call you mother-in-law? You gotta do something. Quick! It's bad!"

"All the young men call me that, dear," I lied. Underfoot, the floor buckled.

We sat on the terrace, the atmosphere tense on my side and hostile on Trinity's.

"Nice view," said Osvaldo, scanning the city.

I turned on the ceiling fans while Trinity brought papaya juice. Daniella reached for Osvaldo's hand. He pulled it away with a strained, "Heh-Heh," and tugged at his dagger necktie.

Hollow seconds passed in which nobody spoke. Trinity and I grieved sensing the intimacy shared by the amorous couple. We were the strangers. Osvaldo recognized our anguish, flipped his necktie and straightened up in his chair as one does in preparation for making a speech. Daniella beat him to it.

"We eloped. Got a civil license."

"You what? When?" I exclaimed.

Trinity slammed her plastic glass on the mosaic table spilling juice. She grabbed her napkin, the lovebirds and mine, and blotted the mess. But it failed to smother her anger.

"When did you do this terrible thing?" Trinity tossed the napkins on the floor.

"We want a church wedding," Daniella said. "When Sofia comes home."

She avoided looking at me, cooed at Osvaldo and giggled like a teenager Trinity's age rather than her twenty-one years. Wounded, I repeated the question about their eloping. I did not deserve the insult and was a good mother, attentive, respectful. And she repaid me with a slap!

"In Arraijan," she said. "Abuelita was the witness. She loves Osvaldo."

My mother. How could she do this to me, to us? I never did anything like this to her. No wonder they slept together in Arraijan; they were married. And to think I brought my family here for my mother's pleasure instead of staying in the US. Trinity twisted in her chair. We both turned to stare at the city as if we didn't see it all day. Refused to look at the couple. I saw nothing, no city, no sky, nothing. A shroud descended everywhere. Trinity's sneaker nudged me, then again harder, her expression serious, a feature absent on Daniella. Chico was spared our misery; he'd gone off with the PDF on a military training exercise. Training for what? War against whom? My people?

The couple left.

"Well, Mom, you're the tough one in this family. Dad won't do anything about it. He never does. What are you gonna do?"

The whole affair left me empty.

"They're married. It's done," I said.

At that moment I smelled smoke. Months earlier I scolded a neighbor for setting fire to a dirty mattress in his yard. The stench: repugnant and vicious, returned, as if yesterday.

We invited the couple for a weekend in the interior to get to know him better. We hoped Daniella, away from artificial city lights and in pure country air, would discover something about her man she'd not seen clearly before. Maybe their age difference.

Soon after we arrived in Penonomé, they argued.

"Food's bad," he said. "I hate country music and all *Cholo* Indians."

She pouted. He walked off. Trinity and I thrilled at the possibility of a quickie divorce. But Daniella pursued her man. Chico shared none of our misery and Trinity and I were too torn to cry.

"It's a done deal. They're married."

Trinity's head slumped.

On their wedding day, a radiant Daniella walked from our house in her white wedding gown to the Catholic chapel to wed Osvaldo. Neighbors and friends, singing and tossing white carnations, led her onto a sweet path of commitment. At Padre Durán's chapel his miniature frogs croaked a rendition of discordant rivets while his pigeons cooed a solemn, sad refrain. We returned to our house for the reception. More than one hundred guests arrived for the wedding brunch. Flashbulbs may have brought on the sad note and caused Daniella to stop smiling and cry. Nobody else cried. Her tears, turquoise as her eyes, heralded a stormy future.

Not hers only, also ours.

8

LAS VEGAS

Years earlier I forced Chico to trash his parachute when he jumped and slashed his face when hitting earth. When he came home walking sideways, crab-style, I suspected he had reneged on the deal. I followed him to the bedroom. He removed his fatigue jacket with the jungle print and sat down without mentioning today's maneuvers with the Panama Defense Force.

He reached down to remove one black boot and moaned with pain. Aware I was watching he mustered a sheepish smile, a perfect hint he swallowed a lie. Spitting on his fingers he rubbed saliva on the tip of his boot to produce a shine. First time I saw him do it aroused my disgust. He insisted his boots required a 'spit-shine' or else. Such demands of cleanliness should have piqued my curiosity to question the inner cleanliness of a soldier. Just then something dropped loud behind me. His boot. He spoke to it directly.

"Someday those men will make top-notch soldiers."

"Who?"

His curt answer surprised me.

"Whom else would I be talking about? The PDF men."

Why snap at me? Was he injured? He confirmed it by skewering a painful face while reaching for his rib.

"Foolish man. I bet that story you told about going on a maneuver was bull. You jumped again. Didn't you? How long has this been going on?"

His dubious answer, "Swimming, I must'a pulled a muscle swimming" did not jive. Swimming soothes.

At breakfast he reached for a tortilla and contorted his face, but stuck to the story.

Mid-afternoon, I sat at the big window in our bedroom and clipped my toenails. Behind me a rainstorm roiled in my direction pushing dark clouds towards our hill. Seconds later sheets of rain hammered the city below. Thunder and lightning brought Trinity in to sit beside me and enjoy the spectacle. The phone rang. It was Chico, his voice drowned out by pounding rain, hitting like a machine gun on our metallic roof. I asked him to yell.

"Las Vegas. Get ready! You're going to Las Vegas. With Noriega's wife. I'll be in Washington with her husband. At the Pentagon."

His excitement failed to enthuse me.

"Me? But . . . But . . . I don't know his wife."

He went on talking as if deaf and as though I had agreed to go. The invitation put me in the eye of another storm. While fixing dinner I broke a dish, burned the beans and added plenty cilantro to camouflage the burn taste. Nobody noticed. Trinity was engrossed in babbling excitedly about Las Vegas.

"Does Vegas only have gambling or do they have Pac-man like Disney?"

Explaining there's no Disney, only slot machines cooled her interest, even when told popular singers perform at the hotels. Sleepless, by midnight the reality sunk in. I was invited to travel with Noriega's wife whether she knew me or I knew her. Or had they already investigated my background of non-descript relatives in Arraijan? Could I say no? Chico would never forgive me. I wondered what she was like.

After sunrise, I called Crystal Voice seeking details.

"I know nothing about his wife," she said dryly which surprised me coming from someone who knew plenty about his mistresses. I had a flashback of a man on horseback, dead-set on taking Sofia away on a helicopter. Crystal Voice lent me a white wool dress. I had given away all winter clothes when we returned to Panama.

Chico walked slightly better, at least straighter and I credited the ice pack. I inquired if the US Embassy approved of my boondoggle trip to Las Vegas.

"Ambassador's exact words were: 'It's great you get closer to Noriega.'"

"For what? Who pays for my part of the trip?"

"Panama's government."

Confirmed. I had become a sponge. No different from PRD people who hang around government offices and PDF Hellquarters pretending to work and doing nothing more than shuffle paper.

Excited about his trip, Chico departed. I passed out chores. Sofia and Trinity were close as fingernail-to-skin, but recently Sofia, our Citibank "executive trainee," had turned serious. The task I left her seemed impossible; curtail Trinity's lengthy telephone conversations at night.

Two days later a taxi drove me to the airport. I checked my bags and waited. Two men appeared carrying hand-held radios; a pistol peeked from the belt on one of the men. Behind them strutted the wife of the commander of the Panama Defense Forces. Big hair over ivory skin, with the carriage of a flamenco dancer, she personified the perfect dictator's wife. Military royalty.

"Her parents are from Spain," Chico had said. My same age, both of us Latinas, and married to a military man twenty-two years. Our similarities ended there. A sea of difference separated us. Her hands: gardenia petals. Mine: skin cracked from housework and gardening; nothing could hide the damaged skin. Well-tended, the woman resembled a porcelain doll. Crystal Voice said her friends called her Muñeca, a real doll. I yearned for her looks, every bit, except for her terrible choice of husband. I approached her and instead of thanking her for inviting me, I spoke nervously.

"Do you like to swim?"

Too late, I cursed my tongue. Only a moron asks a monarch if she enjoys bathing.

"Not much. It ruins my hair."

Felicidad Noriega introduced me to the other two women traveling with us. Standing next to our hostess, the three of us resembled her team of housemaids.

On the airplane I declined her offer of champagne saying I get airsick.

The three women laughed and clinked glasses. Chatting and toasting, they soon asked about me, where I grew up. I said "Arraijan." They clammed up until later when one spoke through her champagne.

"Arraijan doesn't like the PRD," and waited my response.

I dispensed with more comments knowing Arraijan residents never forgave the first dictator for ousting the caudillo, Arnulfo Arias in '68. While my companions slept, I read Rachel Carson's "Silent Spring," about human damage to the environment until the planes' monotonous hum brought slumber.

Landing gear groaned over mustard-colored sands of Las Vegas, its crushed carpet of pulverized quartz a sandbox for the rich. A muscular man met us—Felicidad's bodyguard. Tossing my luggage in my hotel room, I hurried down to the lobby and found my hostess planted on a casino stool—champagne in one hand, gardenia petal fingers clicking a pile of chips. I watched to see if I might gamble. She squirmed, nervous.

"Please don't stand there. It changes my luck."

Embarrassed, I slinked away noticing for the first time the stench of musty cigarettes and rancid beer in the carpets. The coffee shop offered refuge. Stale bran muffins crumbled in my hand while I moped, wishing I'd stayed home.

Daytime, we browsed malls lined with wood statues of American Indians wearing sad faces. Their grim expressions mirrored my frown. Embarrassing. I feigned a smile realizing how pedantic I must seem to my travelling companions, all three as frail as I and yet so different. After all, they were not the ones in military uniform.

Dinnertime, I ate grilled shark while my companions teased about my taste.

"In Panama we throw those awful fish back in the sea."

Another day of shopping and an evening of gambling. I decided to take the risk and play. At a prudent distance from my hostess, I plugged a nickel into a slot machine, then another. Oranges brightly lit the front, a bell clanged. I won!

Exhilarated, I awaited my landslide of money. Nothing happened. I jerked the bandit's arm, then again a bit harder arousing a bouncer's ire. He ambled over, his belly the size of Russia. I said, "I won!" He said, "Cool it," and told me to add more money. I argued the machine owed me money, not the other way around. He failed to understand and raised his masculine voice. My astute hostess heard the argument. From her table, she intervened. Hand extended, she waved a hundred dollar bill at him and called him, insisting.

"*Señor*, please, come closer."

He took the bill and examined its worth, nearly jumping for joy.

She came to my rescue, forbidding the bouncer to mistreat me. I understood why her friends called her *Muñeca*; doll showed no intention of wearing her husband's rank.

I crawled back to the coffee shop and more stale bran muffins and accepted the inevitable. A fish out of water needs to swim. I had no choice: swim at night, outside, while my companions gambled. The pool was heated, but I needed to walk outside the hotel in a bathing suit, wet and freezing. It was time to indulge in something healthy and sane. I tried it. Swam a dozen laps in the warm pool.

Delicious. Walking to the elevator in a hotel robe, dripping water, people gave me strange looks.

The second night the elevator delayed while I stood dripping and teeth chattering. Hotel guests eyed me dripping water on the carpet. Inside the elevator, they kept their distance, avoiding getting wet. Their critical looks were the last drop. I quit swimming. Chico and his companions were due to arrive from Washington soon.

The final day of traipsing through malls, our hostess, in high heels, complained of sore feet. I wore sneakers. After dinner in her room, a suite no fancier than mine, she wore a crimson robe handmade by Gnobe Bugle Indians of Panama's central highlands. A row of appliqués in bright colors circled the garment. Her lustrous black hair crowned the ensemble, transforming her into an Indian Princess. But the lady groaned.

"Aiiee," she reached for her feet, "I need a friend to rub my painful feet."

The other two ladies clammed up. Was I the chosen one? Were all of us too good to touch her feet? She had not looked at anyone in particular. They sipped champagne. Since I enjoy kneading bread, I offered. With baby oil I rubbed one tiny white foot until it glowed pink, softly, avoiding the harsh technique required to knead bread. While rubbing her other foot, the phone rang. She answered; her voice turned syrupy repeating her husband's name. I released her foot.

"*Si, Manuel Antonio, si, mi amor.*"

When she hung up, the other women complained. Her husband called several times a day and theirs not once since we left Panama. Mine either.

Next day Chico and Noriega arrived from Washington with two PDF officers, Colonels Castillo and Barrera, husbands of our hostess's companions. He went to our hotel room to change clothing. A waiter delivered a bottle of iced Dom Pérignon champagne to our room. Chico was delighted.

"Nobody has ever given me such fine champagne."

Our hostess invited us to their room. The men drank whisky and the women champagne. The officers teased each other.

"When was the last time you ran five miles, old man? You can't. Look at your gut."

"Me?"

"Yeah. You eat too many French fries."

They roared. Their laughter bored us women. Following a round of drinks, our hostess, speaking as if nobody were present or listening, said to the general:

"Manuel Antonio, enough. Let's go to bed. You've been with these men for days."

Noriega ignored her, and kept joking with his men. She stood up, walked to the door and stood, arms crossed in front, watching her husband bantering with subordinates.

Taking his cue from the general who ignored his commanding wife, one of the colonels teased Chico. The general joined in needling him too, turning raucous.

"Chico jumps great for an old guy. Don't you think, general?"

Anger swelled inside and travelled straight to my tongue.

"What? Your sore ribs! You lied! Gullible me put ice on you."

He broke his promise never to jump again. And there he sat pain free, laughing, his broken Spanish greatly improved by whisky.

"Hey guys, cut the crap. Jenny doesn't know I've been jumping with Battalion 2000." All of which provoked more laughs and hard slaps on my soldier's back.

On my way out, I left my hostess standing at the door, tapping her pointed-toe shoe—made by man to seduce men but failing to prod the love of her life to bed. My Gringo husband was being sucked into the PDF web. Using his nickname, "El Chico Grande," they kneaded him like bread dough, making him supple. Quite a picture.

Dreams disturbed my sleep: military boots, black and pointed, and Chico cleaning them.

Next morning I tore the pillow off his face. "Fool. You jumped! You'll get killed."

He pleaded jumping was necessary to gain camaraderie.

"Come back to bed and I'll quit," he said.

"Let's make a deal. I'll get in bed if you promise to retire. Now."

He clammed up. I felt jealous and told him so.

"Felicidad is lucky. The general calls her three times a day."

Chico's excitement diminished. "I saw that happen, Jenny. It surprised me."

He paused, "Noriega may have been loving on the phone with his wife but his mistress and secretary were right down the hall from us at the Watergate Hotel."

"That's a Latino for you. That's why I married a gringo. I never understood what made my European grandfather such a dog. He sired children in three towns. My poor grandmother suffered."

Soon as we unpacked in Panama, I baked. At dusk Chico and I dropped off muffins at the PDF commander's mansion in Golf Heights. In the box was an invitation for the couple to dine at our house. A guard carefully examined the bran muffins.

Driving home Chico said something disturbing.

"Our neighbors will probably get perturbed when our street gets taken over by heavy surveillance. Don't tell them anything concerning the invitation. We'll see how they react."

"React? To what?" I asked, alarmed. Just then a screeching siren passed nearby forcing me to cover my ears and close my mouth, cancelling my question and the investigation of the mystery.

9

DECAPITATED

"The neighbors will hate us!" Sofia shouted and rushed from the house in anticipation of our guest's arrival. From outside she yelled again.

"Come see who arrived first!" Accelerating her car she escaped, leaving Trinity sputtering, frustrated and complaining her sister had left. She crossed her arms, uninterested in events outside, but bristled about the development inside. Kitchen duty.

"Now I'm stuck doing dishes alone."

"Alone," she repeated, even though I always washed dishes with her. But to her, not having Sofia, her buddy, was similar to being alone. Even in my company.

As Sofia warned, activity on our street heated up. Strange individuals had taken possession of our hill. Husky men dressed in street clothes sauntered on the sidewalk, communicating on radios and exhibiting supreme authority over the premises.

Our table, laden with English bone china and Peruvian silver, glistened in honor of our special guests. Chico stepped outside awaiting them. Jubilant, he exclaimed at the iron gate: "Welcome general. Felicidad."

The couple entered, theirs an intriguing combination: her, fine as my bone china and him, rough as the carpet at our doorstep. Both found Trinity interesting. Felicidad asked where she went to school.

Trinity boasted, "Maria Inmaculada."

I bragged that our girls were entitled to US schools in the Canal Zone, tuition-free, but we preferred they study in Spanish with nuns.

"It's such a great school." Trinity went on, "When my sister Sofi took the SAT, she nearly aced the math."

My antennas went up at the mention of Sofia to the villain who in Ocú, tried to snatch her away by helicopter. Dinner consisting of cranberry chicken and chatter about intelligent life in the universe mitigated the stories I'd heard about Noriega. *Flan* custard sealed the deal leaving us with a sweet finale.

Our pleasant aftertaste lasted a year. My soldier enjoyed his new job as Pentagon liaison to the PDF while I chased my own dream. I visited distant provinces to observe subsistence farmers. Sustainable agro-forestry was my interest, and the sight of slash and burn agriculture was mortifying. Rampant deforestation drove me to consult with ministry of agriculture employees. They claimed their budget was meager and RENARE, the entity assigned to protect jungles, overlooked the problem. In the field I found one spark of hope: a Rutgers University technician advising cattle farmers to improve grass quality for grazing animals and reduce deforestation.

Soon after, Rutgers learned of my interest and hired me to set up their office in front of the University of Panama. A year later Noriega cancelled the program and the five Rutgers technicians left. Furious, I vented my anger on Chico.

"Why does the government sabotage farmers? Do they enjoy keeping them poor? Doesn't anybody care about the destruction of our natural resources?"

He turned a deaf ear.

Peeved, I returned to Chiriquí to snoop and find out why the military regime crushed the agricultural sector. I questioned farmers who tilled the soil near the Costa Rica border. A Mojica clan member described their uprising two decades earlier when the regime ousted the democratically elected President, Arnulfo Arias. He grew coffee in their province and angry country folk took up guns in rebellion of the coup.

During that same period, Omar Torrijos, the dictator, threw out the US Peace Corps from Panama. They also worked the fields with subsistence farmers at no cost to anyone in Panama. The Catholic priest, Hector Gallegos, was doing the same with farmers in a different province and for this Torrijos had him erased. Torrijos squelched the Chiriqui rebellion and many country folk died. A few peasants escaped through the jungle but troops caught Crúz Mojica. From behind bushes his kin watched his torture. Still alive and moaning, soldiers threw him in a pit and covered him with dirt. After soldiers departed, Mojica relatives dug him out but it was too late. He had suffocated. Soon after, his brother Ramón was caught and tortured. His body was never recovered.

I left Chiriqui, having uncovered the reason dictators crush farmers. In most countries strong agriculture represents wealth and power. Tyranny's enemy.

Still angry over Rutgers' departure, one morning I woke to loud shouts.

"Assassins!" screamed my neighbor, her TV blaring. I rushed to the kitchen and turned on our set. An angry announcer yelled, "Beheaded, a man's body, his feet protruding from a US Mail bag, has been found near the border of Costa Rica. The tortured body matches Dr. Hugo Spadafora. The surgeon was Minister of Health under General Omar Torrijos. After leaving government, he turned freedom fighter doctoring those engaged in fighting tyrants. Eyewitnesses saw PDF soldiers in civilian attire pull the surgeon Spadafora off a bus on September 13, 1985. He directly accused Noriega of drug dealing and launched a crusade to oust the general, announcing he held proof of his drug dealings. "

Trinity rushed into the kitchen. "What's the dead man's name?"

"Spadafora." I said, "Hugo Spadafora. A surgeon."

She sighed, "His daughter's in my class. Did they confirm it's him?"

The announcer continued. Trinity leaned against the counter listening to the TV newsman repeat the gore perpetrated on the surgeon.

"What's all the noise?" Sofia came bustling in and Chico followed. Four of us crowded in front of the tiny screen on the kitchen counter.

"Trinity, doesn't his daughter ride your bus?" Sofia asked. "What's her name?"

"Fifi. I think it was her Dad 'cause she was crying on the bus yesterday."

"Poor thing," Sofia murmured. Annoyed, she addressed her father.

"Maybe now, Dad, your US Embassy will do something about this."

"Not a chance," he bit a tortilla. "The US does not meddle in foreign politics."

"Huh? Isn't that what they do all the time? Of course they meddle."

The savory aroma in our kitchen changed to angry static. Trinity and her father departed with her still talking, "It's not Dad's fault."

For an hour I watched people interviewed on TV until my head pounded. Late afternoon Chico arrived home humming as though he had spent the day playing golf. I asked what the US Ambassador said. His matter-of-fact answer ticked me off.

"About what?"

"Don't give me that. The beheading has been all over the news every minute today. Your Embassy can't ignore murder. It won't go away."

"Face it, Jenny, Spadafora lived by the sword and died by the sword."

"What? Is that what your Embassy decided?"

He washed his hands while I choked on his apathy.

"That's cynical. You believe everything Washington says. They lie. Didn't you learn the truth the second time you went to 'Nam? Men died over there for nothing. Start thinking for yourself. We're dying here at the hands of the military. Some die in the flesh and others in our minds; it's all the same."

A wall went up between us. Over the ensuing weeks Panamanians marched, led by the Spadafora family. Citizens held candlelight vigils and celebrated Masses. Thousands formed a human chain on Balboa Avenue. Brooding under a scorching sun with the Pacific Ocean glistening behind them, solemn faces stared at passing cars, their mournful eyes charged with anger. The collective public demanded an investigation. Finally, a regime judge closed the case claiming lack of evidence.

Spadafora's beheading turned catalyst marking the beginning of a great internal struggle in my country. The infection spread, invading our marriage. We never saw it coming.

Troubled by what I considered Chico's devotion to criminals, my limited congeniality vanished. One morning, he delayed in his 'blue room,' our bathroom lined with baby blue tiles from top to bottom. I leaned against the door inquiring, "Are you reading in there?"

No response meant come in, Jenny. He stood shaving. I leaned against the wall.

"I want you to retire. Right now." I had said it so often it stuck in my throat.

"Still on the Spadafora kick?" He resumed plowing foam and I waited.

"And no thanks, I like my job. I'm not ready to retire."

"You're stubborn as an Army mule!"

Backing up, I banged my head on the sharp corner of the closet door that someone left open; probably me. His face flashed pleasure, making the bruise on my head feel worse. Our bond, now weakened, finally broke when he spoke.

"You Panamanians aren't capable of governing yourselves democratically."

The man speaking was not my husband. His rhetoric came from the PDF.

A punch in the stomach would have hurt less. Perhaps because he was right.

"Chico, even if this were true, nobody, not you or anybody has the right to decide that. We have a right to learn how to govern ourselves. Badly or however, my people are good and proud. Not everyone is a thief or killer!"

I walked out of the bathroom resisting the temptation to slam the door. But in my heart it slammed so hard I heard its reverberation for years. Intuition told me Chico would live to regret his remark.

As the day progressed, his despotic words hammered in my head. By afternoon I was eager to pick up Trinity at Maria Inmaculada. Driving into the parking lot I saw her leaning against a post under the covered walkway. Her undisciplined aspect drew attention to her socks—drooped to the ankles—sloppy socks prohibited by school uniform dress code. Seeing our brick-colored station wagon, she straightened and smiled, more enthused at the sight of the car than at me. She had no reason for cheer. Fifi and her family were suffering the unthinkable. But she had a new love: her driver's permit, which she would receive soon. Already she was making plans to take over the station wagon, excluding her mother.

"Did your teachers say anything about Spadafora?" I steered off campus.

"Yep. They did. But listen to what Dad says. He says when you drive, don't stop at STOP signs."

"Your father told you that?"

"He says I'll get slammed in the rear if I stop."

"So what does he expect you to do?"

"Slow down. Check the mirror. Pump brakes once. Look both ways and go."

In our carport, I repeated, "Dear, what did your teachers say about Spadafora?"

"Biology teacher said PDF killers tortured Spadafora. They took photographs of his tortured body and sent them to civilian doctors to show he wasn't tortured. But our professor says those photos were doctored. The criminals erased the wounds. I heard a friend of Fifi say he was tortured. And on top of that, they beheaded him slowly."

She jumped out of the car. "My classmates are coming to study biology."

Minutes later four girls in the same blue plaid uniform arrived and dropped books on our dining table. A teardrop chandelier over their heads cast an angelic glow on their heads. I served mango juice. Eager as I was to inquire, I hushed, not wanting to interrupt their studies. When one of the girls came in the kitchen seeking ice, I pounced.

"What do your parents say about Spadafora's murder?"

"My parents are afraid, say this could happen to any of us."

In the living room Trinity bragged, "I have a car. Tomorrow. Who's coming with me to hunt frogs?"

Frogs, needed for biology, kept their conversations attuned to dissection and a science that explains, "morbid proof of human similarity to frogs, " as they described it.

Sharing a car posed no problem. While working with Rutgers I ordered an Audi, due to arrive soon. So I stayed home plucking weeds, too uptight to sew for my new unborn grandchild, Daniella's baby. Each nasty root I yanked released a tad of my anger. Observing me from her pool, wine glass in hand, Crystal Voice ambled closer.

"Jenny you act as though a load of guilt hangs over you. Is that why you spend so much time on your knees? I keep telling you, have a little wine with me."

Exactly why I loved her, even though I preferred milk and soursop ice cream.

For months Chico brought home invitations from the PDF and I declined going with him. Our bond broken, we had nothing left to talk about. The man I once called my centurion took on the features of a statue carved in stone.

10

KW CONTINENTE RADIO

Tormented by surgeon Hugo Spadafora's beheading, Trinity and classmates at Maria Inmaculada refused to dissect frogs. When they learned the details of the murder committed by the PDF on their friend's father, they compared their biology class to his torture and claimed incapable of doing dissection. Their biology teacher threatened to flunk them, but behind their backs he took pride in their attitude.

Newborn baby Lulu, Trinity's niece, provided a joyful distraction. She adored the child. As soon as Lulu learned to walk, Trinity taught her dancing the folklore swing in a long skirt to the rhythm of accordions and drums. Baby Lulu in her own pink *pollera* skirt found joy in the dance. Auntie's longer and wider skirt twirled and tangled Lulu. They fell, wrapped in the long skirt, rolling on the floor, howling with laughter.

Chico vied for Lulu's attention and pointed out birds in our back yard. Parakeets, bluebirds and ravens flew daily into our yard to eat bananas. Birds twittered happily until one day a raven destroyed the rhythm of the yard and pecked the eyes of a small bird. Lulu was too young to distinguish the savagery. While ravens kept circling above bad ideas brewed below.

One morning in June 1987, while parakeets pecked fruit in our yard, Noriega's riot-control troops brutally attacked unarmed citizens downtown beating many people senseless. Unaware, I stood hanging laundry outside the kitchen. Trinity burst into the kitchen warning me tortillas were burning. Behind her Chico rushed in. I figured he'd come to rescue the burning tortillas but no, he sped towards the miniature TV on the counter.

Blowing on a hot tortilla Trinity had pierced with a fork, she eyed her father.

"You're bleeding Dad."

Paper, stuck to his chin, showed a spot of blood, the dot identified his reason for fuming. Without response he wiggled the antenna and when adjusted, he commented, "Something important must be happening. Neighbor's TV was driving me nuts."

He was correct. The announcer said PDF troops destroyed KW Continente radio station as punishment for broadcasting Colonel Diaz Herrera's confession.

Chico scolded the announcer, "Troops? You must be mistaken. Impossible they'd send troops for such a thing."

He changed channels.

Trinity pointed the fork dangling a piece of tortilla. She aimed the fork at the TV.

"Da-a-a-d, why'd you change it? I wanna hear. He mentioned Spadafora."

But he kept switching channels. Every channel featured Colonel Diaz Herrera, the ex-PDF Chief of Staff, accusing Noriega, his commander, of thievery, murder, corruption and electoral fraud. When Diaz said, "CIA," Chico angered and turned off the TV.

Trinity complained, "Dad! He said Spadafora. I need to know." She walked over and turned the TV back on.

At last, Dr. Hugo Spadafora's beheading had found a mutineer, one within military ranks. Panama's populace went wild. Great crowds surrounded the radio station airing the public confession. TV showed citizen's blood-stained white clothes. Chico had left the room but the horrid sounds coming from the TV brought him back to watch. In front of KW Continente, Doberman, dictator riot control troops, using hoses, beat the crowd of unarmed citizens. Doberman kicked victims lying on the pavement. Their crude black boots, similar to Chico's shiny ones, kicked soft bodies with a vehemence, sickening to behold. More perplexing was the grim reality: those victims were their neighbors. Naively, citizens misunderstood Diaz's mutiny. They mistakenly believed his mutiny signaled an eminent and impending revolt from the entire Panama Defense Force. Not the case.

Diaz Herrera continued speaking to journalists, "Noriega ordered Spadafora's death and conspired with the CIA to kill General Torrijos." (Diaz was Torrijos' cousin)

Chico growled at the image speaking on TV. "You're pissed, Diaz! Sour grapes 'cause Noriega fired you!" Again he turned off the TV and left.

"Mom, is this happening here? In Panama? I can't believe it!"

Before I could answer Trinity, Chico shouted orders from the living room. "Jenny. Feed the birds. Let's go, Trinity. Traffic will be hell."

I followed saying, "Call me," knowing he wouldn't. Standing behind their car, black smoke from the exhaust pipe engulfed me. When it dissipated, a sinister sight appeared: the black mouth of the exhaust resembled the hole of a gun muzzle pointed at me. To my right, tapping on her window glass, Crystal Voice waved, signaling me to enter.

Inside their large living room her husband feuded with the TV announcer. "Diaz thinks we're idiots, believes we'll fight his battle for him."

"Take advantage, Jenny," Crystal Voice said, "The Catholic Church is passing out tickets to heaven now that they joined the Civil Crusade movement with its forty-seven other civic groups. Did you hear about Aurelio Barría, leader of the Crusade? He went to one of those far-away countries to study Gandhi's non-violent resistance techniques."

Her husband interrupted. "Not so. Don't confuse the truth. Barría went to the Phillipines to observe the presidential election." He continued adjusting the TV.

Crystal kept talking, no longer interested in the TV.

"That Barría is brave. He knows Noriega beheaded Spadafora for opening his mouth, then he had Dr. Zúñiga tortured. Now this Barría dares lead a whole crusade against him! Talk about big! You'd think he's Superman!"

Her husband jumped out of his chair. "Watch the screen! Ricardo Arias Calderon is over there. Head of the Christian Democrats."

A tall, thin man in a white shirt struggled with a Doberman who attempted to clobber him with his club.

"That's his wife!" he said.

A soldier pushed a small woman dressed in white. The camera panned another Doberman chasing a Crusader, catching him and clubbing him to the ground where he kicked him with his crude black boots.

Snow covered the TV screen. The husband fussed with the antenna, blaming Noriega for short-circuiting coverage—which was true.

Who taught the Doberman to hate their own people? This was the first thing that popped into my mind when finally recovered from the shock of soldier brutality.

"Jenny, don't take it personally. But . . ." Crystal Voice sighed. "Blame your husband. The US military taught our sons-of-bitches."

"And they armed them," contributed her husband. "Worse though, you and I pay for all their mistresses."

"Shame, I'm too old to be one," said Crystal Voice. She jubilantly added, "I'd love to dress up, waltz into Banco Nacional twice a month and collect a fat check."

As she spoke, her shoulders trembled in a saucy motion while her husband's glance shot poison darts at her.

"Rabble rouser. You'd make a great Crusader. So Doberman can kick you."

She smiled, as though his cruel desire were flattery.

Approaching our front door, I heard our grandmother clock bong sad strokes, the death knell to Panama's civil rights. Before night fell the Civil Crusade had expanded to sixty-four civic groups. Sofia, Trinity and I gathered on the terrace to watch the mournful panorama hang over our city. Homes below bathed in sorrow as columns of black smoke rose from Civil Crusader cars burned by Doberman. Dusk buried a tragic day; the kind one reads about in faraway lands. My consolation was that our family was safe.

Sofia caught the first criticism. It came from fellow bank employees.

"Co-workers asked me if Dad donated the tear gas and Darth Vader uniforms Doberman wear. I said no but called Dad to verify. He said the Doberman buy their own equipment. I asked if he trained 'em. He said no. Some guy from the Mossad did."

"What's the Mossad, Sofia?" Trinity asked.

"Israeli Intelligence. A friend at the bank told how one of the leaders, General Mike Harari, led an Israeli counter-terrorist team to eliminate a Palestinian Assassin gang called Black September Group. They had murdered a bunch of Israeli athletes at the Olympic games in Munich. Way back when I was in grade school."

"So, what does this have to do with us?" Trinity persisted.

I butt in.

"Mike Harari's here. I met him at the Opera with Noriega."

"Shame on you and Dad, Mom." Trinity said, "for hanging out with bad people."

"You're right Trinity. And if guns didn't exist, none of this would be happening."

Sofia and Trinity were learning the ugly traits of politics and tried to find an explanation for such brutality. Sofia, older than her sister, refrained from blaming her parents while Trinity scolded us, hoping to separate us from criminals.

Sofia tried to explain: "Crusaders say our mental health depends on finding reasons for the lunacy our regime soldiers display in their brutality towards us. They say Doberman are drugged. I think it's deeper than that. Their hate comes from their economic status, a situation that makes their lives less wonderful than ours, both socially and economically. Does what I'm saying make sense to you? I'm the one who studied economics."

Chico found us brooding; none of us had the answer. He served his own dinner. No terrible cacophony came from the kitchen; no angry pot lids banged each other. Not Panamanian, he felt no passion for our country's pain nor shared our occasional temperamental outbursts. He came out to sit with us. One lone candle flickered; its frightened quiver matched our mood. Hoping to hear his comments, we stayed while he ate. The phone rang. Trinity answered.

"It's for you Dad. Osvaldo."

What happened to us? All of us forgot about Daniella! Marriage and a child removed her from our sphere of influence and worries.

Chico spoke and upon returning, sat down and put food in his mouth. Candlelight quivered at his detachment. As a foreigner, he lacked our pain. I blew out the candle.

"Did Osvaldo call just to say Hi?" Sofia asked.

He chewed forever then paused to drink water.

"Osvaldo says Daniella hasn't come home from the university." Another pause. "Wants me to go find her. Students are fired up, as always. He's gotta stay with the baby. The maid's gone home."

He ran his hand over his balding head. "Funny, Osvaldo said he wasn't upset, but he sure sounded worried. Told me to hurry."

Sofia and Trinity jumped up, eager to go find their sister. Their father ordered them to stay and me to come with him. I promised to call. The highway, nicknamed Tumba Muerto, for a no-longer-visible gravestone, took us straight into the melee. I shuddered at the thought of Daniella involved in this revolution. She had a baby at home.

"Let's do the rosary, Chico. I'll pray. You listen."

"Not now. Too distracting. I need to watch what's ahead. Help me see."

University campus. Desolate from a distance. Driving closer we saw debris lumped on the road, vestiges of barricades still smoldering. Nobody appeared, as though the battle had ended. Our Toyota inched around a sofa, car tires, a broken toilet, the hood of an auto, and fifty-gallon drums puffing smoke. Our closed windows blocked odors. White sheets of paper lifted and scattered. Student resistance to dictators existed for years, ever since the military usurped power and repressed citizens. Students learned to throw rocks, barricade streets and break things. Students died, others disappeared but the rocks were too small to eliminate armed soldiers. They never perished.

Campus grounds resembled a battle zone. Unnerving. Student's posters showed pineapples with a knife stabbing it. Noriega's nickname, "Pineapple face," irked him so, that students made it their battle cry, *"Cara de Piña*! Leave town!*"

"I hope Daniella doesn't waste her time on this stuff." Chico said.

I pointed out the School of Architecture and mentioned that our daughter's husband participated in student demonstrations when he studied here.

"Park here." I grabbed the door handle to get out.

"You going in there by yourself, Jenny? I'm not leaving this car here."

I got out and listened, heard a thump-thump. My heart pounded. Didn't dare close the door. Stood there, next to the car, needing urgently to hear a friendly sound. For Chico I was taking too long. He said so.

"Chicken. You make a great target standing there."

I slammed the door and instantly wished I hadn't made the noise. Tip-toeing up the steps, I hoped silence emanating from inside the building promised safety. Or was it dangerous as hell? "Daniella?" The thought of her quickened my step.

Inside the cavernous entrance, pitch-black and threatening, silence hung ominous. Had students left already? Fear throbbed in my ears wishing I'd hear something. What now? I called out.

"Daniella!"

A voice hollered back.

"Aim your rocks!"

I dropped to my knees feeling shooting pains. Nothing moved. Any minute lights would flick on. Big target. Me! Doberman would have shot by now. They don't need to throw rocks. CREAK. It came from somewhere nearby. Maybe if they see I'm unarmed. Who sees? Students, I hoped. I stood up and ran. Jumped the front steps in one leap and crashed into the side of the car with palms open. I expected dozens of rocks to hit my spine any moment.

Chico laughed, having a great time. "Coward! I wouldn't want you in my platoon." He kept laughing.

I jumped in the back seat and hollered "GO!" feeling proud to be a coward.

Our car rolled past the law school. Toyota headlights illuminated a disaster: lamppost lights smashed, burning tire barricades puffing smoke and a regime utility truck tipped-upside-down, one wheel still exuding smoke. The initials IRHE identified the state electricity company, detested by all. Government-run, the electrical company charged a fortune per kilowatt making our electricity the most expensive in Central America. No excuse for the price. Water, the main source for providing electricity, flowed in abundance on our isthmus. Dictators robbed us of everything. For this reason our brave students vented their ire with fire.

Ah, but my mate criticized student's actions. "Irresponsible. Destruction of government property."

"You miss the point. They have a right to their opinion. Students learned destruction from tyrants. Keep driving."

My two husbands, one trained to obey and the other to deny.

Cell phones had not entered Panama yet. At midnight we called Osvaldo from a pay phone. He said Daniella had not come home. We could not give up the search for our daughter.

"Jenny, let's check Santo Tomas Hospital."

"The hospital?" His suggestion and nonchalance appalled me.

The hospital was nearby, its environs dimly lit, visibility poor. Our headlights flashed Crusaders limping past, half-dazed; their dirty white clothing spotted with blood. The wounded leaned on each other, inching towards a door below a pale bulb illuminating the emergency sign.

"Jenny, wait here."

His open door brought in suffocating odors of disinfectant mixed with rotten garbage. The thought of Daniella wounded made the stench give me nausea. By the same token I felt proud. Our Crusaders were true heroes, including my daughter Daniella. Rather than stay home and sleep, she risked facing danger, seeking atonement for her parental complicity. Her father's job favored citizens' enemies, but her involvement renewed our family's honor. Would her husband have done this? He often said, "We can't topple Noriega without guns." He was wrong.

While waiting, several Crusaders walked by the car talking. Some sobbed saying their companions from the march were arrested when they arrived inside the hospital. Chico came out, his physique straight and strong, an embarrassing contrast to the tribe of people I belonged to, now maimed by the cutthroats he supported. He opened the door.

"Daniella's not here." He showed no sympathy for Crusader pain.

From home I called Daniella's house. Osvaldo said she came home dirty and went straight to bed without changing. Then he said something perturbing: "She should quit school." Why? I was too exhausted to ask. Nor did I suspect his comment would bring trouble. After all, he studied at the same university and survived. I dreamt about her running through crowds, flames everywhere.

Suspense over Diaz Herrera, mutineer, holding out in his mansion for several days, kept the country on edge awaiting the explosion. One morning, minutes after Chico left for work at the US embassy, Crystal Voice shouted from her terrace while pointing toward the ocean.

"Look Jenny, helicopters attacking Diaz Herrera's house."

Jubilant, she wielded opera glasses and expressed glee over the assault. I still felt sad about the entire situation. Crystal Voice insisted I come over. My view was the same, but I wished to please her and went.

Two helicopters circled in the distance. Dawn's orange sun bathed the choppers turning them ochre transforming them to something surreal. They resembled pterosaurs, prehistoric predators circling their prey.

"Watch what they do to Diaz Herrera. You'll be shocked," said her husband.

Siege to Diaz Herrera's mansion-house lasted days. He had invited priests and friends to stay with him and his family to await the attack. The Panama Defense Force occasionally took pot shots at his compound buildings. We watched, anxious for the culminating finale. Noriega was capable of blowing the ostentatious mansion sky high, hang his former Chief of Staff on the moon. In his underwear.

No such devastation occurred. Not the slightest pretense of hostile fire took place. Instead soldiers rappelled from helicopters, pushed through a window, grabbed trembling

Diaz Herrera and took him to Noriega. We imagined he scolded his mutinous subordinate for being naughty, "Get out of town and never come back." No spanking involved.

"See what I told you?" Crystal Voice's husband said. "You thought they'd cut his head off or at least his balls. Diaz Herrera initiates his mutiny, Crusaders take the beatings and it's the same old story. Criminals seldom punish their own kind. Honor among killers."

11

MARCH

Freedom's voice died for Panamanians in June of 1987. With KW Continente radio destroyed, regime troops attacked and closed all opposition TV and radio stations and dismantled opposition newspaper La Prensa. The country hit bottom.

Civil Crusade leaders reacted. They began their leadership task: getting the news out. No matter how. On-foot and by-hand, news bulletins circulated, distributed by brave young men, the *Canillitas*. They dashed through traffic, their brown legs seen flashing between cars, handing out free information sheets delivering the credo: The Military Must Go!

Wasting no time, Noriega blamed the Civil Crusade for all havoc in the city. A mysterious and clandestine radio station, the voice of freedom, broadcasted the truth and demanded justice and democracy. This voice was silenced.

Calm reinstated itself in our tropical paradise. Superficially. The lull in opposition demonstrations coincided with our twenty-fifth anniversary. Chico bragged to his subordinates, "Jenny and I made history together from day one. Back in October 1962, John F. Kennedy was president and my unit was ordered to prepare for deployment to support the Cuban exiles' invasion of Cuba. We lived at Fort Sherman, Panama, on the Atlantic coast, a jungle warfare training post where ripple-back caiman roamed creeks near our quarters. Alligators wandered around freely. We told our wives to stock up on food and water in case those crazy Russians decided to launch the missiles they posted on Cuba and attack the Panama Canal."

I recalled the grim event. I collected water, filled the bathtub and added my tears, willing to sacrifice to stop Castro. Our brand-new baby Daniella, born at Coco Solo Hospital, cried 'cause her diapers were full. I kept filling pots. When the US backed out of the Bay of Pigs invasion abandoning Cuban exiles to die on the beach, my tears dried up. I learned to distrust politicians and never cry again.

Voices chattered out front; Daniella and Sofia talking. Elated, I thought Daniella had brought precious grandbaby Lulu. Not so. She walked in dressed in lightning white.

"Mom, Sofia and I came to get you. Come on. Change clothes. The Civil Crusade march starts soon. Go put on something white."

Sofia shot past me, announcing she left the bank early to join the march. Stupefied, I wondered aloud when this drastic change took place. My daughters converted into political dissenters? Their father would dislike it.

"Okay. I'll change clothes." Trinity began pulling off her green t-shirt to go.

"Not you, Trinity," Daniella said, "Too dangerous. Mom's different."

"If it's dangerous, why are any of us going?" I asked, deliberately dallying.

"Don't worry. Sis and I will take care of you." Daniella bared her teeth, struck a karate pose, cutting air with her hands. I winced, recalling the night we searched for her at the university. I never asked if she concocted Molotov cocktails. She might say yes.

Sofia came out of her room completely in white insisting: "Mom, what are you waiting for? Change clothes."

Intrepid. The sisters who marched for fun with their school band now intended to march for love of country disregarding danger.

A taxi dropped us off at Via Argentina. Malt aroma wafted from the brewery. To our right Panama's National University stood deceptively tranquil. Student fury had subsided, and those same war-like students now dressed in angelic white. Many mingled in our Crusader crowd, converts to non-violence.

Steeled with determination following the attack by Doberman at the radio station, nobody around us smiled. I was scared and tightened my belt to overcome my fear.

Hundreds more Crusaders in white apparel and waving white handkerchiefs joined our group. We marched toward Via España. Acacia trees divided the double lane; their leaves trembled at the sound of our chanting Crusader Credo, "*Que se vayan!* Get out of town! No more tyranny!"

From high-rise balconies aged residents waved white handkerchiefs and threw kisses. Below them all first floor shops were bolted tight. Strange, why did stores close early on a Friday afternoon? Did they expect trouble? Our white flags stood for peace, and victory, never surrender.

Thousands shouted.

"Out with the military!" And the chant repeated from front to rear of our crowd.

Was I the only one in doubt Crusaders could force the PDF to leave town for fear of our white flags? Could we, the Quijotes of the impossible dream dislodge tyranny by our determination alone? Without a fight? As if answering, megaphones bellowed.

"*Un pueblo unido jamas será vencido;* A people united shall never be defeated."

The statement was the direct opposite of a PDF slogan: divide and you shall conquer. We strolled towards our destination, El Carmen Church. Minutes into our marching a loud sound rumbled our way. Vibrations increased. I looked all around realizing reverberations came from above. Ear shattering.

WHUMP! WHUMP! Stopped our march. The crowd, aghast, stared up at two helicopters hovering, rotor blades slashing at palm fronds.

Shots fired in the midst of terrible noise drowned Crusaders' screams. Confusion and despair took hold. A voice yelled confirming.

"They'll kill us!"

Terrified, I grabbed my girls. People charged in every direction. Crashed into each other. A man next to me yelled, "Doberman! Coming our way! From Via España!"

People panicked, stumbled and fell. We three clutched, hanging onto each other. Marchers searched for a way to escape. Crusaders screamed, "Hide! Run!"

But where? From the crowd a man in white recognized Sofia and tugged on her arm to lead her. She stood firm.

"Wait, Roberto. I can't leave my mother."

She pulled me and Roberto latched onto Daniella. The crowd blocked our way. Shots whizzed above us. White hats flew, rolled underfoot. Desperate, marchers charged at store doors, struggled to twist open the doorknobs. Found them locked. Chaos everywhere and no way to escape. Terrified out of our minds, all screams were lost in the thundering roar from shots and helicopter rotors.

Daniella shouted, "My friend lives over there. Follow me!"

Roberto used his body to push through the frenzied crowd. We reached the alley and climbed stairs. I tripped; nearly fell. Sofia lifted me apologizing.

"Sorry we brought you, Mom."

I recalled her father's teasing: "Youth thinks it's indestructible. That's why we send young soldiers to the front lines. None fear death. But fifty-year-olds aren't fit for war."

Daniella knocked on the door. No answer. She pounded with clenched fists.

"Please. Let us in. It's me. Daniella!"

She turned to us. "She has two little kids. Gotta be there," her eyes showed panic.

A sliver of light ran up the doorjamb. A young woman opened, recognized Daniella and allowed us in. The small living room, packed with Crusaders, smelled of vinegar. Tossed salad? Hardly. Crusaders carried handkerchiefs soaked in vinegar, a lesson learned at KW Continente Radio Station where Doberman attacked with tear gas.

We found a corner and slid down to the floor. The door closed. Heavy drapes plunged the room into darkness. In that room I learned, fear smells of rotting flowers. Someone whispered: "God help us . . ."

I forgot Him when I needed Him most and recalled Padre Durán's words.

"When bad things happen, terror overpowers our senses and prayer escapes us."

He was right. Inside the room was an abyss of darkness. Outside, boots pounded, running past, chasing our fellow Crusaders. We heard horrific sounds. Screams. Cries. Incessant pounding of clubs beating on our march companions. Hearing their suffering made our refuge a hellhole. Doberman shouted, "Stop!" Then more clubs pounded on dense bodies. Defenseless Crusaders.

Doberman barked, "You want us to leave? Take this! You Shitty Crusaders!"

"Civilistas de Mierda!"

Spanish, the language of love, fouled in the mouths of devils. I covered my ears. Sofia rubbed my arm.

Another Doberman yelled, "Grab him!" And many more boots ran, then a scuffle. Again the sound of Doberman clubbing humans caught in their path. Screams of pain, then moans. Inside the room, a woman sobbed, "Please, no more. Don't hurt them anymore."

In the dark someone whimpered, "They're killing them down there."

Daniella gripped my arm. In the dark room, all of us stared at the thin line of light etched around the heavy curtain. The window to death. A door opened, bringing light. Those of us on the floor jumped, frightened. The young apartment owner exited her bedroom carrying a little girl clutching a doll. A barefoot boy followed, tugging at his mother, his other hand in his mouth. He studied us, asking why we were there.

"They're part of a movie cast," the mother said picking her way through Crusaders' feet stretched out on the floor. The boy stopped to study us.

"Mama, I don't see the camera."

Hours passed; at least I thought so. Later, I learned we hid sixty minutes. The apartment owner came out again and opened the door for us to leave. A woman complained.

"How can you send us back out there? Outside is hell."

Her husband hushed the Crusader while helping her rise. The owner continued holding the door ajar, her eyes glued to the floor.

We descended the stairs. Cautiously. At the door to the street the smell of sulfur asphyxiated. Tear gas. We burst into the venomous haze of a tainted afternoon. Via Argentina deserted, and us at the mercy of Doberman. Daniella pulled us uphill towards La Salle High School; a tranquil scene spared the attack. We hurried towards Transisthmian Highway.

Roberto departed. We three alone rushed onto the main artery and scurried past car dealers, Riba Smith Supermarket and Banco Nacional. Only one car had gone by. The soles of my feet burned. I collapsed to the curb. Daniella and Sofia paced back and forth. Nervous and tense, hands on their hips, they flipped their heads around at every sound.

"Please Mom, let's go. We're targets in these white clothes."

We reached the last stretch, Main Street of Bethania, and slowed our pace under the cool, *guayaca*n trees, once famous for their annual yellow blaze of flowers. A TV blared a program in Spanish, canned laughter. It appeared residents knew nothing of the attack, that freedom had been trampled, Crusaders mangled. Not one word on the news that our country fell to tyranny, our liberties destroyed. Affecting everyone.

We trudged uphill to our house and unlocked. The sound of clanking metal brought Chico out.

"You look terrible." His first words.

"What happened?" Trinity walked around us fingering our dirty clothing.

Daniella and Sofia slipped around their father to the kitchen. I followed. We gulped water and went to the terrace to inspect our city under siege. In the distance, smoke spiraled, staining the sky.

Sofia told Trinity, "That black smoke is Crusader cars burned by Doberman."

Chico came up behind me. I stepped aside, uncomfortable with his nearness.

"Don't you see what this could do to me Jenny? I'm about to retire and you're jeopardizing my future in Panama."

"I did what every Panamanian should."

"I have to work with the PDF."

"That was your choice."

Daniella rolled her eyes and left. Her sisters withdrew.

"Jenny, what makes you think the Civil Crusade is any better?"

"They're not in the street shooting people. Your friends are. Five years ago you said you'd change Noriega. Wake up!"

"Are you blaming the US for what's happening?"

"If the shoe fits, wear it."

"Jenny, stay out of it."

"This is my country. You stay out of it."

Without uttering another word I went to shower.

A loud ring woke me. I switched the light on. Midnight. The phone kept ringing.

Chico answered. "*Hola,*" then he listened. "Tagamet?"

He looked at me then turned away talking. "Sorry, I can't do that."

He hung up and went to the toilet. I followed asking who called and why. He answered with a yawn.

"Marie's husband was arrested at the march. She wants me to take ulcer medicine to him at Cárcel Modelo Prison. She should call a priest to do that."

"I'll come with you." I began to change my nightgown.

"I'm not going. That's not my job."

He turned off the light and snored before I finished punching my pillow. We knew the jailed man. I planted thousands of cedar and teak trees on his property for a pilot project intended to prove how easily cedar and teak trees provide substantial income to its investors. Now held prisoner, his wife asked for our help, and we refused.

12

DOBERMAN TAKE MY DAUGHTERS

Saturday, July 11, 1987, most of the population wakened in shock, sad and frightened by the horror of the previous day, Black Friday. Worse yet, we could not imagine the war had only just begun. Otherwise my daughters never would have dared leave home. Sofia and Trinity were driving down Via Brazil to check on their friends from yesterday's march when dictator dogs attacked them. Seeing is believing and since Trinity had not been allowed to march the previous day, the torturous Black Friday, she nagged Sofia so much that sis gave in and off they went. Trinity could not visualize the true meaning of the term Black Friday. Intrigued and only sixteen, she possibly confused it with Halloween and all its witches. Or perhaps she was introduced to horror movies at too young an age when her father took her to see Jaws. It desensitized her. Fact is, she convinced Sofia and off they went.

Trinity tells her story

It's all my fault. I never should have stuck the white flag in the Volvo. And now six Doberman ambushed us and they're taking us prisoners, dragging us somewhere in this damned pickup *chota*. Who knows where.

Six Doberman. Eight of us hardly fit in this awful *chota*. They smell bad. I don't see a way to escape. Every time the truck careens around a corner I bang my head against the metal wall. I'm glad my classmates can't see me. Arrested . . . How embarrassing!

We left home around noon, but it feels like we've already raced through the rest of our lives. We pulled into Hellquarters. My only hope was Dad would be here. He's always here. And to think he's so proud of these men. They fooled him Big Time.

Across the road Cárcel Modelo Prison looked frightening. We knew Crusaders arrested yesterday were getting tortured in there. Sofia's friends called for hours telling about the horror. That's why our phone was cut. And now what will happen to us?

Doberman ordered us to get out. Told us to follow them. My hope of seeing Dad vanished when we didn't see him immediately. He really likes going to Hellquarters. No sign of him, maybe he'll be inside. We went in. Terribly dark. Blurred figures leaned against the wall. When my eyes adjusted, I recognized Crusaders scrunched together, their white clothing dirty. Frightened faces. For sure, I looked the same, but Sofia looked her usual cool, like nothing was wrong, until she whispered something terrifying.

"Don't let anybody separate us." Then I knew she was scared shitless, like me.

A Doberman led us down a dark hall. I imagined the other Crusaders went down the same hall. They probably got interrogated and then paid a fine for marching or some other wild concocted excuse. That's why they were sitting out there waiting. Crazy thoughts ran through my mind, anything to calm my panic.

Doberman stopped and talked to another soldier at a desk. Both looked us up and down, like examining. I felt like our own dogs when we take them to the vet and they pee from fear. Only now everything was backwards. We were the strays Doberman dragged into their pound. I wanted to scream, but no sound came. I grabbed Sofia's hand.

I kept thinking: why doesn't Dad show up now?

Two Doberman led us to a room without windows or chairs except for a camera on a tripod.

Doberman growled, "You! Stand against that wall," and pointed at Sofia.

Doberman snapped a bunch of pictures of her. More than fifty shots. Why so many photos? Those bright lights burn the eyes. She didn't blink or complain. How could she stand it? I couldn't have.

Then Doberman ordered me to stand against the wall. He took more than twenty shots and my eyes burned. My clothing stuck to my skin. My hair itched. Wanted to complain but didn't dare. I saw their rifles leaning against the wall. I couldn't stand it. I yanked off the band holding my ponytail and pulled my hair over my sweaty face.

Doberman got mad and yelled, "Don't do that!"

I ignored him. Left my hair right there. That's when Doberman's fist went up, threatening. He moved closer. I cringed and closed my eyes, expecting the blow.

"Stop! Don't touch her." Sofia screamed.

She kept screaming. So unlike her. You know how she is, Mom. Never yells. Like Dad. But now she kept yelling like she was out-of-her-mind. She ran over and stood smack between us. She had turned red with fury. She's taller, but they had guns. Doberman stepped back. Sizing her up. For sure he planned to hit her. Everything slowed down in front of me. Like in movies when death is coming and the victim knows it. How could I stop them? No way. They were going to kill my sister. Punch her to death or shoot her.

Doberman turned around real slow. Looked at his gun in the corner.

I snapped. Lost my cool. Screamed and couldn't stop.

You demons! I'm gonna tell my father! Tell him how bad you are! He'll punish you for this! Wait and see! You're in big trouble!

Doberman froze. Mouth open. They didn't know who we were. We hadn't told them. To protect Dad. Doberman stepped back. Looked at each other, as if wondering: Who the hell are these women?

Then I knew we'd had it. They'd crack up laughing if I told them Dad's name. Mr. Nice Guy who likes all soldiers. Dad's a real sweet officer.

Not Mom. She'd shoot 'em quick with her pistol she keeps loaded all the time. I've seen her a couple of times chase men with her gun. I didn't dare look at Sofia. She knew Dad well.

Doberman turned and walked over to his rifle. Done. We were dead!

He picked up the gun. I closed my eyes, waited for the bullet. Nothing happened. I peeked and saw Doberman signal the other and the two were out the door. The lock clicked. Didn't dare look at Sofia. Scared she'd be mad at me. She walked over and poked my arm.

"Hey kid, you're really something. I'm proud of you. At least we won't go down like wimps."

I felt worse. I wanted to save us. Not be a dead hero. That sucks.

She made an effort to laugh. Sounded more like one of our dogs choking.

"Trinity, cool it. If they'd wanted to kill us or rape us, they would've by now. They want to terrorize. Let's just hope . . ."

A sound. As if someone were trying the door. Doberman? The key clicked. I grabbed Sofia. Too late to pray. The door opened.

Back home

The phone rang. Sofia? Trinity? I dashed, picked up and heard a hoarse voice, strangely friendly. Not Chico. The caller spoke Spanish.

"*Señora* Stone. This is Colonel Leonidas Macías. I have your daughters in my office."

Macías? I considered him our friend, cooked for him and his wife and flew in a helicopter with them. I pictured Macías smiling—nice, white teeth. I'd fix him.

"Why are they there? Who gave you the right? Good Panamanians don't do these things. You and your men betray the country."

He hushed, breathed into the phone, each breath becoming more agitated, furious. He took an eternity to speak.

"Now I understand why your daughters are revolutionaries." He hung up.

What had I done? Endangered my daughters. I slid down the wall to the floor. Chico was on his way to Hellquarters. I had no way to tell him where to find our girls, or that I chewed out Macías. Damned poisoned tongue.

13

PRISON

Cárcel Modelo Prison, Avenue A, El Chorrillo. Chico went directly there searching for his daughters, to the torture chamber, a Calvary for Civil Crusaders these past days. He ran into a Panama Defense Force lieutenant we knew well as a student at West Point, during the period Chico taught astrophysics there. The lieutenant told Chico Colonel Macías had our daughters, easing his fears. He had worked with Macías, considered him a good man. He ran, hoping to find an apologetic Macías, ashamed of PDF atrocities.

Five long years Chico enjoyed a glorified salute each time he entered Hellquarters. Soldiers addressed him as, *Mi Coronel*. Officers called him *El Chico Grande.* The days of fanfare and salutes ended. Upon arrival a guard blocked his entry, held the rifle high across his chest, as though confronting the enemy. Hands at his side, Stone put his nose smack up to the soldier's snout and ordered.

"*Apártate cabo*; step aside corporal."

Corporal stood firm. Seconds passed—humiliating moments. Chico repeated the order, his voice guttural. From inside Hellquarters a voice boomed with a new honorary title for the US Colonel:

"Let that *Gringo Cabrón* come in."

Later Chico would describe the humiliation he endured as "unbefitting an officer of the US Army. The soldier acted as if I were a lackey."

Betrayal hurts, and worse when it comes from one's colleagues who honored him for many years. Carrying the wound, my Gringo Cabrón husband now demoted to the rank of political pimp, bastard, S.O.B., all the insults defined by the title Gringo Cabrón, ran upstairs to the Chief of Police's office to rescue his daughters.

"Hey, Dad," hissed a voice from the shadows near Macías office. Sofia and Trinity huddled in a corner.

"Wait here," he said, easing their fears while he turned the doorknob, entering unannounced.

Coronel Macías, sitting at his desk, watched Gringo Cabrón come striding in. He had no idea Macias called our home to notify me. Sphinx-faced, Macias showed annoyance over recent events. But Stone had bigger bones to pick.

"Leonidas, why are my daughters here?"

"A white flag was confiscated from their vehicle."

"So what's the offense?"

"I called your wife. She insulted me," he winced, as does one who's been slapped.

"I'm sorry. She's upset. She knew your men took my daughters. Please forgive Jenny. She's hot-headed like most Panamanians."

Coronel Macías did not invite Gringo Cabrón to sit. He left his long-time counterpart standing. Stone inched close to the desk.

"What's happened, Leonidas? You told me the PDF would change. You would permit political parties to exist. The country would move towards democracy. What happened?"

"We believe in democracy."

"Will you hold honest elections next year? Clean elections?"

"Yes." Macías blinked.

Stone leaned on Macías' desk, bent forward getting closer to his face.

"Leonidas, if Christian Democrats win, will you let Arias Calderon take office?"

Macías flipped his chair around, turning his back on Stone to answer him.

"Never! Arias Calderon will never be president."

Arias Calderon, exiled years earlier by the first dictator, Omar Torrijos, was a philosophy teacher and respected political leader who dared challenge military rule.

"Is that your idea of democracy? I had hoped democracy would come from within the military and your troops would return to the barracks, like we've talked about, and exactly what the US agreed upon with Omar Torrijos. What happened?"

Macias spun his chair around.

"Don't kid yourself, Stone! Panama needs a strong arm, especially now. Your Pentagon agrees. Democracy yes, but without losing control."

"You mean by muscling the outcome, like PRI in Mexico. They hold elections but never lose."

"No. I mean a controlled democracy, our kind of democracy." Macías stretched his arms, as if bored with the interchange and tired of listening to the nagging Gringo.

"You're kicking the shit out of Panamanians, your people, and you call that democracy?"

"Wait a minute. Tell me this. Since when did the US care?"

"I'm sorry, Leonidas. Truly sorry I gave you equipment you're using to hurt civilians. They have a right to demonstrate."

Stone stalked out and waved at Sofia and Trinity to follow. At the guard's desk he asked for his Volvo keys. The sergeant snarled.

"Come back later."

Gringo Cabrón slammed his fist on the desk. "I want my car now!"

Without a reply the sergeant left. Sofia and Trinity lost whatever joy came with their father's arrival. They had heard the exchange between their father and Macías and now feared he would become an enemy. Long minutes passed. The sergeant returned, tossed the keys on his desk and sat down. Stone grabbed the keys and charged out without asking where his car was. His girls hustled behind him, nudging each other.

Outside the sisters cautiously glanced around; sunlight was not a bother but the noise was outrageous. The sound was a combination of crashing cans and crude music. The cacophony came from dreaded Cárcel Modelo Prison across the street from Hellquarters.

Sofia whispered, "Do you think the noise is a cover-up for Crusader screams?"

They hurried, sensing piercing eyes watching them from behind tattered curtains. They hustled between ramshackle buildings in Chorrillo, the ghetto surrounding Hellquarters. Residents received crumbs from Hellquarters. These people saw and heard the torture, but overcome by fear, they accepted in silence regime brutality in their neighborhood.

Chico spotted the Volvo and handed the keys to Sofia.

"Go straight home, I'll follow."

His coldness deepened the anguish the girls had endured earlier. They drove home in silence. The Volvo varoomed happily into the driveway, for any mother the sweetest sound in the world, it heralded her daughters' return from terror.

Running out to greet them I saw Sofia's eyes glued to the steering wheel. Trinity stared at the blank wall ahead. Frightened, I wondered if they'd been hurt.

"Are you OK? What happened?"

Neither looked my way. Sofia silently opened the car door and walked past me into the house. Relieved at the sight of them, I followed.

"Please say something."

Sofia turned; her face etched with sadness, she scolded me.

"How could you, Mom? You? Of all people? We could'a been hurt because of you. Yes, because of you.

Macías called you trying to help us. After you scolded him, he threw us out of his office. Then we really got scared."

Trinity walked past me and then came back. I thought she came to hug me, as always. No. She sidled past towards her father who had driven up in the PDF car. He crossed the yard to the rear of the Volvo. She followed and stood observing him inspect damages to the auto. He ignored her.

"Dad? We didn't do anything wrong. Those men are evil."

He hustled around the Volvo, mumbling something about busted headlights, and rearview mirrors. Trinity blocked him.

"So?"

"You're OK. That's what matters." He spoke without removing his eyes from the car. "I'm retiring next month and don't want any trouble with the Panama Defense Force."

Stung, Trinity stomped past me, her expression taut. Red blotches, like hives, marred her cheeks. Nearly out of sight she grumbled, "Wish I could pick my parents."

Following the girls to their bedroom, I apologized from where I stood in the hallway and watched their blue jeans hit the floor. Still wearing prison dirt, they slipped into colorful Guaymi dresses made by the Ngobe Bugle highland Indian women. Similar to the garment Felicidad Noriega wore in Las Vegas years ago. Sofia lay on her bed. Trinity on the window seat examined her toes as if they were wounded.

"Why all those pictures?" she asked Sofia.

I asked what pictures. They ignored me again so I stayed in the hallway, listening.

"Sofi, I hope you're wrong and they don't use all those pictures to identify us. Come after us, like you said."

"Quit worrying. You saw all those Crusaders they arrested. You were phenomenal. You saved us when you yelled out who Dad was. "

"Dad doesn't deserve our protection. We should have screamed who we were right from the beginning."

"Speaking of beginnings, when did you put the white flag in the car?"

"Just before we left. Sorry."

Sofia lay staring at the ceiling. I wished they would scold me more so I could act wounded and enter their room. No luck. Rejected, I went to my room, not knowing how to console my daughters and certain they needed it. I had no idea how. My own mother never gave me attention, or my father. Trinity was the only person who did, hugged me often when she was a child. And now grown up, going through a crisis, she needed me for consolation and affection. I wanted to, but didn't know how.

14

SOLACE

Twenty-four hours after Doberman arrested Trinity, she was still angry at her mother. Unable to sit still, Trinity switched US radio stations and local TV channels from one program to another searching for news of Panama's crisis. Her military roots had been torn to the core. Born in Old Cadet Barracks at the US Military Academy at West Point, she joked being a cadet by proxy. Child of a long gray line of high-ranking officers, she trusted men in uniform. Her unwarranted arrest conflicted with her beliefs, her family image, all trained in the principle of honor. To complicate her sentiments further, she possessed all the mannerisms of a Latina.

She vented her anger directly at the US military TV program announcer on Channel 8, the only US owned channel in Panama.

"Why do you guys pretend nothing's happening here? Whose side are you on?"

Sofia tried using psychology to cheer her.

"Trinity, check out this scenario. The US has powerful telescopes to spy from Ancon Hill. They can see El Chorrillo and Hellquarters, clear as their navel. Yesterday they saw these two women, you and me, dragged into the Doberman's hellhole. Bet'cha they're desperate for details. Let's go over there and clue them in. Come on!"

She stood up to leave and Trinity laughed.

By nightfall Trinity had forgiven her father, but not her mother. While in grade school, he combed her hair into ponytails each morning and took her to horror movies. She received tenderness the rest of us Stone women missed. Mother's duty was disciplinarian: "Eat your broccoli. Brush your teeth." And Mom was in the doghouse.

Worried about our daughters, Crystal Voice brought grizzly details of jailhouse abuse. She told how the military encouraged convicts to abuse and rape prisoners. She mentioned a mutual Crusader friend, the same man whose wife called our home at midnight on Black Friday. She asked Chico to deliver Tagamet ulcer medicine to her husband in Cárcel Modelo. He refused. Desperate to avoid rape by inmates, Tagamet Man pulled a shrewd business deal to save his ass. Robbed of his fancy shoes, he stood barefoot in the filthy cell and watched hardened criminals divide his personal belongings. His belt with the gold buckle, initialed LRH, a convict looped through his own trousers. Another convict slipped on Tagamet's wristwatch. One con emptied his wallet, trashing medical and ID cards and pocketing the money. Next they turned on Tagamet Man for the final piece: prison rape. He talked directly to the crusty one who appeared to be group leader, an inmate they called, Liculí. Tagamet Man convinced Liculí to trust him, promising he'd bail him out if Liculi protected him.

"Check the business cards you threw out, the ones from my wallet. My brother's card is there. He's a lawyer. He'll get you out of here."

Behind Tagamet Man dozens of Civil Crusaders cowered. They scooped shit off the floor and rubbed their clothing and skin with excrement to discourage rapists. Shit dressed their lesions. Blue-green horseflies buzzed at their cuts and foul white clothing. Tagamet's would-be rapists took his word, and sealed the deal with a filthy handshake.

The morning after Doberman arrested them, Sofia asked to skip Sunday Mass.

"I can't go. Today I'll pass out and this time I won't be faking, Mom."

Trinity steamed up. "Only in church. You only have these weak moments in church. I don't wanna' go alone," then she pointed disdainfully at me, "With them."

She added strength to her argument. "Don't make me go alone. Anyway, Sofi, how come you didn't faint when the guy at the golf course stuck a knife in your back? Huh? Please come to church with us."

Walking to church Trinity kept teasing Sofia about wrestling the knifer.

"I don't understand why you returned his knife after you knocked him down. Come on! You had already taken it away! That's dumb. Bet they didn't teach you anything sweet in karate!"

Sofia winced, our brave martial artist who faints in church held her tongue while we entered the chapel.

Padre Durán, son of a marine from Ferrol, Spain, criticized the regime's brutal treatment of citizens. He repeated the need for justice. Mass ended. Holding the chalice, Padre walked past us unaware of Trinity's whisper to her sister. The priests' comments delighted her.

"Dad won't like it. He says priests shouldn't meddle in politics."

At the exit I told Padre of our daughter's arrest. He put his arm around them and questioned Sofia about her job at Citibank. He raised his hand blessing them, then squeezed Trinity's cheek, a gesture she disliked.

"Girls, pray always but never quit struggling to achieve justice. Nothing's automatic."

His statement left me cold. I expected consolation for their arrest, not applause for the dire incident.

"Do you condone civil disobedience, Padre?"

"Jesus was a revolutionary. He advocated justice. Not for a select few. Prayer is essential but action makes the difference. Remember, God does not solve our problems. Justice must be pursued but never with violence."

Padre turned to Chico asking if he saw an effective solution to the military problem. His response bothered me.

"I don't know. The fact is the PDF won't let up. They're trained to stop civil unrest. Do whatever it takes; however necessary."

We stood in awkward silence until another parishioner tapped Padre's shoulder. Chico wore the blasé expression required to deny the obvious, an expression my neighbor labeled: "A face that hides guilt; *Cara de yo no fui.*"

On the way home Trinity kicked pebbles. A loud ping confirmed a stone hit target and bounced off a parked car. Sofia approved the gesture.

"Hey kiddo, Padre's blessings went to your head." She grabbed yellow flowers from the honeysuckle tree, piling them on Trinity's hair. Then she praised the priest.

"Durán's the only priest I trust." Sofia reached for more flowers.

"Where did this distrust for priests come from?" I asked.

"He doesn't spend collection money on fancy chairs for parishioners. I don't exactly enjoy sitting on folding chairs, but I admire his love for the poor. When I was little, Dad used to say we shouldn't give much money 'cause priests stole the collection."

"I said that?" Chico's voice rose to soprano and he stomped off.

We sauntered past Crystal Voice's house, a facade humble as ours with the real mansion hidden inside. Six bathrooms. We had four. And her house had a huge pool. By the time we got home, Chico had changed into shorts and stood munching a peanut-butter sandwich. Criticism directed at him never pierced his armor. Golf bag on his shoulder he mumbled a goodbye.

Next morning, Trinity announced she would skip school. "I have a headache."

Sofia would have none of it.

"You're a hero, kid. Someday teachers will find out we were arrested for carrying a white flag, and they'll reward you, give my sister all A's for the day."

"Betcha some already know. But what if some dumb girl whose father works for Noriega makes fun of me for being arrested?"

"Then you tell Mother Superior. She's tough. She'll stick up for you."

After school, Trinity sashayed into the house, her mood buoyant.

"Nuns are wonderful." She flung the book bag, popped in a cassette to *Amor Verdadero* with Willy Colon singing. Her white knee socks draped around her ankles. She wiggled toward the kitchen, her skirt swishing east and west to Salsa music.

"Nuns were super nice, didn't scold me for having drooping socks. Somebody must'a told them about my arrest 'cause they were all smiling at me. Remember the old nun Nolaska who never laughs? Even she smiled at me. Such great nuns!"

Another privilege we enjoyed were the nearby US military posts. Going there was like entering an oasis. A far cry from the assaults and horrors taking place on the streets of Panama; crimes perpetrated by regime Doberman, especially on 50th street. A US Army post was like being transported by satellite to a world of peace and tranquility. They had a Post Exchange, bowling alley, fifty-meter pool, library, shopette, post office, and golf course. All the best. On the other hand, Panama City life had lost its sweet flavor; even heavenly scents of flowering plants at night vanished. Their sensuous names, "Lady of the night" and "Lusty love" lost their pungent scent, suffocated by tear gas and replaced by terror.

Blaring music vanished from cars, a sign of collective mourning. After dark the Doberman assaulted civilians at bus stops; people wearing white became targets. A fellow parishioner nurse told how nurses and beauty shop operators caught hell. Caregivers had no immunity from beatings and rape. Warned to change into colored clothing, caregivers became obstinate and angry, refused to switch, risking everything.

Friends and neighbors never accused Chico of complicity, at least not to his face. Although they hated the PDF, they respected Chico's loyalty to his job. But they despised the US attitude towards the dictatorship, particularly overt displays of friendship.

Sofia turned informant. At dinner she unloaded bank gossip. Told who got dragged to the airport and deported and who went to jail. Cowardly, we adopted an attitude of tolerance and accepted totalitarianism. We deceived ourselves; tyranny could not last forever and would go away by itself.

These changes happened over time. When peoples' liberties disappear in increments without entirely destroying their status quo, they adjust as we did. So long as an entire street of people are not annihilated in one sweeping blow, humans take comfort in eating breakfast with loved ones and huddling together at night. When the dictatorship deprived us of everything, including electricity, the flicker from a trembling candle took its place. The candle became our faithful beacon.

One drizzly evening Sofia came home angry. She bypassed the stereo and her habit of flipping on salsa music. She yanked the telephone from the wall, threw it down and kicked it.

"All phones in town are tapped. Ours too! Trinity was right. Our bank technicians confirmed it today."

Trinity's nose went up. "I told you so! I pointed out INTEL truck parked at the same pole for weeks. Dad said I see witches everywhere. Just like my grandmother."

The noose tightened, strangulating everyone. The regime prohibited meetings in public places and nobody dared have groups in their houses, unspoken martial law. Crusaders practiced caution, adjusting, never imagining total anarchy loomed. The dictatorship found ways to further drain citizens' finances. They arrested prominent citizens and accused them of being Crusaders. Their relatives were forced to bail them out at enormous cost. The offense was always the same: conspiring against state security. One terminology covered all accusations: sedition.

Sofia joined the vigilante groups. Her classmates from Maria Inmaculada would pick her up. Giggles kept low, their car coasted downhill in neutral, lights off and the radio mute. They found solace in small groups in different homes, all of them childhood friends. Night checks confirmed everyone's safety. Trust united them. If someone disappeared, they mobilized Crusade lawyers. Even so, Crusade supporters were unveiled and deportations and exiles increased.

Trinity and I sought solace by swimming a mile each evening at the US base, Fort Clayton. Driving home one evening, Trinity hung her head out the car window to dry her long hair. Near the exit gate, a line of cars delayed us allowing the opportunity to read a sign propped inches beyond the sentry. In bold letters the sign warned of danger downtown. OFF LIMITS —AVOID 50th STREET.

Trinity took offense to the message.

"See that sign, Mom? On Channel 8 TV news the US never reported when all of us were arrested and dragged to jail for carrying white handkerchiefs. Now look at this! The same people tell us to stay away from downtown. They're hypocrites!"

15

DANTÉ'S INFERNO

Civil Crusaders received a message from Noriega and his cohorts. "Money for friends, beatings for seditious Crusaders and bullets for the enemy." The edict received praise from the military and PRD party followers. Civil Crusaders responded by banging pots, honking car horns and waving white flags, "In-your-face". At designated hours pot banging broadcast citizen's harsh lament. The cacophony threatened to shatter eardrums. Regime threats had increased Crusader unity and fueled non-violent demonstrations.

Critics always exist. Chico labeled Crusaders naïve and meek because they scheduled demonstrations only on weekdays. Come weekends Crusaders relaxed at home or at the beach. Chico voiced his favorite litany. "Candy-ass. You Panamanians are willing to die for your country from Monday to Friday—but never on weekends." Then he added, "If your people want democracy, they better dodge bullets fulltime."

His cruel criticism diminished my desire to cook. One day he asked for tripe, his favorite dish, prepared for him by his Mexican grandmother. "Menudo" they called it.

"OK, I'll fix tripe tomorrow if you take me to 50th Street to watch marchers. Today."

Anxious for tripe, he accepted. On July 2, 1987, he took me to the most important site of the freedom movement: 50th Street, Panama's equivalent to Beverly Hill's Rodeo Drive, a hotspot avenue. Crusaders chose it to demonstrate. One hundred-thirty international banks comprised the financial center and contributed to the prestige of 50th Street. Crusaders felt safe there, a fallacy.

Daily at high noon, Crusaders swarmed the avenue to march. Bank employees and finance center technicians, men and women of all ages and color, wearing sophisticated and fashionable attire, chanted their demand.

"The regime must go! *Que se vayan!*"

Confetti descended like snow from skyscrapers, dousing hundreds of dissenters bellowing in unison. Long strips of white toilet paper streamers festooned the avenue and its reveling Crusaders. For a short while they enjoyed the privilege, deceived by their international high-finance façade of protection from repression. The regime took photos of the festive demonstrations and published them worldwide using the propaganda to show Panamanians enjoying freedom of expression.

Perhaps the regime believed Crusaders would tire of getting sunburned while tromping on cement in high-heeled shoes and office attire and hoped they would quit. They were wrong. Participation grew in number and fame. Doctors in scrubs, teachers, businessmen and the common laborer exploded onto the avenue. Inside regime Hellquarters tempers boiled.

By coincidence we arrived on 50th Street when the pseudo-celebration was about to turn vicious. We parked in front of La Mansión Danté, an establishment owned by relatives of the director of the opposition newspaper La Prensa. To avoid recognition, Chico remained in the car while I joined the crowd waving at the curb. Marchers bathed in white confetti falling from skyscrapers passed in review.

"Noriega get out! *Fuera Noriega!*" Crusaders chanted, assuming themselves safe.

Secretaries in spike heels sashayed in tight, tailored uniforms, performing their saucy catwalk. Businessmen in neckties bellowed, teachers waved, all chanting the slogan rejecting the dictatorship. My head spun with delight, until a piercing female voice hollered my name.

"Jenny, why are you here? You're a Gringa!"

Rita. Her inked roots, Madonna style, plus anger made her appear fierce as a lioness. I mustered a weak smile, hoping she comprehended I shared her anguish and understood the reason for her hostility. Her brave Crusader husband, Alberto Conte, a golfer at Chico's club at Cerro Viento, had been arrested. He accused the PDF of atrocities and they sent him to the penal colony on Coiba Island, a deadly place. Few men returned and Alberto suffered horrible torture. A first-class citizen, his bravery and patriotism cost him dearly. But at this moment his wife had not finished scolding me.

"Don't tell me your husband's here too." Rita said. "Why? He's one of theirs."

She marched off. I watched her backside trudge away fast. Dazed by the insult, I imagined a message came from her physique as she stomped off. Her hips tightened by anger became hard fists. Each fist punched back and forth throwing punches at me. Distraught, I ambled back to the Volvo, blaming Chico for the insult.

"I'm labeled a traitor, because of you."

He stroked his balding head. "Her husband's a nice guy. But Alberto should stick to golf. Not risk his ass playing patriot games."

I stepped inside Danté to browse the lovely clothing. Still disheartened by Rita Conte's admonishment, I went back to the car and must have dozed. Something startled me awake. Chico had slammed the car door. A loud noise coming from underground caused the car to shake. The rumble kept moving in our direction. Two large trucks, military type, pulled up adjacent to us. Armed Doberman in black uniforms jumped out running past us into Danté. Several uniformed men carried large cans. What for? Their haste and suspicious antics frightened me enough for a wild thought to flash through my head. Did the regime send troops to destroy Danté?

I recalled words the dictator's wife, Felicidad, uttered years ago while we shopped in Las Vegas. She had to quit shopping at Danté and missed it. "Danté sells exquisite things," she said. "Shame I had to quit buying there when La Prensa published terrible things about my husband. The owners of the newspaper own the store."

Dictator goons had already destroyed La Prensa newspaper installations. Was Danté next? Frightened, I turned to check why Chico hadn't started the car.

"Let's go! Hurry!"

Our escape was blocked. To our rear cars jockeyed trying to get away. Panicked, I opened my door to get out. He yelled, "Are you nuts? Get back in! You'll be killed!"

A car nearly hit ours when he tried backing up. Screaming citizens ran past us. Soldiers followed. An explosion came from above. Glass from second-floor windows of Danté shattered around our car. Sounding like hale, chunks of glass hit our Volvo. Flames whooshed above our car. Bursts of fire spilled from gaping holes in Danté's windows. Debris rained on us. Smoke enveloped the store and us. Danté's Inferno.

As we pulled away, flames and smoke from Danté consumed elegant men's suits, dresses, cosmetics and European shoes, destroying a first-class store. The regime chose to burn Danté in plain daylight while marchers vociferated their opposition. Regime arson sent another deadly message, one that outdid the previous one: "Money for friends, beatings for seditious Crusaders and bullets for the enemy." They added fire to the mix.

Our Volvo inched through chaos. People stumbled in front of our car trying to escape. We finally reached Via Brazil. Feeling safe I turned to accuse Chico of fiddling with the steering wheel while Danté burned. "Because of you we were nearly killed."

"My fault? Your fault for asking me to bring you."

There we were, nearly victims and I mirrored regime aggression mentality. I fell victim to the regime scheme: divide and you shall conquer.

When the ashes of Danté's Inferno cooled, Crystal Voice came to visit. Like many Crusaders, she worked seditious opposition behind closed doors far and away from fiery scenes. But this time she acted strange, as if something she ate settled wrong. Her usual charm missing, I waited quietly for her to dish out her discontent.

"Jenny, I haven't seen you pluck weeds lately. But I'm sure you have a reason. I came to bring toxic news. The regime is killing us via our stomach."

"How's that?"

"Just what I said. Chico's friends. They're selling us contaminated milk products. Yes. Radioactive. The Panama Defense Force and their cohorts in the PRD party bought Russian toxic milk real cheap. Those cows ate contaminated grass during and after Chernobyl's nuclear breeder explosion. Our neighbors in Central America rejected the cow's milk, same stuff that killed tons of people in Russia. And now Panama consumes it."

She paused to relish my horror and added, "Watch out. I never touch dairy. Who knows how long you and Trinity have been swallowing poison? Only fools drink milk. I prefer wine."

Trinity heard and joined us.

Undaunted, Crystal Voice continued, "Our local scum bags, the military, pulled a double whammy. They make millions and get rid of Crusaders in one quick cash flow."

Satisfied she'd scared us to death, she left.

Trinity rejected the warning. Leaning on my shoulder and pushing me aside at the kitchen sink, she filled a glass of water and rebuffed our neighbor.

"What if it's a lie? A terror tactic like Dad always says? They spread the lie our milk's full of radioactive substances to make us paranoid. Then you and I panic and leave Panama. They'll have the whole country to themselves."

She pulled *Guanabana*, soursop ice cream, from the freezer and heaped a dish, licking the spoon with her eyes closed.

"I'm too hot to quit ice cream."

I never returned to 50th Street, but staunch Civil Crusaders did. By the thousand. Rebellious and fearless, they raced out there, knowing they were targets for killers. Reassessing the tactic utilized to provoke the regime, Crusader's new strategy required a speedy getaway—by car, no longer marching. Not on 50th Street. To avoid tipping off G-2 informants, *sapos,* Crusaders communicated by word-of-mouth. No phones, they were all tapped. Success prompted Crusaders to repeat the seditious act over and over. In response, the regime switched from birdshot to solid slugs, sending their loyal civilian lackeys to infiltrate Crusader auto demonstrations on 50th Street. Driving alongside the Crusaders, civilian traitors shot at them.

A Crusader friend caught a bullet in his foot when the slug penetrated his car door. He didn't quit; dissident to the bone, he returned to 50th Street with his foot heavily bandaged. Many times.

Sadly, I identified one dictator follower, a civilian, who shot unarmed Crusaders from his 4 x 4 Toyota. He was a neighbor. The bilious color of his auto was a dead giveaway. He also belonged to our parish. I never told Padre Durán, fearing he would use the conclusive evidence to reprimand the sniper and use my name as proof. A criminal in saint's clothing, he and his family attended the same Mass I went to every Sunday, at Padre Durán's chapel.

16

TRINITY BATTLES

With Danté's Inferno the regime sent a clear warning: 50th Street was designated a shooting gallery with Crusaders as targets. Equally appalling was Chico's insistence in taking Trinity to survey the former Crusade parade ground during its most dangerous era. Not once, but each time the sophisticated avenue smoldered following a demonstration, they went in the car loaned to him by the PDF. Accustomed to her father taking her to horror movies including "Jaws" when she was a child, she didn't flinch. I stayed home during both encounters.

On 50th Street Trinity crouched as the Toyota zigzagged between fiery barricades. She peeked at Crusaders fleeing, desperately running to escape armed Doberman pursuing them. Nipping at their heels were newsmen and my Stones right behind. Such dangerous evidence of regime criminality should have quelled Trinity's desire to march. The opposite occurred. She figured, "No big deal. It's just another movie. I'm safe."

She became desensitized to danger while Daniella, Sofia and I quit marching.

Our own, Colonel Charles B. Stone, US Army, still marched, but to a different drum—a soldier's dream—the sentimental journey into his last horizon. Retirement. Thirty years of honorable service released him from duty to country to conquering golf courses.

No celebration planned, a perfunctory ceremony took place in the US Ambassador's office at a time when none of our daughters could attend, mid-morning. On the ambassador's office wall hung a portrait of President Ronald Reagan wearing his lop-sided, Hollywood smile and signature red tie. Mr. Ambassador leaned on his billiard-sized mahogany desk, smiling through a bristle-brush moustache that tickled his teeth.

Straight as a sword, Chico stood tall in his tropical green uniform. Mr. Ambassador pinned the Defense Superior Service Medal for career achievements on the puffed-up chest. A dull ceremony, we shook hands with his fellow workers and went home to enjoy cake with our daughters later, with music.

Golf filled Chico's days. Trinity had recovered from the trauma of being arrested by Doberman for waving the white flag. One afternoon she bounced into the kitchen handing me a scrolled-up sheet of paper.

"I found this sheet shoved into the iron loops of our front gate. Our Biology teacher mentioned this march. The Civil Crusade plans to march at San Antonio. I wanna go."

Whoa! March? Instantly my mind pictured a magnet named Flavio. Perhaps her real interest was him, who by coincidence lived at the starting point of the march, Barrio San Antonio. Flavio was special, brought her fat frogs, presents for her biology assignments. He further impressed her by driving many hours to Ocú town to dance with Trinity when she reigned as carnival princess.

For Crusaders, the idol that drew them to march so far out of the city was a priest. Pastor of the church in Barrio San Antonio, Padre David Cosca was young but had already made a name for himself. Though small in stature, the energetic priest loomed gigantic from the pulpit when lashing vituperations at the regime. His invitation stirred spirits all over town. At supermarkets, gas stations and bus stops people whispered, "Padre Cosca . . . March . . . San Antonio."

I dismissed it. Come Sunday as we ambled out of Padre Durán's chapel, Trinity tugged at my sleeve.

"San Antonio march is today Mom. Aren't we going?"

I had quit marching, resisted the idea, but with her sticking close, acting her old self, chummy, and giving me attention again, I wavered about going. While fixing lunch, Trinity hovered near me, insisting. Chico edged sideways through the kitchen carrying his golf bag. It nudged my spine. Ladling hot soup, I offered him a cup. He stopped.

"Hot soup in this heat? I'll never understand you Panamanians."

"Dad, we need to go with you," Trinity said. "Please take us, Dad."

"To play? You wanna' go play golf?"

His excitement and our lack of interest clashed midair.

"Will you drop us off at San Antonio?" My mouth spoke before my mind kicked in. I tripped into the worst calamity ever, as accomplice.

"What for?" His enthusiasm crushed, he lost interest in us.

Bewitched by Trinity's sweetness, my mouth spoke under the influence of love, knowing her interest was not me but her admirer. "There's a march starting at the church there. Padre Cosca will lead. We'll be safe."

"You're coming all the way back to the city marching? Damned far."

"We'll take a bus home," I said.

I succumbed to Trinity's innocence and the contagion of dedicated Crusaders struggling for democracy. White handkerchiefs pitted against guns were an integral part of the national bewitchment. Each time the Civil Crusade said, "Follow Me," echoing the words of Jesus, we obeyed. Some smarty once remarked, "An entire crowd of people cannot hallucinate over the same idea." Wrong! We were living evidence. An entire town hallucinated.

Crusaders decided to change another rule. Broke with the established tradition that Sunday is the day for fun with family and friends. They scheduled a march on Sunday, the day for tilting a beer to the sound of music and relaxation. They tossed out the window the habit, "Never On Sunday," along with the empty beer can. The political situation demanded it; Crusader bewitchment sponsored it, and Chico condoned it by dropping us off at Barrio San Antonio.

White-frocked Crusaders milled around, choking the entrance to San Antonio. The barrio was the opposite of wealth found in 50th Street's business metropolis. Military supporters would certainly stay away. Here lay the sophism: Noriega portrayed himself as devoted to the lower class and pushed the lie that Crusaders were rich whites and not true Panamanians. We all deceived ourselves in different ways. I believed the aura of a Catholic priest leading our non-violent march bestowed the necessary protection to keep the military away. If this were true, why were so many Crusaders sullen-faced?

Fear. Yet more Crusaders kept arriving, hundreds in seditious white. The priest appeared and our crowd cheered, "Padre Cosca!"

His Indian features and Mother Earth complexion conferred distinction on Padre—invested him with the authority necessary to bestow celestial energy into our rebellion. This was the contradiction that left the military statements flat when they broached the subject. They argued racism existed among Panamanians. Our "man of the people," Padre Cosca, initiated a song declaring fraternal love.

"Together as brothers; *Juntos como hermanos.*"

"We the people are at it again," Trinity said sarcastically, not realizing the accuracy of her words, "Look at us, pitting God against the devil."

Her eyes remained glued on the street to Flavio's house, anxious for his tall frame to appear. I felt deserted and wondered why I had come, but shook off doubt to sing along.

Our Crusader horde gulped miles of road as if a banquet awaited us. Past the entrance to Club de Golf where Chico had gone, concrete pavement began to sizzle, tiny coils of heat rising, attempting to escape scorching. To our front the familiar sight of Crusaders in white hats bobbled, resembling a field of cotton. Determined people spurned forth by the body electric.

Trinity suddenly looked peeved, perhaps realizing too late the choice to come was wrong. "Dumb Flavio. He should'a come," she kicked an empty can. "I hate him."

The only way home now was to march—the Crusader way.

Speeding cars blurred going past on the other side of the median en route to Tocumen airport. Several cars slowed; passengers cheered, "We Want Democracy! *Viva la democracia!*" Exhilarated marchers waved white handkerchiefs and threw kisses. We passed an abandoned wood cart piled with gutted coconut shells resembling human skulls. Buzzards circled. We walked faster.

An hour later, thirst strangled us, intensifying our tedious uphill trudge on the last stretch to our destination, the road crossing at San Miguelito. Rocky, harsh terrain on the knoll forbids even the poorest man to build. Alone at the summit, a bust of US President Roosevelt presided over the small park named after him. Climbing closer I detected a strange group in baseball uniforms. Odd—no baseball field existed nearby. Footsore, my thirst and aching feet erased any suspicion of foul play. I craved water. Nor did I sense alarm when four cars arrived. Out climbed men wearing bright shirts and bandanas on their head. Thirst blinded me; we had arrived at our destination. Nearly . . .

Trinity's thirst kept her from spotting Flavio, taller than everyone. Waving his hands above the crowd, the giant sidestepped Crusaders to dash our way hollering.

"*Hola* Trini!"

"Flavio?" Trinity growled, "You think I'm glad to see you? Now?"

He hugged her, sweeping her off the ground. Her feet dangled, doll-like. Suddenly his sweet-apple-pie smile became a grimace, framing his shout.

"Shots! Those are gunshots!"

A slew of firecrackers exploded nearby. Flavio dropped Trinity and yelled.

"Shots! Someone's shooting!"

He grabbed Trinity and stretched out an arm reaching for me.

"No! You're wrong!" I yelled, bravely moving out of his reach. "Can't you tell the difference between firecrackers and . . ."

Just then, another voice yelled my name. Who? Where? The voice called me again, sounded like Chico.

"Jenny! Get down! They're shooting guns!"

Flavio yanked Trinity's hand and ran left away from men in colored shirts charging at us. One headed straight at me, his pistol aimed over my head. Confused, I mistook the man for a Crusader gone crazy from thirst. In a rage, I charged at him yelling, "Put that gun away! Act like a Crusader! Before you ruin everything!"

Chico saw my outburst, grabbed me, pulling us from the gunman's path.

More shots! Nearby! In the mayhem Chico disappeared. Many Crusaders ran past. Wrong direction? No. Down the same hill we had marched up. Flavio pulled Trinity. I followed, perpendicular to fleeing Crusaders.

Ahead the road plunged downhill. Flavio let go of Trinity to scan the scene. We separated. Trinity and I broke away, ran to a tree and wrapped our arms around the only palm tree on the hill. Flavio yelled at us.

"No! Get away from that tree! Hit the ground!"

He bolted back, tore us from the tree and pushed us into the ground. I tasted dirt, salty, needed to spit. Lifting my head I saw feet overhead, running past. Attackers! Shooting started again. Crusaders screamed. Before ducking again I glanced around, looking for Chico. He left no trace. I noticed a thick log nearby. Was the log there before? Thumping feet ran past my head, and finally sounds faded away.

"Let's go! They'll be back." Chico yelled. "It's the Dignity Battalion!"

Where had he been? He stood up. He was the log I had seen. He rushed over and pulled on my shirt. Flavio pulled Trinity. We ran towards an approaching truck that kept coming at us. Men jumped out wielding baseball bats.

"Go, Jenny!" Chico yelled. "Get out'a here!" He pushed, ordering Flavio to take us while he chased after the assailants wielding bats. I stopped to see.

"Colonel Stone," yelled a bearded man. "You shouldn't be here!"

The bearded man jumped back in the truck, and speeding away, left the men with baseball bats to work us over.

A man with a red bandana lunged at Chico, swinging his bat. Chico grabbed the bat. Another man ran from behind swinging a bat at Chico's head. A Crusader in white grabbed the bat swinging at Chico and struggled with the assailant, wrenching it away. The bat-slinging coward ran off. Chico yelled, "Thanks Pierre!" to his rescuer.

Flavio yelled.

"Quick! Run! My car's downhill, around the curve!"

We ran downhill and found a huge blaze engulfing Flavio's car. Flames silhouetted Flavio throwing punches at the air, shouting. "My car! My car! Sons-of-bitches!"

A lame name to describe criminals. The towering inferno burned hotter than hell! But Flavio kept lunging at it. He tried over and over to get close, to rescue his mother's car from the saffron flames. Chico grabbed his arm and said something in his ear. Patted his back as if stroking could console. The two walked away from the inferno with Trinity and me trudging behind, downhill.

Chico urged, "Keep going!" Trotting for a long stretch we saw no cars and worried when the Volvo failed to appear. Further down it stood, dented badly. Chico yelled.

"What the hell? I didn't leave the Volvo over here!"

A man came out of a house nearby saying he'd pushed our car downhill to keep arsonists from burning it.

Trinity yelled, "They smashed all the windows!"

Newspapers protruded from the gas tank and under the hood. Chico removed the evidence. "Shit! They were gonna come back and burn it! Couldn't get the gas out. That man saved it by rolling it away from Flavio's."

As we opened the car doors, crushed glass from shattered windows sprayed us. Shredded glass covered seats. Glass crunched when we sat. We needed to escape, quickly, sitting on glass. The Volvo started. Rolling downhill, the breeze blew more glass into our faces, cutting us. The sensation of Flavio's suffering combined with Trinity's anguish filled the back seat—a melancholy atmosphere detected only at funerals. Sulking, two innocent teenagers caught in an unjust war lost their innocence along with their trust in the human race.

We bypassed the main road and zigzagged through modest residential sectors to avoid meeting Dignity Battalion goons. We paused to ask directions from residents. Curiosity spurned them to step closer to the car and seeing all our windows smashed asked why. Residents had no idea our march was attacked a mile away. The destruction of our car infuriated them. Several raised their fists yelling, "Justice! Justice!"

Sad, we drove in silence the final long stretch.

"Colonel Stone, stop here," Flavio said. "I'll get out here."

Standing in the sunlight Flavio's dark hair, seared by flames, had turned burnt orange. He asked Chico, "What is the Dignity Battalion?"

"Convicts. Murderers. Noriega rounded up delinquents and gave them weapons."

Like a wounded animal returning to its corral, the Volvo gave a roar entering the carport. We drank water as though our mouths burned; nothing assuaged our thirst. Neighbors, seeing the destruction to our elegant car, began coming over.

"Hide your car," said one.

"If they see it like this, they'll take it away," said another.

Chico grumbled. "Nobody's attacking us again. Not while I'm here."

His words startled me. Where else did he expect to be?

Just in case, Trinity and I dragged plywood up from the storeroom. Chico sawed the wood while we held plywood in place. He pounded three-inch nails into raw plywood covering the pretty amber glass panels framing our front door. Plywood: three-quarter inch thick, our shield for stopping bullets. Doubtful, but it gave us the illusion of security, especially for Trinity.

The phone rang. Flavio. He arrived home safely. His mother did not blame him. The phone rang again. Chico answered.

"Hello Pierre. Thank you again. You saved my life. That Dignity Battalion hoodlum would have split my head open. What did you say? No, I didn't see it happen. What's his name?"

Hanging up he said, "That was Pierre, the one who saved me from getting my head cracked with a bat. He says Armando Morán was murdered by the Dignity Battalion. Remember the bearded guy who showed up at the march? The one who brought men wielding baseball bats? He's Lucho Gorilla. One of the leaders of the Dignity Battalion. I know him 'cause he's a PRD legislator. He's bad news. We'll see how he covers up the killing."

Then, as an afterthought he added, "Oh, he also said that truck with the hoodlums tore down the Roosevelt statue and it's disappeared."

Again the phone rang. It was Flavio saying his mother was called and threatened for marching. We could not understand. She hadn't marched. It was Flavio who went to the march with his mother's car and Dignity Battalion goons burned it. The caller threatened to burn her house.

Trinity got upset.

"Burn your house! Your mother didn't even march!" She stuck her head in the corner repeating: "I'm so sorry, Flavio" and hung up. She turned to us; her young eyes lackluster as the pitiful dark holes in the Volvo windows.

I collapsed into the sofa, palms pointed up expecting help from above. Hands, spotted with dried blood but painless. These fingers once cooked for Noriega and massaged his wife's pretty feet; hands made to sew, cook, pray and work hard. But not created to handle brutal repression aimed at my docile people.

17

WAS THAT DENI?

Grotesque, the half-inch-plywood barrier covering the amber glass frame around our front door gave proof of our desperation. Our participation with the Civil Crusader took its toll and the price was high. How can people resist threats of armed attack without resorting to the preposterous? Trinity deemed the barrier security; a phantom to help her believe plywood can stop a 5.62 caliber slug. Not so, but if she thought it did, then ugly was worth tolerating. A gun expert would say three-quarter-inch plywood couldn't stop a projectile similar to the ones used by the Dignity Battalion. Our phone lived in the corner guarded by raw plywood in need of sanding and varnish. And the phone was ringing.

Trinity, faking nonchalance, sauntered over and sat down, leaning against the plywood, her ally. She answered the phone.

"Hi Daniella. Uh-huh, I'm all right," she sighed. "I guess."

Was she? Our backgrounds made us different. Chico never brought a gun home, had no reason to; he had the whole US Army behind him. I grew up with guns; my father obsessed over weapons. A civilian accountant for the Panama Canal Company, he kept an arsenal in the closet at our front door and it reeked of gun oil. He enjoyed hunting duck, deer and wild pig. He belonged to the San Juan Hunt Club. Trinity never saw all those guns. Only one. Mine.

Come nightfall, we ate leftovers. Trinity pushed her spaghetti around, avoiding the tomato sauce. The phone rang; her lackluster greeting quickly switched to panic.

"Mom! Quick! Turn on the TV. Flavio says PRD legislator Lucho Gorilla, the one who brought the villains to beat us up at the march. He's on TV. He's accusing Dad of being a Crusade advisor."

We three crammed in front of our miniature TV to watch the bearded legislator.

"This afternoon, I personally witnessed Colonel Stone from the US Embassy lead Civil Crusaders marchers at San Antonio. Armando Morán died there. Stone is responsible."

"Liar," said Chico, turning off the TV.

The answer to Chico's question as to how Lucho Gorilla planned to hide Morán's murder came across clearly. He hung the corpse on Chico. The accusation killed my sleep.

Next morning, he dropped off the Volvo at a body shop. Retirement robbed him of prestige. Now Mr. Ordinary Guy had to trot or taxi around our hot metropolis. Yet, he was luckier than Padre David Cosca, the leader of our march. His friends snuck him out of Panama overnight, fearing Doberman reprisal. In our ignorance we considered Chico safe, protected by the US Embassy and US troops.

His cutthroat accuser, legislator Lucho Gorilla, made news again when he punched an opposition legislator. He slugged a lawyer, Guillermo (Willy) Cochez, during a national assembly session and it was caught live on TV. Regime maniacs in the PRD could punch opposition legislators at whim. An assault by them went unchallenged; all courts were run by the regime.

Flavio's mother crumbled when Dignity Battalion thugs threatened to burn her house. Terrorized, she spent the night checking windows. Her hyper-vigilance took its toll and she suffered a stroke. Industrious Flavio helped his Mom with expenses. He invented a business. Each dawn he squeezed fresh oranges to sell juice at a men's spa before rushing off for senior class at La Salle High School.

Trinity did the opposite: withdrew from society. She studied late, rejected friends' invitations and seldom spoke.

At dinner one evening she announced: "I've decided to be a butcher and slaughter cows. Slit their throat."

Sofia gagged, concealed it by swallowing water then asked, "What about your dream to dance *pollera* professionally? I like that better. Butchers get bloody. Is it 'cause Mom never buys meat? Want a steak? I'll buy you a big one."

As she left for work at the bank, Sofia gave me money and I went to GAGO for filet mignon, purchasing an entire tenderloin strip. At dinner the girls tore into the steak. We women enjoyed the novelty and overlooked Chico's noticeable lack of hunger.

That night he punched his pillow digging a spot for his head and grumbled.

"I have no future here. I'm PDF's persona non grata."

Nothing I said consoled him but his misery settled in my stomach. Not his. Everything I ate turned acid, while he could eat leather and be fine. Cream of wheat became my steady meal; the only food I tolerated. Discomfort drove me to my knees. I knelt on the hard tile and begged.

"Please God, take my life," then cringed, waiting for the merciful end. Nothing happened. I persisted.

"If you don't take me, please Lord . . . Remove Chico from Panama."

To make certain my plea was heard, I repeated the same litany for days until calm settled on my stomach. I told nobody of my prayer.

Crystal Voice invited me to have green tea. After all these years, she accepted I was no wino. I related how Chico's attitude had affected my digestion. She mused a while before commenting.

"Watch out, neighbor. Confucius said the happiest day in a man's life is when he turns widower."

"Are you sure Confucius said such a cruel thing?"

She rolled her eyes.

"There you go again, Jenny. No wonder your husband complains about your passion for conspiracy. Don't let things get to you, lady."

I could not and continued my routine ignoring her advice. A sad Trinity continued to isolate. Flavio's orange juice business reduced his frequent visits and she stopped smiling. Only when Daniella brought Lulu to visit and they danced and sang did Trinity laugh. Their skirts tangled as they twirled to their favorite folk song, "*Ay Lucy querida*; Oh, dear Lucy" And the accordions whined and drums rolled.

Often, posters publicizing diversions appeared everywhere in town. "Fair," an event orchestrated by PDF civilian lackeys excited Trinity. She already had in mind what she wanted her *pollera*, the typical dress, to look like: fine linen, lace and blue embroidery. We planned to buy one as nice as Sofia's.

We stood in line outside Atlapa Convention Center. The Pacific Ocean splashed behind us. The smell of fish and brine swept over us and other Crusaders standing in line. Persons in front of us talked loud enough for us to hear.

"Do you know why the dictator sponsors these spectacular events? Roman leaders did the same. They distracted their rebellious plebeians by giving them a Circus."

Crusaders still had plenty of fight left in them. They commented that inside the fair we'd see PRD people pretending to be nice citizens. "Tomorrow they'll order Doberman to beat the shit out of us."

Entering Atlapa Hall we left behind a 94-degree temperature. Inside we would enjoy air conditioning set at 74 degrees, an impact comparable to leaving the country. We wandered between hand-carved wood jaguars, ceramic urns and hand-embroidered textiles. Beautiful women in lace and embroidery *pollera* dresses danced on stage, their male partners performing a soft-shoe step as nimbly as a fighting rooster. They twirled. A dancer lifted her *pollera* in one hand and the delicate lace fanned high and wide, its gossamer texture indescribably fine. The sensual rhythm of drums and violins hypnotized us. The regime succeeded in subduing us, the persecuted rabble, with a circus.

Trinity picked a *pollera* in royal blue appliqué. I bought a shorter version of hers in white. She approved, and while driving home fondled mine, made in Guararé. She joked about mine.

"It's too narrow and short to twirl. Where will you go in this?"

I spoke without thinking, "Oh, someday I want to be buried in it."

"Oh M-o-o-o-m," her voice dropped, "How sinister. You ruin everything."

It did not occur to me that I hurt her. My attitude was part of the drama we lived. Everything around us reflected the taint of repression.

We women were lucky; we could enjoy frivolous fancies while poor Chico continued under surveillance. TV stations pursued him for an interview. He refused, knew anything he said would be twisted against him. I forgot about it until the day the chain at the front gate rattled loud. Caught off guard, I went to the door.

Outside the iron gate stood three strangers; primly attired in white shirts. I nearly mistook them for Crusaders until I remembered TV stations wanted Chico's interview. I gave them a courteous hello.

Their curt, non-response, alerted my suspicion.

"*Coronel* Stone?"

The man speaking gave me a stern look. He showed impatience, gave no courteous Panamanian, *Buenos Dias*. His shoe scraped the cement, as would a dog gearing to fight. I scrutinized their white shirts, pleats down the front, all uniformly identical.

"*Coronel* Stone?"

What grated on me was the question mark he hung on my husband's name. A good reason to suspect they worked for DENI, Panama's FBI.

I asked, "Who wants him?"

Stern-face puffed up his chest, "*Coronel* doesn't know us," and turned to his companions for confirmation. They nodded, convincing me these swans in white shirts were impostors, too well rehearsed. Their gestures sent heat waves up my spine. "Why do you want him?"

They turned to each other as if asking: do we need to respond to this woman?

Stern-face pulled on his ear. Another clue, none of them wore a moustache, the symbol most prevalent on Panama's men when I was growing up. When the military took power, civilians changed, removed facial hair hoping to be less noticeable. These three men at my door were clean-shaven.

Stern-face said, "We need to speak to the *Coronel,* invite him to our TV station."

Chico had refused all interviews. Radio and TV were controlled by the regime. All requests for interviews had been by phone. These men were here to muscle him.

"My husband has nothing to say."

One of them had not yet spoken and opened his mouth, "We need to speak directly to your husband."

That was it! I turned in silence, as if going to fetch him and closed the wood door leaving them on the other side of the iron gate. I heard them speaking.

"*Señora*, tell him we'll bring him right back."

How in hell did they know Chico was here? Was their vigilance so astute they knew when he took a shower?

Miserable men! I needed to get rid of them. Now! Before Chico gets out of the shower and pulls rank on me, as always. I felt suffocation. Empty-handed nobody negotiates well. I learned it growing up in Arraijan. My mom forbid me from having girl friends. No choice but to play with boys, my brother and cousins. Fights all the time to wrestle the ball and play first base. Terrible life for a girl, but I never dropped the ball.

Chico and I collided in the hall. Bathed and cool, he smelled of cinnamon. He hugged me, said he heard talking and asked if it was Padre Durán. Urgency gripped me. Fear they'd take him; must do something to stop them. My colonel would never cooperate with me. Never. He was my commander.

My commander asked about the voices at the door, "Who's here?"

"Some guys." The magic word: 'guys'. He lunged towards the front door with me behind. I reached for his hand. He pushed it away and grabbed an iron bar on the gate, shoulders taut, either from tension or whatever. It was me who wanted to barf. Did he know them? No mention.

Stern face lost the supremacy attitude when my gringo appeared. He invited Chico somewhere with the vague excuse, "We need to hear your impression of what happened at Roosevelt statue."

No mention of the TV station.

"Where will you take him?" The strangers and Chico ignored my plea. My commander moved his body in front of me, blocking my view. I poked his ribs.

"Don't worry, Jenny. I know what I'm doing."

Like hell! After all the trouble I had caused him. Not a chance.

Water spots on Chico's t-shirt from the recent shower raised my shackles. Was he sweating from trepidation? Stupid question. Not my soldier. He was a ranger, skydiver, and Psychological Warfare Commander . . . But what if those goons were armed and killed me also?

I charged back inside—to my closet. Groping, I found it, grabbed what I needed and slid the weapon into my skirt pocket; great feature about wide skirts. Holding the piece tight, I ran back to the wood door and stopped. On purpose, I drew the weapon, letting them see my extra-long-barrel-six-gun in full view. Then I walked towards them.

Chico, with his back towards me, had not budged.

What if these men came armed? I'd know soon. Stern face and company dropped their jaws open. Six arms flew straight up. They came unarmed!

"*Vete*! Go!" I yelled. "Get out'a here! Now!" My growl failed, voice squeaked. Damned girlie voice. Nervous, I knew any minute Chico would scold me. Screw up my courage. Try and take my gun away.

Chico hushed. I raised the gun to waist level. Weapon heavy for scrawny arms. The strangers edged backwards, away from the gate. Half-hidden by Stern face, a culprit to his rear spoke.

"*Ey Señora*," both his hands still raised, "Put that thing away. We came to talk."

"Get out of here!" I said.

I knew my weapon well. Hollow bore. Capable of scattering a bear's guts a quarter mile. Ruger six-gun. Once belonged to my brother. Taught me well. Only .22 caliber but the power lies in the hollow-bore bullet. Dynamite. Explodes inside the victim.

Guns make great negotiators! I glanced at Chico, perfectly calm. I switched back to Stern face, thinking: try me! You'll be first. Then I'll drag your body inside. Chico will help. My hand began to tremble. Gun getting heavy. Damned stand-off taking too long. My flabby arm threatened to cramp. Atrophied muscles from washing too many dishes. Now Jenny! I inched the gun around.

Chico's body relaxed, the soldier in him loving a combat situation. I inched closer, his back exuded heat—not from the gun—from having fun! His life was men and guns but never under these circumstances. Not in a million years would he have dreamed—his wife.

"*Vete!* Go!" I shouted to camouflage the tremor in my voice.

Chico still hadn't moved, but his shoulders said it all. They softened with pleasure. Stern face walked backwards, lost his balance, tottered. Then the three ducked into our carport. One shouted from behind our car, "*Vieja de mierda.*"

Me? Old bag? They took off.

Chico, silent and still facing forward, slid both elbows into the space between the iron bars and leaned comfortably. Seconds passed, minutes—a lifetime—he still hadn't turned my way. Water spots on his t-shirt had dried. Lifting his face to view the top of our ficus tree near the curb, his eyes burrowed into the lush green.

"You know, Jenny, we need to trim the top of that tree. It's awfully close to the high tension wires."

Bliss filled the air. I stored the gun and ambled back to the kitchen. My knees flirted with the idea of kneeling, giving thanks. Out of nowhere I coughed. Could not stop. We had survived again and the enormity of it was asphyxiating.

Trinity came home from school. Her smiling father asked about her day.

"Not bad," she said tossing the book bag on the sofa. "Hey Mom, I have some ideas for clown suits for Lulu's birthday. But where are we gonna hide all the cars? You know we can't have cars parked out front. Nobody can. Doberman will come swarming at us thinking we're having a political meeting."

I sighed. If she only knew . . .

18

CORONADO

When foreigners and Panamanians entered DENI installations for questioning, anything could happen to them. Chico knew it and had not thanked me for saving him. At least he could offer to oil my weapon. Soldiers know sweaty hands are death to a barrel's blue. But he did grasp the message sent by the regime. He was a marked man and the visit from DENI was a warning.

Two sorrows darkened our home. Daniella's marriage disintegrated. Months earlier her husband Osvaldo began nagging her to quit school and get a job. The couple attempted counseling. I told her to salvage the marriage however possible for the child's sake. He claimed she partied too much. I heard secondhand that he would disappear from home. Who was right? Either way, I warned, "Don't plan on moving back home."

Arguments continued. The day came when little Lulu sadly lugged her toys across our threshold weeping for Daddy. She and her Mama moved in downstairs, near us but separate, a one-bedroom apartment with a big living room and small kitchen. The design was such that their apartment could view spirals of smoke from cars burning, torched by Doberman on 50th Street.

Often Lulu sobbed, calling for "*Papi.*" She tugged on Daniella to take them home. Lulu quit sobbing soon as Trinity turned on drum and accordion music to dance with her swishing their long, *pollera* skirts.

Chico did not mind his colleagues called him Gringo Cabrón. He claimed his Mexican male relatives were proud to be considered a Cabrón. What saddened him was the treachery to Panama's citizens by those paid to protect everyone. And he had been their adviser.

In the midst of the two sad situations, Trinity came home one afternoon rain-drenched and announcing *fiesta,* "My friends are going to Coronado beach. Can I go?"

"We'll all go," I said. "I'll call Coronado immediately and rent a place." An hour's drive away, the resort sported a golf course for her father's pleasure.

Lulu went to her father's for the weekend, and Daniella came with us. The drive to the beach induced a visual calm: quaint little houses surrounded by chickens, cows and horses shaded by tamarind and mango trees. Children sold scorched cashews at road stands. At Coronado, Daniella dragged us to a party and the cruel reality of politics followed us from the city. Upon entering, the sweet and pungent scent of pineapple greeted us. The centerpiece on the table consisted of two pineapples pierced by a dagger. Unsavory joke. A thought, sounding much like Crystal Voice talking, seemed to coax me: relax woman. Have a drink. Try pineapple with rum.

Trinity asked to go across the street to another party. An hour passed. I worried. Another hour came and went and no Trinity. Alarmed, I went searching for her and while walking past houses overheard a conversation. "Did you know there was a killing last weekend?" Another responded, "Yeah. A PDF soldier shot a guy in the chest for shouting, Pineapple Face, *Cara de Piña.*"

I felt the dagger from the pineapple pierce me and ran down the street calling Trinity. Out of breath, I slowed down and walked for who knows how long. A salty breeze in the dark brought her sweet, melodic voice. Under a dim streetlight her trim silhouette approached.

"Hi, Mom!"

I snapped, furious at her for causing my distress. I lunged, grabbed her arm and punched her frail bicep. My precious girl. She recoiled, astounded by the brutal aggression. I hung on, punched again. Bystanders gasped, probably her friends. Trinity held still, head down, accepting my venom. I humiliated her, destroyed what Doberman and Dignity Battalion hadn't annihilated—her trust.

Damage done, she walked away crushed. Friends huddled around her like young pups eager to lick the wounds of their loved one. Chico stood silent throughout my attack. Nobody rescued Trinity from my unwarranted tirade. Her sisters had been spared such treatment when they were teens, perhaps for lack of war and my torment.

In the car on the way back to Panama silence and sadness impregnated the air. With each curve I sensed their condemnation. For sure she did not deserve such treatment. Once home the three unloaded their bags and disappeared. I hid in a dark corner and grieved over my treachery to my youngest. Chico went to bed. Later when he got up to pee, he interrupted my insomnia. I went after him.

"You should' a stopped me."

Groggy, he slipped past but I followed, needing to hurt him as I ached.

"I should'a taken my gun to the beach. I'd been less worried about her."

He halted, bristling, "You're crazy. Guns never solve anything."

"Look who's talking? You provide guns to my people's enemies. Criminals."

He backed off. I felt better. I scored, hit him where it hurt and forced him to say what he never accepted. Guns ruin everything.

"Jenny, you've lost your head. Maybe it's Noriega who's done this to you. But I warn you, keep up this Crusade stuff and his men, as Panamanian as you are, will come here. Shoot you with your own gun. Everybody thinks they're right. Look where you've ended up, fixated on guns."

The war had shifted. Now we were enemies. I lay down. For a long time his words buzzed around my head, menacing: "Shoot you with your own gun."

Tired, I got up. Cool tiles licked my warm feet. Sticking my hand deep in the closet I pulled out the Ruger. Always loaded. I pointed the long barrel straight down. The time had come—awful. I headed back to the bedroom. In the dim moonlight I contemplated my husband's sleeping profile at peace. The big nose; open mouth. Sound asleep. I stepped closer. His bed squeaked. Did he hear me? See me? I whisked away. Swallowed by the dark tunnel of our long hallway, I ran.

"Where are you going?"

"Go back to sleep, man. I'm going for milk."

Before I could turn the corner, he flicked the light on. He saw my weapon.

"Stop right there, Jenny. Where are you going with that gun?"

I rushed into the kitchen and switched on the light, he was close behind. I knew he'd never come near a loaded gun, especially in my hands. I opened the garbage container and pointed the muzzle into the center. Pulled out the cylinder pin, rotated the cylinder, hearing the sweet clicking as it turned and each bullet dropped into the trash. Six slugs. They slid, disappearing into the kitchen garbage. Twenty-five years I kept this gun loaded in the house. It protected us four women when he was gone.

"Why are you doing this?"

"My life and Trinity's are ruined. All you care about is the military."

My words sounded hollow, same as our lives in the hands of a destructive regime. I grabbed two plastic bags and placed the cylinder in one bag and the mainframe of the pistol in the other, separating the six-gun so nobody could reassemble it again. Ever.

Turning off the light I left the kitchen. He followed. I forced him to think, get upset and call me crazy. If such were the case, why didn't he fear I'd shoot him? In bed I sulked for having trashed my deceased brother's gun. My only sibling, dead at twenty-one in a plane crash at Rio Hato. He burned fatally. His friends called him Pooky. Trinity looked exactly like him: same lips and sharp nose. Both individuals sweet as honey to me and I rewarded Trinity horribly.

Confirmed. Justice must begin at home. If not, where does one find it?

19

DARK

My nuclear family boycotted me for hitting Trinity, and rightly so. Innocent, she acted like a typical teenager, testing her independence. Her favorite friend, Flavio, was shipped out by his parents soon after Dignity Battalion goons torched his mother's car. No small wonder Trinity hungered to be a butcher. The menu inside and outside her home consisted of gore.

Shame drove me to hide under the dense canopy of banana and mango trees I had planted in our back yard the year the first dictator died. Hummingbirds zipped straight for the bird of paradise flower, *heliconia*, to drain flower's sweet syrup. Periodically, they twitched my hair. I reminded them, "Those *heliconias* you suck I planted for you."

My mother's generation considered trees their enemy and axed them with a passion. To counteract the damage I volunteered in our parish to promote agro-forestry in the hinterland and took Trinity. Barefoot, we waded across the river slipping on slimy rocks at Rio Pacora. I chatted with subsistence farmers trying to convince them to preserve trees alongside their tobacco crop. Trinity complained but never quit coming. And I had rewarded her violently.

Padre Durán noticed her deep sorrow. He chose her and five others from thirty students in confirmation class to work alongside the poor. They carried rocks and sand for nearly a week in El Salao, a community so rural that only a dirt road accessed the families established there. Trinity accomplished her chores without hesitation, but shunned the outhouse and ended up constipated.

Returning from camp Trinity was still sullen and Sofia noticed it. She brought home fresh coconuts and they sat on the terrace sipping with straws, sucking juice directly from the husk. The noisy sound of air sucking and Sofia's jokes made them laugh and Trinity loosened up.

"Sofi, do you think Flavio was shipped out 'cause of me?"

"Course not. He went all the way to Japan to study how to make sushi. When he comes back he'll serve us."

Trinity laughed. But Sofia had other plans and stood up.

"Just a minute," and returned jingling keys to her new sports car. "Here," she tossed the keys. "Drive carefully."

Trinity gaped at the keys to Sofia's new sports car. Soon as she bought it to drive to work at Citibank, Trinity dubbed it, "Batmobile." Now she caressed the keys as one does a strand of Mikimoto pearls. "Wait till my friends see me."

Sunday arrived. Lulu went to her father's and Daniella came upstairs midmorning wearing a jacket. Her apartment had solid glass windows making it impossible to live without air conditioning. So she froze and had to wear a jacket. Her hands cuddled a cup she carried upstairs, most likely hot coffee. Sitting uncurling her cold toes she watched blue birds dart to the feeder where her father set out bananas each morning.

"How's it going dear?" I dared call out from the kitchen, knowing my daughters still resented me for hitting Trinity. I pursued. "Sell any cars this week?" Her part-time job selling cars forced her to attend night school; exactly what Osvaldo wanted while they were married. She removed her coat, warmed up by our sultry equatorial heat.

"Life is unfair. I make money at the expense of Crusader misery. Doberman burn their cars and I sell them a new one. Worse still, my classmate in architectural drawing got hit with birdshot in both eyes. Doberman were hiding when the kid hung a dummy of Noriega on campus. They shot him for that! Now he's blind."

Feeling her sorrow and yearning to improve my image with my girls for what I did to Trinity, I decided on the spot to do something big for the blinded student and me. I blurted, "There's a Civil Crusade march at San Miguelito. Can I borrow your car?"

For the first time since I hit Trinity, Daniella smiled at me, a gift I did not deserve.

"You're going to the march?"

I nodded in confirmation.

"OK," she said. "I'll have a classmate pick me up. Need to work on a design project together anyhow. Mom, don't forget; take the Crusade paraphernalia out of the trunk."

I hurried away hollering, "I'll do better. I'll switch license plates."

Our Audi plates came with a 26 prefix—different from cars owned by locals. Marked for quick identification by the regime, all diplomats and military of foreign countries stationed here had distinctive plates. My reason not to take the Audi to a march. Daniella's car was registered in Arraijan with local license plate numbers. She had lived there making it easy for the regime eye to overlook the car.

Wielding a wrench, I sprayed the rusty screws of the Audi license plates with WD40. Nearly finished, I caught a glimpse of Trinity waltzing home from visiting her favorite friend, the Chinese girl who lived up the street. She snubbed me and went inside to talk to Daniella. Suddenly she came running back outside, agitated about something.

"Daniella says you're going to the march!" her first words to me since I hit her.

"Uh-huh." I wiped a puddle of WD40 from the garage tiles.

"Why are you doing this terrible thing, Mom? It's suicide."

I dropped the wrench, mumbling, "I never liked men's tools. Only my gun."

I continued listening, loving her raging over my safety.

"I'll be fine, Trinity. Thousands of Crusaders will be there."

"Why? We were nearly killed there! Same area! Don't go!"

I concentrated on bolts, Trinity's shrill voice music to my ears. I crossed the yard to Daniella's Datsun parked at the curb and switched plates. Trinity watched, pleading. I went inside to change clothing with her on my heels, heckling me, a heavenly sound.

"Mom, I'm going, too. You cannot go alone. Too dangerous."

"No. You said it yourself. Too dangerous. Good reason for you to stay home."

Wearing white, the regime's nemesis, I tried to sit on the bed and put on sneakers. Trinity blocked me. Everywhere I moved she was there, threatening to go with me.

"I'm not letting you go." Then she disappeared. I quickly donned sneakers, headed for the hallway and found her blocking my exit. Hands up and arms stretched to reach the doorjamb; she resembled Spider Girl. Her face flushed from pressing her hands hard against the doorjamb.

I asked her to move. She frowned.

"Little girl, I'm going 'cause I love you. My mother's generation should have stopped the first dictator, Omar Torrijos."

Holding tight to the doorjamb, her armpits vulnerable, I tickled her. She folded and I ran to Daniella's Datsun. Too late she grabbed the car door handle I had already locked. The car rolled, she tugged at the door and then chased alongside the auto, her face distressed. Soon she fell behind. Through the rearview mirror, I saw her stare in my direction, hands covering her mouth. Then she looked up at the sky and did something strange: shaking a clenched fist she threw a punch at heaven. She blamed the wrong entity.

20

SAN MIGUELITO

En route to San Miguelito traffic was light. It gave me pause to ponder the gift of forgiveness. Could Trinity bridge the gap in the complicated process of forgiveness? I aimed Daniella's Datsun towards my goal, the march in San Miguelito, a home to a million people. Passing USMA, the Catholic University, next Machetazo Department store with its machete-slashed prices, I turned onto the Transisthmian Highway. Lined with low-income houses and robbed of trees, the road unfolded onto a barren gray strip, so different from the tree-lined boulevards of my childhood where trees formed a canopy as their branches interlocked over the roads.

Light rain smeared dust on the windshield and fuzzed the true picture, tricking my eyesight. Moving in my direction a blurred, enormous blob of gray emerged. A moveable mass of Crusaders. Marchers dressed in white created an illusion—a band of ghosts. Ominous. I turned on the windshield wipers and the image dulled more.

Narrow shoulders on the road forced me to park the Datsun halfway into a ditch. I joined the marchers chanting a hoarse refrain, "Tyranny Must Go." Their voices sounded like someone who has cried much. Missing was the effervescence of our first march with journalists conducting interviews and photographers clicking pictures. None today. Many journalists had been threatened and beaten, others deported. Also absent was the usual male majority. Doberman beatings and arrests had knocked men out of circulation, some permanently.

Women wore sullen faces. Anger resonated from them. With a vengeance they waved white handkerchiefs. These stubborn women came wearing their best threads for San

Miguelito. To my front a woman's rhinestone pockets sparkled with every step.

A man wobbled between crutches, precarious, but he came well accompanied. Women in white marched on either side. More women marched behind him. Next to them a women's foursome waved white hankies with a ferocity that could only be rooted in fear.

I joined a group and they read my thoughts as to where our leaders were. They said in chorus: "Our leaders are up front." I verified. They were there, walking tall.

Crusade march leaders set the tone, roaring *"JUSTICIA!* Democracy Now!"

For sure love of country propelled them to march at such great risk. In my case Daniella's sorrow for a classmate blinded by Doberman birdshot motivated me. This march commemorated a hero, Hugo Spadafora, surgeon, guerilla doctor, liberator and martyr par excellence. His ideals and actions infuriated the dictator and for this he was tortured and decapitated by Noriega's troops. To my front the leaders continued yelling.

"JUSTICIA!"

I recognized march leaders: Carlos Iván Zúñiga, Andrés Culiolis Bayard, Ricardo Arias Calderón, Guillermo "Willy" Cochéz, Bruno Bemporad, Winston Spadafora, Delfin del Busto and Carlos Efraín Guzmán Baúles. All of them Civil Crusade leaders and Christian Democrat Party officials. Brave men clubbed by Doberman in the past came unarmed as always. Fear never stopped them.

Missing at this march were onlookers. In past marches they cheered us on, gave us vitality and courage and offered us water. At barrio San Antonio a resident came by toting a pitcher of juice full of ice. My thirst craved some but I didn't dare, not knowing who she was. Here, closed windows and roadside kiosks presaged trouble. Why were beer sale kiosks closed? Why weren't the men dancing in the doorway hugging a baby? As they often did. Or cuddling a cold beer; but dancing all the same. Where was the ever-present loud salsa music, especially on Sunday?

We marched past one of the famous Blue Bird busses, 'Red Devils,' parked on the roadside dazzling with bright hand-painted artwork. One portrait in particular on the rear door of a bus caught my eye, the torso of a bearded young man. Its script, *Corazón de Jesús*, identified Him. Magnetic eyes, long hair draped over his white robe; his fine hand pointed to his bleeding heart. His doe eyes followed us with concerned tenderness.

The heavenly gaze soothing me was interrupted by a masculine voice yelling my name. Demanding. "Jenny! Jenny!"

The voice sounded like my husband. Here? Why? Where? Again he yelled. Closer. But in the crowd I saw only women. Seconds later he charged straight at me, pushing.

"Jenny, we're leaving! Right now! Trouble's coming! Let's go!"

"How'd you know I was here?"

"Trinity. She's upset. Gotta get out of here! Let's go!"

Crusaders marched past frowning at the sight of a man pulling my arm. I could not understand why he was acting so strange. I shook loose, ran back into the march and got between two women. Turning back, I saw Chico scrutinizing the environs. Looking left and right, searching for something or someone. He yelled.

"Please, Jenny, please. Let's go." His sudden plea was incompatible with the man.

A shot rang! BANG! Then another, as if ordered by Chico to impress me.

He hollered, "Holy shit! It's too late! They're here!" And pulled my arm.

Women screamed and ran in every direction. More shots. No guns visible anywhere. Marchers howled, tripped and crawled over each other. Women grabbed their heads as if hands can protect from a bullet.

Male voices screamed from up front, "They shot Carlos!"

Another voice yelled, "He's dead!"

We couldn't see what was happening up front. We ran away from them. Chaos. People crashed into us. The man on crutches fell. His companions helped him up. Behind us cars honked, trying to get through.

Chico pulled me and bulldozed through the crowd. What if he hadn't come? We plowed through panicked Crusaders scrambling to get away.

More shots! Confusion! Terror! Marchers crazed and desperate to escape.

Chico had not stopped looking around. For what?

"Where's your car, Jenny? Where'd you park? We'll go in your car. I'll leave the rented one here."

I pointed in the direction of the ditch where the Datsun was parked. We ran, stumbling over rocks, leaving marchers screams and shouts in the distance. We reached the car. I threw him the keys. They fell. He scratched gravel till he found them. Finally we were inside and safe. We pulled onto the road but cars blocked us.

"Honk!" I yelled.

In the seconds we delayed, most Crusaders disappeared. We had been left alone. I shoved my palms into the dashboard as if to help push the car, yelling, "GO!" He nailed his eyes ahead and suddenly released the steering wheel. The car stopped moving.

"We've had it, Jenny."

I looked up front and saw what terrified him. Four men in street clothes armed with shotguns and pistols strode our way. Sauntering they came, owners of the road. They came directly at us, blocking our escape. Chico studied them.

"Dignity Battalion. I knew they'd come."

His voice changed, now tender, sounded lost.

"I'm sorry, Jenny."

They came straight at us. The apocalypse four. Three feet from the car, two of them lifted their rifles and lunged, gun butts aimed at the windshield. The impact burst the glass in front of me! Exploding glass flew in my mouth, nostrils, and hair. I closed my eyes in time and spit glass.

Another gun butt pounded the window on my right; it exploded next to my ear. Deafening.

Crash! They attacked the rear window, several gun butts at once. The explosion was horrendous. Then another. I screamed but heard nothing. A blanket of shattered glass covered me.

I turned to grab Chico. He sat stiff, hands down as though dead. I touched him and he blinked, a sign he was alive. Then I saw why he didn't move. A pistol pointed at his head, inches from his left ear. My mind screamed again but I heard nothing. I read his attackers lips: "Gringo. *Bájate del carro*! Get out of the car!"

He obeyed immediately. I turned to get out but couldn't. The muzzle of a shotgun blocked my exit. The gunman pointing the shotgun at my stomach had opened my door but I never heard it. He ordered me to get out but kept the gun against my stomach. I was stuck. He inched back and waving the barrel signaled me to get out. Then, as if unaware of what he did, he put the gun right back, nearly poking me. Was that his intention? Shoot me in the gut. Whether he was cynic, drugged, stupid or all three, I had no idea.

Finally, my assailant's shotgun backed off and I got out. What a horrid sight! The gunman's pale blue shirt was blood-splattered and his eyes spacey. My ears popped and I heard sounds. Slurred voices came from Chico's side of the car. He spoke Spanish to his gunman, broken pronunciation.

"Crusaders have a right to march and demand democracy."

What gall. Fine time to proselytize the killer holding him at gunpoint. Gunman lowered the pistol he had pointing at Chico. But my gunman kept the shotgun on me close to my stomach. He backed up slightly. I slid out of the car and deliberately dropped to the ground hoping he'd move. Face down; pebbles stabbed my cheek. Inches from my gunman's shoe, I tasted dirt, just like at San Antonio. With luck my gunman would tire of the slob on the ground and abandon me.

Noise came from Chico's direction. Gunman's black shoe moved away from my nose. He too was interested in the scuffle of footsteps crushing pebbles and approaching the rear of the car.

"Gringo, open the trunk."

Aeei! The trunk! I needed to get up. Daniella warned me to remove Crusader paraphernalia from the trunk, and it was still there. Gunmen would think we were Crusade organizers. Shoot us for sure. Chico kept talking, calmly. Unbearable calm.

"I love Panama. That's why I married a Panamanian."

Disaster! How could I stop them from opening the trunk? I rose to my knees and again the gunman aimed his shotgun at me. I heard a woman's voice. The woman begged. Where was she? She begged for mercy. Who was that woman? Sounded like my voice. Was it? Yes! It was my voice!

"Please. I beg you. In the name of God, please don't kill us," I repeated.

All hell broke loose. The leader gunman, the one at the trunk with Chico, slammed the trunk without looking inside and barked, ticked off. "Who put that woman on her knees? Get her up! Right now!"

My personal gunman nudged my shoulder, this time with his hand, not the gun. I felt two eyes burn the side of my head and sensed it was the leader. I needed to see his face and rose to peek. Not the face of a killer. What does a killer look like? This one had gray curly sideburns as gray as his moustache. He had a soft expression like Chico's. Both matched my neighbor's description of military men— face of innocence, guileless. And I got this other one: a bloodstained louse pointing a gun at me as if I was his prize. He'd been scolded for it and still had the bead on me. Wacko!

"Get out of here, Gringo. Go!"

The leader pointed his pistol up the desolate road towards town indicating we were to go on foot. No sign of other Crusaders. The Don Quijotes vanished leaving us.

I stumbled towards Chico. He took off, me behind. Not a leaf moved. We had ventured about three minutes when behind us a car door slammed. Daniella's car?

"Hurry Jenny," again he took off fast. I tried to keep up. Further on, Daniella's Datsun drove past us, turned left and disappeared down a dirt road. We walked past the spot and caught a glimpse of her auto behind a high dirt mound.

"You're too slow, Jenny!"

He moved fast again. I skipped, ran between gasps, not catching up. My chest heaved. I wanted my husband to walk behind me. Shield my back. No chance Jenny. This is not a country walk. Men watch out for themselves; cover their ass. Even if the cover-shield happens to be their wife.

"Slow down," I yelled, needing Chico to pull me. About to die, I wanted to catch up with my mate, hold his hand or at least keep up with his flaccid fanny and thick heavy legs. It should have been easy. I was light, but unfortunately, untrained. He ran miles in heavy boots and now my man left me behind.

"Keep moving!"

Was that all I deserved? Ribs aching, I saw white spots. Suddenly, an explosion burst from where our daughter's car disappeared. Flames shot straight up, then billowing smoke. The Datsun!

Chico looked back and yelled, "Jenny run!" and charged off. A heavy feather moving further away. I alternated skipping, then running. Every breath hurt. Finally I gave up, slowed down, and then staggered. He got further ahead, then stopped, turned, and barked for me to keep moving. He probably thought if he slowed down, I'd quit moving. Exactly. Damn soldier.

I wanted to hold his hand and apologize for getting us here. But he was far ahead. Forlorn by his abandon, I ignored a strange sound. "Psst." Then heard it again and looked around. Did somebody call me? On either side of the road stood a few humble houses, but doors were closed. I saw no owners. How sad, these people were the reason I came and now I was in trouble for it. Did I hear a door slam?

Chico yelled, "Hurry up!" I bolted. He finally decided to wait for me, probably heard the same sound and thought we'd be ambushed. Again.

A voice called out. Subtle, at first. Then came a shout. A man yelled in Spanish.

"*Oye! Vengan aca!* Hey! Get over here. They'll return. Shoot you in the back."

Chico rushed in the direction of a ramshackle dwelling where a man stood in the shadows. The man waved. "Come! Hurry!"

I hurried towards the stranger; his smile eased my fear. He held the door to his house open, shooing us in.

"Quick! Get inside. Those killers won't find you here."

We obeyed and entered. He nodded to a woman, must have been his wife. Her smile said welcome. She reclined in a hammock nursing a baby. One brown breast lay over the closed eye of the infant. Behind her hung a thin, multi-colored curtain held by a string, sagging across an open doorway. No other door.

Absorbed by their game, three small boys sat on the cement floor playing with Speed Racers. Teasing each other they ignored us. A window opened to the highway we had just left. The scene of the battle. A scent of sweet, ripe mangoes came from a container under the table. The woman ordered someone to bring a chair. I scanned the room. Barren. A small TV on the only stool. The man pushed the thin curtain aside and came back with a chair and offered it to me. I sat and felt aching bones.

Two thin girls giggled near the window; one leaned against the sink chopping yucca roots and the other stirred the pot on the stove. Their lives thrived while war raged outside. A sweet existence went unperturbed by vicious politics nearby. One girl poked her elbow into the other and used her knife to point at my dirty white clothing. I wanted to ask the girls what grade they were in. Tell them all of my girls had gone to María Inmaculada. My tongue parched, I could not speak. The girls kept staring. The mother also appraised me, perhaps wondered why I was filthy. Chico conversed with the father about the hostilities outside.

The mother ordered the girls to bring me water.

Water. I guzzled and when the glass emptied, I marveled at the greatness of water and sadly recognized the inadequacy of its protection. Chico's eyes swallowed the empty glass. A gush of water from the faucet resonated. A girl asked me if I desired more. I smiled and it hurt where my cheek burned from its harsh encounter with pebbles on the road.

The men's conversation gravitated towards a shameful subject. Our hero spoke of the abuse by the military if residents refused to heed their dictates.

"Wearing a white shirt around here would be crazy. Suicidal."

He reminded me of my motives for being here and the bumpy path that led me. Absent was the cheer from the residents I came to be with. Mistakenly, I thought they had abandoned us, the people of San Miguelito. While we marched, their doors were closed and nobody cheered us at the onset. They hid, same as our rescuer's family hid, wanting to escape Dignity Battalion repression. As he spoke, he became incensed.

"Those goons with guns are encouraged by their mayor, Babylon Herras."

Apart from having our daughter's car burned, we were rewarded for coming to San Miguelito. A family with few assets gave us more than money can buy. Their gift was a great sacrifice. They jeopardized their lives to save ours.

21

DANIELLA'S TURN

Our hero from San Miguelito drove us home in his dilapidated truck. It shook, rattled and rolled. Busted sharp springs in the seat poked me. I squirmed, grateful we were alive, thanks to him and his family for rescuing us. They put their lives in danger. He ragged on about the regime leaders controlling his area.

"Our barrio is the Dignity Battalion base. Those two, Gorilla and Babylon, know most San Miguelito residents dislike them, but you think they care? We don't march, but they punish us to keep us scared." He returned his eyes to the road enjoying his captive audience. "Hey, you Crusaders are brave. You make me proud." He slapped the steering then returned his eyes to the road missing Chico's expression of disdain for being called a Crusader. Our rescuer was the real hero, regardless of his driving habits. He went on.

"Look at me, I solder iron doors, window bars, whatever people want. You saw my living conditions. The military rips off all my profits. They call it protection. Everybody who has a business out where I live gets the same raw deal. It's hell. Damned bloodsuckers."

The rattling truck pulled up in front of our house. We got out and Chico handed our hero fifty dollars. He stepped away from the money and raised his arms in a gesture of surrender.

"No, you Crusaders are my friends." He wished us luck not noticing Chico's shock at being called a Crusader. Twice. Our rescuer left.

Shattered glass inside my clothing cut, making me miserable. I thought of Daniella and her reaction when we tell her they burned her car. As Chico unlocked the iron gate, he thanked me. "You saved our lives. I could never beg."

Stepping out of the shower I heard Daniella's voice out front. Vibrant and eager she shouted, "Anybody home?"

She must have noticed her car wasn't parked on the front curb and thought I was still gone. She had no inkling.

I hurried out and observed her outside the iron gate digging in her purse for keys. Usually, I'd grab the key hooked on the doorframe and rush to open. This time I waited, indulging in her temporary bliss, unaware her car was burned. Chico walked up behind me, my skin heated up from his closeness. He also needed a cold shower to get rid of the fire and heat from our heinous attack. Daniella saw us and smiled.

"Thank God you're safe! Trinity told me Dad went to rescue you, Mom. Did you hear someone was shot? You're lucky!"

Lucky? Perhaps. Our rescuer said the villains planned to shoot us. Daniella came in, joyous to find us safe. She pulled me to the sofa, her hair smelling of gardenias.

"When'd you get home? I've been calling."

She studied me then her father, perhaps thinking her terrible news had shocked us and tied our tongue. "Did you know about it? Mom, it could have been you. Anybody."

"We saw it happen."

Daniella failed to grasp the significance of her father's words.

"Dad, you took a big chance. You know they're watching you."

She squeezed my arm as one handles an expensive purse.

"Daniella, I'm sorry to tell you. Dignity Battalion burned your car. Practically with us in it."

She jerked upright and twisted so fast her knees hit mine nearly knocking me off the sofa.

"He's kidding, isn't he Mom?" Her blue eyes shot straight though me. I took her car. How I wished my hand were burned, finger cut, anything to prove we struggled.

My voice returned. "A stranger hid us. Took us in his house. Drove us home. Wonderful people in San Miguelito."

Her father cleared his throat to get our attention.

"I'm warning you. The Civil Crusade doesn't stand a chance. They're up against Dignity Battalion killers. Not professional soldiers."

His compromising words upset me and momentarily I ignored Daniella's dilemma. I turned to him.

"You mean trained soldiers have a license to kill?"

It went right past him. Next to me Daniella recoiled, pinched her shoulders and studied her hands, mumbling: "And I had just bought new tires," as though her delicate hands might rescue the new tires from the fire. She rose, her heels clicking all the way to the terrace railing where she stood and studied the city. Lights began turning on, sparkling, one by one as they came to life.

"What will I do?"

"You can have everything in our bank account," I said, "It's only three grand."

She sighed, "I'll borrow. Thank goodness you're safe." She kissed us and left.

Sofia and Trinity arrived and hugged us. Then Trinity scolded me for going to San Miguelito. Her father interrupted to describe the horrible attack by Dignity Battalion killers and how they burned the Datsun.

"I told you not to go. Now look what happened!" And she went to her room.

Sofia came to my rescue condemning the attackers, casting blame where it belonged, on the criminals.

Next morning, local TV stations under the regime thumb skipped over the details of the march stating only that Carlos Efraín Guzmán Baúles, community representative of the Civil Crusade, was shot dead at the march. No mention of who attacked the marchers. I called a Christian Democrat I saw marching near Guzman and he said the killers stood on the overpass, shooting down. I still had no inkling whose blood was on my attacker's shirt.

Chico and I drove the Audi to San Miguelito and retrieved the rental car he had abandoned there. Still traumatized I failed to recognize the blessing for me. Burned in all the horror was the license plate on the Datsun, the one I took off the Audi. I had switched plates to drive to the Civil Crusade march. When the Dignity Battalion burned the Datsun, they burned my Audi license plate; the one marked by the Panama Defense Force with a 26 prefix. Now on the Audi was the license plate from Arraijan.

Gray skies matched the national mood until one day Trinity came home from school full of cheer. *Fiesta*, she said and talked about the fabric we needed to buy for making costumes for her class group.

"My group theme is we'll be a rainbow. Come on Mom, let's go buy shiny, rainbow colored cloth." She attempted a salsa move and froze. Gone was the effervescence that accompanies festivities. Talking fiesta was one thing but having to dance required joy.

Maria Inmaculada nuns showed brilliance; they made great attempts to keep student morale high. Nuns invented programs with music among the girls, no boys or public invited. I wished I had done the same thing.

Our losses whittled Chico's morale and diminished his enthusiasm for golf. His colleagues in the PDF, those he promised to change, betrayed every principle he believed in. The only glow he preserved was his faith. Untarnished.

Not so with Crusaders. Hungry for news, they exercised cunning to communicate by word-of-mouth. They made contact in church and supermarkets, both key places.

We recovered our Volvo busted up by Dignity Battalion at the San Antonio march. New glass in all the windows improved its appearance but the shine was gone, it lost the luxurious redbrick sheen. My soldier also turned dull; lost his desire to care for the ferns he once pampered. In the past he squirted the ferns that hung from the rafters on the terrace. The water spray made them spin and twirl on their chains. For him they danced like carnival queens all 'agush' with pleasure from a cool spray of water.

My soldier, the gardener, renounced his love for the ferns. I rescued them, hosed the ferns wishing I could douse him and revive his wilting spirit. One day I caught him sitting on the terrace staring into his cup of coffee, oblivious to his favorite view of the city. I yakked nonsense. He continued staring at his empty cup, perhaps seeing his future dark as coffee.

Finally, he looked up. "Immigration. They called today, yesterday too. They want me to go over there."

His alarm, subtle but real, was lost on me. I busied myself with the details for Lulu's birthday party in the back yard. Too late I would realize his angst and plea for help. I paid no heed, lost in the frivolity of preparing for the toddler's party. Pushing aside his dark mood and wanting his attention, I tested him by posing a nasty question.

"For Lulu's party will you help me buy some alligators and carry them down to the backyard to play with the little kids? Do you think they'll bite those toddlers?"

He mumbled, "OK. Anything." confirming his despondency.

22

DON BOSCO

Daniella replaced her Datsun burned by Dignity Battalion goons. As salesperson for Ricardo Perez Toyota car agency, she bought a new one and sold another to Sofia. Both were exhilarated until days later when Sofia called from Citibank. I expected talk about her sporty, new black Batmobile. Not so. She asked, "Mom, did you hear about the machete?"

"What machete? Mine are all here. Do you want one for your new car?"

Her tense laugh was incongruent with her personality.

"No thanks, but please, Mom, stay home today. My co-workers are upset. Noriega came on TV waving a machete during a speech. Anyway, I gotta get back to work. Stay home. Make *flan*. I love your custard."

She hung up leaving me perplexed. *Flan*. Why did she request custard? She knows sugar just adds pounds. It gives energy but doesn't calm panic. Well, if my daughter is nervous because of killers on the street, it's nothing new. She should have told me to pray or gather rocks just in case. I cooperated and assembled the required ingredients for a perfect *Flan*: eight eggs, canned milk, vanilla, and a handful of sugar for caramelizing over direct heat. First, singe the sugar to a dark brown in the bottom of the custard pan. The other essential item called *baño de maría* in Spanish is a pan for hot water which goes in the oven under the custard pan, vital to prevent bubbles from forming in the custard while baking. I made this same *Flan* for Felicidad and Noriega when they came to dinner. They enjoyed it.

Trinity arrived from school repeating the story of the same wild man waving a machete on TV. The moment she caught a whiff of the *flan* she rushed to the kitchen.

"*Flan!* I want some."

While she ate her second dish, I told her about the garbage men, whose starting salary was $176 per month, such strenuous work for so little pay.

"Mom, you jump from one subject to another, too fast. Did you already forget the machete madman? And now you're concerned about the garbage men. When I leave for school, do you spend your time chatting with the trash man? How? They race past you. You'd have to run as fast as them to ask about their salary. You see what I mean? I understand they're friends of yours from Arraijan, but you can't change the world. Don't go looking for another reason to march!"

She relaxed when I said I'd only go to church. Churches were packed daily. A feature non-existent when the country was at peace. Trinity went with me several times to Cristo Rey Church where the priest Villanueva celebrated. Crusaders flocked to his Mass dressed in white and anxious to hear the small priest lambast the regime. He urged the opposition to keep up the struggle and disobey the tyrant's illegal mandates. Pigeons seemed fascinated by his rhetoric and flew in and out of rafters; happy to have us underneath so they could drop their organic bombs. When Mass ended, Crusaders left. Pigeons wanted to leave but got stuck. They had no idea how to retrace their entrance flight. I felt the same: cornered by the regime with no hope in sight.

A memorial Mass for Carlos Efrain Guzman Baúles was scheduled at Don Bosco Basilica. No need to invite Trinity, she had converted studying into her religion and was engrossed in books. When I sidled past her bedroom, my sneakers squeaked. New sneakers. Dead giveaway. She came out to check and sounded the alarm.

"M-o-o-m! Just where do you think you're going dressed in white?"

"Mass, at Don Bosco."

Satisfied, she returned to study. I was nearly out the gate when the phone rang. Trinity yelled, "Answer it". I feared Sofia would urge me to stay home, but it was Chico. His tone, less authoritarian, had been softened by fire. It purified him, cured his sick devotion to the local military. He called from the US Embassy saying he finished writing a detailed report about Guzman Baúles's assassination at the Crusader march. He asked if we needed milk. I took advantage of his weakness to invite him to the special Mass.

"Don Bosco Church is located close to the US Embassy. Mass commemorates fallen Crusaders."

"When I retired, the ambassador made it clear—avoid Crusade activities. You should do the same."

"Sweetheart. Nothing can happen. It's a Mass. Church is safe."

"I wish you wouldn't go, Jenny."

"Aw, come on. God will take care of us."

"Never, never, put God to the test."

"You're right. We'll stick to prayers. Especially since the US government doesn't care how often people get killed here by the military."

He remained silent momentarily, then, "Meet you there, Jenny. Wait at the door."

The taxi driver smiled when I said, "Don Bosco." He pointed to a rosary hanging from the rearview mirror. Back then taxi drivers protected Crusaders. Several died for our cause.

Basilica Don Bosco stood imposing in red brick, a contrast to the crumbling building across the street, a two-story house sporting wet laundry hanging on the balcony. Droves of Crusaders in white streamed past me, their long faces as somber as their colorless clothing. At the Basilica door their right hand drew the sign of the cross. Some did it twice.

Aside from our suffering and burned cars, I felt blessed. My gringo had finally stopped praising our local military. My mate had denounced the military's cruelty, turned against them and communicated it directly to Uncle Sam. A celebration was needed and church the perfect place.

Another victory for Panama stepped out of a car. Her pedigree preceded her, Arthur Davis, the US Ambassador, was her father. His daughter supported the Crusade overtly and with passion. She came alone and gave the Crusade movement a morale boost each time she appeared. Crusaders saw and buzzed around her like bees to a flower. Her father, a widower, could not stop the divorced mother of three.

Crusaders whispered, "I bet the ambassador doesn't know she's here."

Chico alighted from a taxi and nobody noticed him. Mr. Nobody. But for me he was a brave, renewed person. He grabbed my hand to enter church. We halted when the sound of heavy equipment roared behind us. Frightful sound. Something huge approached, unpleasant to the ears. I turned in unison with other Crusaders to see PDF Army trucks barreling in our direction.

"What in hell? Why?" Many voices whispered.

I let go of my husband's hand; sorry I had invited him. He knew only the PDF operated camouflage, two-ton trucks in town. He dropped his head with shame; these trucks were US manufactured. His counterparts in the Panamanian military had killed the pride he held for them. Certainly they did not come to participate in the Commemorative Mass.

Crusaders slurred a collective, "Doberman devils."

Chico whispered icily, shaking his head, "A whole platoon."

Doberman leaped from the trucks and assembled in formation. Riveted, we watched forty riot-control soldiers line up facing us—three ranks deep, a wall of heavily armed soldiers. Sinister in black fatigues with helmets, boots, shields and rubber hoses, they carried rifles and sawed-off shotguns. Who did they plan to attack? Unarmed Crusaders?

Two soldiers held cameras and pointed these at Crusaders. Same terror tactic they used on our daughters when they arrested them.

Crusaders repeatedly drew the sign of the cross on their face and chest.

We joined people moving into the church. The huge door suddenly seemed very narrow for so many frightened souls who came to honor a hero.

Soon as we sat down a priest crossed the altar and began singing. For a long period he sang alone. Then, without warning, the rumbling of a motor coming from above drowned his voice. The roar moved closer, growing louder. Chico leaned over and whispered, "Rotor blades".

The Whump-Whump of helicopters hovered above and all heads stared at the ceiling now in danger. The troops in front of the church were not sufficient. Very high up, the church ceiling displayed an ethereal motif in turquoise-green. The design, intended to be serene and pretty, under the circumstances disturbed me. In carved wood and medallion-shaped, the turquoise sheen failed to resemble sky. For me it represented a coffin's lid with a turquoise satin lining.

Helicopter reverberations caused the roof and walls to vibrate. Crusaders trembled as glass windows rattled. Their heads shifted from one window to another watching helicopters pirouette above. The roar drowned out the spoken word. What type person could order such a thing? When Crusaders marched on the street, we could run. Here they had us boxed in.

The priest continued celebrating Mass. Nobody heard a word, but we knew the ceremony by heart and followed. The homily was short and a total loss to congregants.

The priest raised the Host, then the Chalice with wine. Hundreds of eyes glued to him, more attentive than ever. When he finished consecrating, Crusaders broke with decorum and pushed forward, fixating on the altar, not the terror above. A second priest assisted in distributing the Body of Christ. Everybody went up for the Host. Inside the church there were no sinners. Mass ended and the priests disappeared. As if cued by the devil, the two helicopters departed.

Crusaders sat in silence. Torturous seconds passed. A few sighed, barely audible. Nobody dared move. A woman asked: "Did the Doberman out front leave?"

Not a soul budged. Finally a brave male Crusader rose saying, "I'll go see." Everyone turned to watch him. He rushed back to say in a sad voice, "They're out there. Waiting for us."

A pathetic moan rose, rousing terror known to us many times.

A masculine voice ordered, "Let's go. Right now."

Shoulder to shoulder we jammed the aisles. Willing to face the worst, but together. We inched closer to the huge door. Who would go out first?

Packed tight in the entrance, several men with their women leaped together. Intrepid souls. No sounds. Nor shots. Then many more congregants left. Our turn came. We stepped out into a timid sun.

Something was wrong. My vision blurred. Unable to gauge my step on the cement below, I grabbed Chico fearing I'd fall. Glancing at the spot where Doberman had lined up I saw dark blobs. Nor could I distinguish the string of laundry hanging from the rickety balcony across the street. Something flashed. I asked Chico. He said, "PDF cameras are capturing us on film."

Our hushed crowd swept us along with them like the tide. But why couldn't I see? I asked Chico if we were passing Novey's hardware store. He growled a yes saying "Hurry." I calculated we were still within shooting range. Further ahead Crusader's white figures began disappearing. At this point the reality hit me; I could not see.

He pulled; I tripped and nearly fell, clutching him in time. Large, dark blobs passed by, probably cars. I asked if we had reached Transisthmian Highway. He said, "Uh-huh." Then yelled, "Taxi."

I felt shame. Chico had come to rescue me again. Poor guy. A dark object pulled up. "Taxi's here." He pushed me inside. The taxi smelled of cigarettes and musty upholstery but not offensive. Grateful for the smell, I felt fortunate we were alive and rubbed my eyes. "I can't see."

He didn't answer. I elbowed him.

"I heard you the first time. Face it. You're at war. You chose to be a Crusader. You gotta be tough. We had plenty of your type in Vietnam. Brave men. Tough soldiers fell apart when they faced a near-death situation. Their eyesight short-circuited. It spared them from seeing death coming. You came to church knowing what happened to us in San Miguelito. You're a hardhead. But fear is nothing to be ashamed of. It's healthy. Proves you're not crazy. You saw it back at the church. Thousands of Crusaders just like you, willing to die. You're problem is you're getting soft. *Floja.*"

"Mean guy!"

"Look. Oh, sorry. Forgot you can't see. Listen, since you can't see me laughing at you, just listen. Back at the church, I knew PDF had no intention of shooting anybody. Noriega's too smart. He knows terrorizing civilians can ruin the whole movement. It's a great tactic. Destroys morale. Breaks cohesion."

"What? You flatter them? They're cowards! Whose side are you on?"

He laughed, "Militarily, the PDF is doing a great job. Look at you."

Anguish overwhelmed me, and I lost my desire to argue. After all, I was the one who couldn't see. When the taxi slowed down and stopped and Chico was paying him, it meant we were home. I began to see again. I got out, walked up the sidewalk admiring my plants, especially, 'mother-in-law tongue' shaped like a knife blade and always straight up. But as far as seeing anything else, I couldn't stand the sight of Chico.

Sofia came to the door, Trinity on her heels. She softly pawed my dirty clothing. "OOOH, poor Mo-o-m . . . Not again. You must have fallen; look how dirty your white clothing is."

Later, everyone in bed and Chico snoring, I lay in the dark thanking God. Top on my list was gratitude Trinity stayed home from church. I thanked heaven we survived. Again. Then I squeezed my eyes and visualized a court of law, putting Doberman on the stand and listed their crimes. In the imaginary trial going on in my head, I put the PDF and PRD and all their lackeys on the stand together, prosecuted them with witnesses, accused them of unjustified arrests, torturing people, men and women, and beating them deliberately on the kidneys so they'd die slowly in great pain; the many murders and decapitation of a brave surgeon. An unending and terrible list. I was severe. Accused them all equally and sentenced them the same. Every single one.

Forgive the criminals? As Padre Durán said, forgiveness will be granted after those villains serve a jail sentence. A very long one.

Finally, I had a conversation with Jesus. Told him Crusaders went to Don Bosco Church looking for Him and instead faced an armed confrontation.

As I spoke to Him, something happened. Out of the dark came a strange sound, at first not clear. Then softly a masculine voice laughed. Distinct. Who was it? I put my ear near Chico's mouth. He snored. But the laugh continued. From where? Inside my head? But who could be inside my head, reading my thoughts and laughing?

Only God.

23

THE CAPTAIN

Blindness is depressing, even if momentary. If blindness is caused by abuse of power during the solemnity of the Catholic Mass, it is a criminal act. Equally perverse were dictator lackeys, civilians, who turned a blind eye to the aggression at the basilica.

Trinity still had not regained her cheerfulness. Ever since her own mother punched her physically and morally. Sofia came to her rescue as always. Although six years apart, they were close as skin to its fingernail. Sofia would ignore her friends and new sports car to stay and wash dishes with Trinity. Then Trini sang.

To the tune of clinking dishes the boisterous duo belted their favorite song: "*Mami, yo no sé lo que quiere el Ne-e-o-o-o-gro;* Mom, I don't know what the black man wants." A far cry from the rhetoric Noriega told his followers. He said the upper crust of society, White Tails, and locally called *Rabiblancos*, disliked people of color and claimed these White Tails made up the main core of the Civil Crusade.

To confirm the lie, our populace latched onto the song and sang it everywhere, wooing the black-man in retaliation to the racist lie. Color-blind to the extreme when it comes to music, white girls historically have crooned men of any color.

Returning from the grocery store one afternoon with the car full of groceries, the Audi radio blared the same song. I cruised along Tumba Muerto Avenue. Through the rear-view mirror came a police motorcycle tooling behind the Audi. I hadn't broken the law but the cop stuck there, tailgating. His siren screeched, scaring me so bad I almost hit a Red Devil bus. Innocent, I kept going in abeyance to Sofia's instructions to Trinity.

"Don't stop for a cop. They're all gorillas."

Gorilla cop on motorcycle turned off the siren and pulled alongside motioning me to pull over. Caught, I obeyed and pulled over. Pot-bellied in a tight uniform and wearing shiny black boots up to his knees, he swaggered toward me. In passing he slapped hard on the metal chassis of the Audi. Twice. Gorilla cop walked past my open window hissing, "Open the trunk." A sneer proved he enjoyed his duty.

I stayed put and opened the trunk from inside. Confused as to what he searched for I expected him to find nothing, slam the trunk shut quickly and leave. I had no intention of giving him the usual bribe money. Not a dime. Gorilla dallied endlessly at the rear of my car.

Watching him from the side and rear-view mirrors, I saw him lift something. My machete! He unsheathed it, checked the sharp blade, fingering its razor-sharp edge. Please slice his finger. He slammed the trunk. Gripping my machete he walked past hissing, "*Arma blanca*; Lethal weapon."

He climbed on his motorcycle taking my machete. Flabbergasted and speechless, too late I yelled, "Hey! Stop! Thief! Don't steal my machete!" He drove off.

The louse had no idea how often I needed my machete on the property my mother had abandoned in Arraijan. Angry as hell, I drove home recklessly, groceries colliding and complaining in the back seat.

"Damned Gorilla!" I said, unloading groceries at our door.

Trinity came out to help with groceries and heard my outrage. "What's up, Mom?"

Still livid, I spoke incoherently and complained so much she retreated into silence.

I kept talking without explaining, "What if Gorillas come here? Take whatever they want? Who can stop them?"

She lifted her eyebrows. "Do you really think they'll come here and take one of us? That's terrible!" Looking more despondent than when I drove in, she answered her own question. "Why does that surprise me? They arrested Sofia and me. For waving a white handkerchief."

Reliving the sorrow, she kept quiet and went to study. I left for church.

Padre Durán's Santísima Trinidad Church was a source of emotional support for many, us included. Parishioners sat on metal chairs as a reminder that poor people needed a helping hand. My interest was the décor behind the altar. Unique in simple design, flat cedar slats rose from floor to ceiling in the shape of a giant arrow pointing at heaven. Modern and elegant. On either side glistened two vertical rows of portraits in bright colors. Confectioned with glass chips these jewels of artwork depicted Biblical images designed by local artist Alfredo Sinclair.

Not alone in my political angst, worried citizens flocked to our church praying for a miracle called democracy. One evening after concluding the Mass and still carrying the chalice, Padre came around front to the foot of the altar and announced Archbishop McGrath needed our support and we should go to his residence tonight.

"Please accompany me. His Excellency received a threatening phone call warning him his house will be tear-gassed. Tonight."

Padre ambled away. I sat still; flat refused to be gassed along with McGrath. From my seat I saw my favorite neighbor with hair whiter than Crusader hankies, Flori Castillero. Twenty years my senior, she was busy engaging other women to go. Knowing she'd invite me, I slithered out and nearly reached the car when her words struck me from behind like an arrow to the spine. A divine arrow.

"Jenny, you're coming with us, right?"

For her, I would go anywhere, but not for Archbishop McGrath. I was oblivious to his patriotism and photographs of him marching with protestors when the young priest, Hector Gallegos, disappeared in 1971. Perhaps the tallest man in the country, McGrath's stature would make a huge impact. I needed his image to boost my courage.

No doubt the archbishop's behind-the-scene accusations aggravated the regime. Why else was the regime eager to punish him with tear gas? Monsignor McGrath was a native, not Padre Durán. He gave everything for our country, but marching guaranteed the regime would deport him back to Ferrol, Spain. Nobody invited Durán to march.

Tense-faced, Flori waited for me to volunteer to get gassed with her. I lied. May my spouse and God forgive me for lying. "Chico is sick."

My soldier had never been sick in his life, except in Vietnam when he came down with malaria. He often claimed soldiers eat rocks without wincing. His wry humor and her belief I had courage were too much. And there she stood proud of me, believing me.

"OK. I understand. I'll pray for your husband's health."

At home I found Chico tense. Immigration had called again pressuring him to go there even though his papers were in order. Their harassment had a purpose and the tactic worked; my spouse lost his confidence. Worse still, I missed the cue; did not react to the gravity of his situation. Disassociating from reality, I invited him for pickled raw fish, *ceviche,* at Don Samy's, as if distraction and a dish of spiced fish was the solution.

The Volvo had been repaired for the second time and we drove it to Don Samy. Near the restaurant stood Paitilla Park. A zealous university professor planned to speak there, condemning the infamy of the revolutionary process of the past 21 years. And I was drawn like a moth to flame.

My poor Gringo, his worst ally was his wife. But not intentionally.

Driving past Paitilla Park, we saw people milling around carrying placards, an activity strictly forbidden by the regime. Like two fools we drove closer.

"Drop me off, dear. I just remembered that a professor from the National University is scheduled to speak. Don´t worry about me. I'll take a taxi home."

Usually he'd have scolded me. But like a web woven by circumstances including the evil calls from immigration, all the wicked pieces of the puzzle wedged together and dulled his wits. He lost cunning and failed to react astutely. Gone was the shrewdness that kept him alive for two years in the Vietnam War. He gave in to my whims and said OK as if compelled to endure the ordeal awaiting him.

I got out of the Volvo. Chico turned his head automatically to check approaching traffic before pulling away. Then he noticed. People in the park wore the forbidden white and carried placards with the bold word JUSTICE. He hollered, "Jenny! This is political! Come home with me. You're not safe!"

"Don't worry. It's a small gathering. I'll be fine. Go home dear."

Again he obeyed and proceeded to leave. Charging towards the park I heard a piercing siren and stopped. The shrill siren came closer. The small group behind me in the park dropped their placards and ran. I looked around and panicked at how far away I had gotten from Chico. The siren came from a *chota,* the dreaded pickup truck, same kind Doberman used to drag our daughters from the Volvo for carrying a white flag. *Chota* drove straight toward the Volvo, blocking its exit.

"That car's had it!" shouted a man crossing the park.

Siren stopped screeching. Chico got out of the Volvo and with the gait of a soldier trained for conflict, walked back to the *chota*. Then he changed, smiling as though about to greet a friend. Did he recognize the individual? The uniformed officer climbing out of the *chota* was young and handsome. Sour-faced, the junior grade soldier walked towards Chico who had his hand stretched in the captain's direction, "*Hola Capitán Pug.*"

I recognized Captain Pug but with less enthusiasm than Chico. He had sent Pug to the US for military training and had raved about his military future. I ran towards them suspecting the worst. Nor could I read the man's intentions on his face, but I recognized the lack of sincerity, similar to louses in Arraijan where I grew up. No transparency there. My open-toed sandals swallowed pebbles, piercing my feet as I ran to rescue my naive husband. Close enough to confirm suspicion, I read hypocrisy on the captain's face, my husband's protegé.

"How are you, *Capitán* Pug?"

My husband practically flirted with him. No smile in return.

He repeated the soldier's name with a fondness that made me jealous. My colonel's extended hand still hung mid-air.

"*Coronel* Stone, I'm taking your car."

Stone dropped his hand as though wounded.

"What did you say? Take my car? What for? I can't believe what you're insinuating."

His voice quaked with anger and shame for having trusted the officer.

"There's an anti-government rally here. Your car is arrested for participating. For sedition."

He might as well have spit on my husband.

"You can't be serious. Are you saying I'm seditious?"

To add to our predicament, not a soul remained in the park.

Capitán Pug raised a hand to beckon a Doberman in the *chota* to come forward. He turned back to my colonel.

"Give me your car keys."

My soldier reacted obediently. He plunged his hand deep into his pocket. Anger faded making his vibrant tan turn to gray. His rage cooled instantly as he recognized a combat situation, not the ridiculous "war game," so hawked about. Stone assumed the posture he trained for. Win or lose. The table turned. He held the keys, the desired bait. You want this key Pug? You come get it! His eyes drilled through the captain, eyes cold, watching and waiting. His hand remained deep in the pocket.

Captain Pug kept calm, knew all the military tricks. All this happened so fast an ordinary observer would not understand the profoundness of the contention. It was a duel. My war veteran felt no urgency; he understood the odds and they were all against him. The captain wanted his key but the colonel intended to enjoy the impasse.

Recognizing the Gringo's intentions, Captain Pug relaxed.

I stopped walking. Aware the two men were in a duel. Not my place to join the fight. Never would be. My soldier would swallow his poison alone as he had during his entire military life. Anger kept me standing. A young punk intended to destroy my king. The sad thing was I begged him not to take the job with the Panama Defense Force, the worst slime ever to rule my country.

Captain Pug exemplified perfectly what it entails to serve a military dictatorship and he intended to prove it. He signaled the Doberman to hurry. I figured they planned to either kick my colonel to death or shoot him. The order to the Doberman was, "Get those keys."

The captain intended to enjoy the spectacle of the young Doberman struggling with my Gringo Viejo. Doberman would knock him down while Pug watched Stone eat dirt and his Panamanian wife drown with pain and guilt. To make matters worse Stone's father still lived; a US Air Force three-star general, rank earned during world war II. General Stone would suffer the dishonor perpetrated on his only son, crushed at the hands of a corporal in the country he chose as his own. A crime ordered by the victim's chosen pupil.

I changed my mind, abandoned good judgment and sprinted towards the two soldiers yelling, "Oye!" fully intending to help fight that SOB. Do anything to forbid those two scumbags from destroying my noble man. Never in our years of marriage had I needed to defend my soldier. He was a gentleman, "By Act of the US Congress," as he always said. The other two men had no idea what that meant. Perversion was their military motto.

Neither one heard me shout when I approached. Three yards from the captain my husband pulled his hand from the pocket and showed the keys to Pug to teach him something. He raised the keys. Did he intend to fling the keys or wait to be attacked?

Captain Pug expressed distaste, twisting his mouth impatiently. His expression reflected a phrase valued in Panama. 'Satan is wise because he's old, not 'cause he's the devil.' In the captain's twisted mentality, the devil held the keys.

My mate tossed the keys and smiled when they hit Captain Pug's chest. Chico chose to protect me from sorrow. To keep his daughters from suffering more, he swallowed his pride. For us. Great man my soldier. The Captain picked up the keys and tossed them at the Doberman. He jumped in our Volvo and drove off, barreling down Via Cincuentenaria in the direction of Hellquaters.

Chico watched his chariot zoom away for the last time.

"Best you go now," advised the traitor.

Grabbing my arm, he pulled me across the same double highway the Volvo took. Cars honked. In that harrowing moment, I promised myself that Captain Pug would face justice. Ha! When had I ever seen justice served in Panama?

Anger ran through the fingers digging into my arm. He waved a taxi. Settled in the taxi I dared not look at my unfortunate husband's face. I feared seeing his expression reveal the inevitable question: what misery will my Crusading wife drag me into next?

24

CHAINED

Never again was the Volvo mentioned. Chico suffered the same loss many Crusaders did: their cars and other properties. Many suffered abuse beyond that. Women, young and old, beaten and raped in Cárcel Modelo Prison continued to Crusade for democracy. Shocking but true. Their passion to establish democracy in Panama endured horrors. Some lost everything. My neighbor's male cousin, arrested for marching with the Crusade, was imprisoned and repeatedly raped. The young man committed suicide.

Chico changed but he paid dearly for awakening so late. Having his own protégé rip off his Volvo demoralized him and left a mark. Depressed, he quit shaving and gray stubble made his countenance mournful. To add to his misery his former Panamanian colleagues published the statement that he grew the beard to hide from them. As if such trivia could be true. A ghost of the former warrior, he stood out more.

I returned to daily Mass with a heavy load on my conscience. When Mass ended, Padre Durán walked down the altar steps and smiled, thanking parishioners for accompanying him to Archbishop McGrath's house the night his residence was gassed by the PDF. Wow! Ashamed for not going a doubt occurred to me. If I had gone to inhale tear gas along with Archbishop McGrath would our Volvo have survived disaster? Both attacks occurred during the same afternoon-to-evening.

Slumped in my folding chair, I snuck a glance at Flori talking to other pious women; her white hair a natural halo of silver. But Padre Durán wasn't finished; he lingered in his long white vestments.

His message: "Archbishop McGrath urgently wants dictator attacks on the Civil Crusade to stop. He suggests the Crusade consider dialogue with the regime."

Congregants hushed and bowed their heads. Not a peep was heard. But soon as Padre left to remove his ceremonial garb, women voiced anger.

"Never! Our church joined the Crusade to oust the regime! Never dialogue with the devil!"

The group headed for the exit. Within seconds their heated defiance switched to the rising cost of food and electricity. Their fury dissipated. I surmised my fellow parishioners willingly marched under gunfire but never rejected church authority. True followers but reluctant leaders. None considered opposing a church mandate. I walked away formulating my rejection. By the time I reached the car, I had planned my revenge. It required a brave driver for my getaway car, preferably male.

I found Chico sitting on the terrace gazing at the city; his somber face lacking the love he showed in the past. I offered to bake chocolate brownies and hurried to the kitchen. Later, while he munched hot brownies with milk, I related Archbishop McGrath's recommendation.

"Will you drive me to church tonight?"

I often went alone so the question should have struck him as odd.

He kept eating while I laid out my retaliation plan. Sweetened, he nodded. Not until I mentioned "black paint" did he sound off the alarm, shooting the question, "How can you do this to Padre Durán? Does anybody else know your plan?"

At midnight I piled tools in the Audi trunk and we headed for church. Chico drove. Desolate and dimly lit by tall lampposts, Padre's temple lent itself for my message to the Archbishop. Its huge white surface was perfect. I planted the stool on the rocky asphalt and leaned it against the white church wall. Under my feet the stool trembled. I dragged my shaky hand making a scraggly black line. Big awkward letters—six of them—spelled out: NO DIAL. I rested my arm preparing for the next letters.

The roar of a car coming startled me. I jumped off the stool and lay flat on sharp rocks poking my chest. Returning to my mission, perspiration and paint ran down my arm to my pit. Bold black letters marred Padre Durán's pristine white church. NO DIALOGO glared ugly from the ivory wall. I expected a rush of satisfaction. Nothing.

After collecting my tools, I climbed in the car hoping my accomplice would congratulate me and erase my guilt. He drove in silence. My morale sunk lower. Did I deface Padre Durán's Spartan church we parishioners loved? We worked hard to raise money for its construction. If I had approached Padre and said, "Crusaders reject dialogue. We want the regime to go." Would it have made a difference? Would Archbishop McGrath have backed off knowing Civil Crusaders refused to barter and wanted only one thing? The military and their political party, the PRD, must go.

Early next morning, I drove past Santísima Trinidad Church. Already a man stood rolling white paint over my black art—a message rejecting dialogue. I felt neither shame nor pride. Backing the car into MOMI Bakery parking space to return home, I was certain the message was received.

The interesting feature of my message was I never asked for permission or sought anyone's opinion for what I did. All Crusaders were potential leaders of the movement. This perception made it successful. When a prominent Crusader was exiled, ten more filled the vacuum. I repeated, "Never tell Padre Durán what you did. Someday we shall celebrate together."

During afternoon Mass Padre said nothing about the black paint, but in closing his words held the key. "Forgiveness is essential. But we cannot accept regime atrocities. Justice must be achieved. Remember, the only sin not forgiven by God is loss of hope. Despair is a rejection of the Holy Spirit. We all inherited the Holy Spirit and carry the Spirit inside us."

No mention of dialogue with the devil. Never did he mention it again. Nor McGrath.

Strange, Chico's sadness made me happy. Captain Pug finished the job of betrayal initiated by the Panama Defense Force leaders. In celebration I cooked his favorite dish, Gnocchi a la Romana. He probably preferred having the tripe dish menudo made by his maternal Mexican grandmother. I ate tripe so often growing up in Arraijan I never craved it and yearned for a different dish.

He barely ate. His sad soul was destroying his morale. Our civilian friends continued treating him with respect. Nobody said, "I told you so." Only his wife. For years friends swallowed their hurt and pride while Chico huffed proudly saying the PDF promised reform and clean elections.

The regime controlled people's well-being but not love for music. Our perfect example, Sofia arrived from the bank, turned on music and harmonized to Ruben Blades, "*Como huracan llegó. Como huracán se fué;* Like a hurricane it came. Like a hurricane it left." At dinner she talked about Danté's Inferno and how THEY informed the owners that if they dared repair the store, they should expect arson again.

"Who are THEY?" her father asked.

Trinity contributed, "Da-a-ad, everybody knows THEY are the enemy."

"THEY," Sofia said, "Are the PDF. Crusaders fear their lunacy. One minute they set a rule, and next day they use it before notifying the public. And Zap! They arrest Crusaders for breaking the unknown rule!" Sofia's cynical grin lasted the entire explanation as if she were on stage mimicking the cruelty enjoyed by the regime.

"Opposition lawyers, teachers and leaders have an escape mentality, attuned to the slightest sounds. Every strange noise alerts them to run. One dentist heard heavy boots tromping past his office and jumped out a window to safety. Crusaders plan their lives based on the future. Postpone everything: weddings, vacations, and house remodels, until the crisis is over. Many don't sleep at home anymore. They hide in friend's homes; sometimes even in stranger's homes. Terrible life."

Sofia's commentary failed to console her Dad.

My mate's betrayal by his PDF military colleagues augmented my good will towards him. I invited him to a spectacle in front of a church. A journalist, a zealot for freedom of speech, planned to chain himself to a huge Corotú tree outside Guadalupe Church on 50th Street. He agreed without hesitation. We arrived early to park within walking distance from the huge tree. Traffic was light perhaps due to fear. It was siesta time; the neighborhood was so quiet one could hear a dog snore.

As we admired the immense Corotú tree, the brave journalist arrived dragging his chain. To honor us he rattled his chain on the cement.

He announced, "*Soy periodista*; I'm a journalist."

Chained journalist stopped before the Corotú tree and studied its wide trunk, appreciating its girth and the unrealistic challenge it presented to chain himself to such a wide tree. He smiled at us. Obviously, he expected a crowd but was grateful for an audience of two. He stuck a hand in his pocket and withdrew tape and cleared his throat as if preparing to make a speech. To further shock us, he stuck the tape across his mouth and bowed. Then he turned to a post nearby and wrapped the chain around his healthy paunch then fastened it to the slender metal pipe.

The drama was now complete: press censorship that bound and gagged journalists. Perfect metaphor! And I forgot my camera.

Engrossed in the event, we failed to notice the arrival of an old woman. Faded as her clothing, she ignored the chained man and pulled a white handkerchief from a plastic bag and approached Chico. "My niece," she dabbed her tears, "disappeared four months ago. Doberman dragged her from a march. I was like a mother to her. We haven't seen her since. A Crusade lawyer offered to help for free. He never found her."

So she pressed her hope onto a foreigner. Chico's gray beard made him appear what he was not. A diplomat. Or at least she thought he represented the US.

She cried again, her grief contagious, filling us with sadness and impotency.

"We Panamanians have nobody to help us. The church is useless; the press suppressed. Can you help me find her? God will pay you with blessings."

The chain clunked loud on the cement behind the sad woman, but she only had eyes for the bearded Gringo. The journalist's face turned pink. He attempted to communicate something. Tape on his mouth forbid it and we were ignoring him. Where was the crowd he expected? Why wasn't the church packed by now?

The woman kept pleading, "What can we do? I live in San Miguelito. That place is hell. The mayor runs the Dignity Battalion. Please, help me."

Before Chico could speak a car drove up, honking incessantly. A man jumped out waving his arms and running in our direction, yelling.

"Blas, let's go! Run! Mass is cancelled. Doberman convoy coming!"

Cancelled? No wonder nobody showed up to celeb Blas. Until that moment we had no idea his name w⸱ Panicked, the journalist jerked his chain. It stuck. ⸱ tugged, "Blas! Why the hell did you lock it? key?"

179

Tape over Blas's mouth blocked his response. His friend grabbed the tape and tore it off sending a sting through my skin. What agony.

We charged at the Audi and left the three behind.

"What's wrong with you Jenny?" Chico growled. "You wanna get us both killed?"

I deserved the scolding.

25

DEPORTED

Crystal Voice came over to criticize the journalist chained to a tree.

"Jenny did you say the chained journalist was fat? I know a fat guy named Blas, but he wouldn't dream of putting an iron chain around his neck. The man you saw is trying to get himself killed."

Until now she had supported the Crusade movement from afar. Her new attitude was suspect.

"Jenny, I think he's nuts. He causes problems for all of us. He's tempting the devil's ire."

Why contradict her? She wasn't acting her usual self. She got up to leave and I latched onto her arm, checking her closely. "Let's have some tea."

"I can't. Gotta run some errands with my old man."

Recognizing my mortification, she half-smiled. "You must quit putting yourself in danger. Nobody can predict what the regime will do next. And poor Chico."

On her way out through the vestibule, a cross-breeze hit and whipped her yellow skirt up, leaving her 'tooth-pick' legs exposed thigh-high. For years she had joked about her skinny legs.

"See what I mean Jenny. That sorcerer Noriega knows I'm talking bad about him. Makes fun of my scrawny legs."

Enjoying her theatrics, she missed seeing her husband walk up behind her. His European fairness and husky body contrasted her olive skin and svelte figure—she the Queen of Sheba with her Viking. He came close and I invited them in. He declined saying, "Crusaders are getting nowhere, Jenny. You tell the leaders for me. When they're ready for guns, I can get 'em, quick. From Europe."

Guns? Civil War? Was he insane? No. Money mad. Guns would bring Crusader annihilation. Exactly what THEY wanted: justify their sweeping the streets with guns. Reason I trashed my gun. In all this where the hell did Crystal Voice stand? She knew guns meant civil war. So quick to scold me for flattering the chained journalist. What about her kids? She calmly stroked her thick curls to avoid looking at me. Where was her tongue now? She should slap her Viking for wanting to sacrifice Panamanians for money. Could her husband's shameful business deal have caused her to talk so crazy earlier? Chained journalist deserved her praise, not criticism.

Crystal Voice turned completely away and in so doing, her plush velvet hair I so admired faced me. Gone was its luster. It reminded me of wire scrub pads.

Behind me the phone rang. Trinity answered brusquely, perhaps she heard the neighbor's gun talk. At her parochial school, teachers kept students informed of the injustices taking place; her teachers were Crusade sympathizers. The phone call did not interest me. I chased after my neighbors.

"The Crusade has said it a million times. Non-violence is the only way. Never guns."

The Viking stomped away. His wife, more diplomatic, made excuses. "Pay no attention. He thinks he's a great businessman. Men are all the same."

"Not my husband!" I said and suddenly doubted everybody.

Aware her husband dropped a bomb, Crystal Voice hushed. I said, "Weren't you going somewhere with your husband?" She drooped her head, wordless, and picked her way across the lawn on her stick legs. I went inside seeking strong tea, gunpowder type, and found Trinity watching me, tapping a pencil against her book.

"He's a pain, that neighbor, Mom. It's a shame, too 'cause he's a great cook. I loved his tomato soup but I'll never eat it again!" She continued, "That phone call was immigration again. Why are they after Dad?"

I didn't understand why either, but she needed reassurance and I invented something. "They'd probably quit pestering him if we paid a bribe. That's how it's done here." Reassured, she trotted off. I hurried in for tea, doubting every word I told Trinity.

Unaccustomed to Chico's gray beard, it surprised me each time he appeared. He came in waving his residence card like a flag, a document that gave him legality in Panama. He pointed at the photo and asked, "You think I look better in real life than this photograph?" I lied. Didn't have the heart to say the gray beard made him look forlorn. He said the insurance company kept searching for the Volvo instead of paying up.

One evening, Sofia's friends, Luis, Tony and Virginia came over. Virginia graduated from Maria Inmaculada with her. They stayed in touch while Sofia studied at Rollins College in Orlando. Our home had always been packed with our daughters' friends, but with martial law social life in Panama changed. Music low, they all arrived in one car planning to leave soon, adhering to the rule they set for themselves to meet in public places. This pattern removed the focus from private homes.

The trio went to the terrace and chattered; their cheer traveled all the way to the kitchen. Trinity joined them as she had since childhood and they loved including her in their parties. They inquired about her studies and joked about nuns. "Are the nuns still cool?" Trinity laughed and their glee inoculated the house.

City lights blinking, the taller man, Tony, a lawyer, asked, "Can we see Cárcel Modelo jail from here?" They all squinted searching the distant lights and he added, "I spent the entire day there trying to rescue my friend." Virginia interjected, "Did you get him out?" When the lawyer shook his head, she grumbled, "How awful. He's probably going through hell. Somebody's gotta get rid of Noriega. Now!"

The telephone rang. Sofia crossed the living room to answer; her dark slacks made her look taller. She said, "*Un momento,*" and hollered, "Dad. It's immigration. Why are they calling you at night?" She stiffened, the question hanging mid-air, awaiting an answer. Behind her the crude plywood barrier covering the amber glass to protect us from villain bullets appeared abrasive as the caller.

Chico picked up, his Spanish more broken than ever. "I have it here." He had pulled the resident card from his wallet. "There must be some mistake. I'm holding the card you sold me. It permits me to reside in Panama legally."

Sofia, back on the terrace, heard the alarm in her father's voice and returned in a flash with friends close behind. Lawyer Tony said, "I don't like it. Calling so late."

Chico argued, "My wife's Panamanian. Yes, your office issued the card." He paused and shook his head, "That's not my problem." Trinity, Sofia and friends sat on the sofa bunched together watching him. I pulled up a chair. Six pairs of eyes drilled through him, trying to guess what immigration was up to.

His scrubby gray beard concealed the angry tightness in his jaw. He planted his hand on the wall in front of him and leaned forward—head touching the wall as if about to vomit. "All right, I'll go first thing in the morning."

He seemed to settle, then jerked upright exclaiming, "Are you saying come tonight?" He glanced at his watch. "It's past nine. Why not tomorrow?"

"No! Say no!" I jumped up and ran to his front, "You can't go!" Virginia tugged Sofia's arm, "Don't let your father go. Not at night. They'll hurt him."

"OK," He hung up, turned and avoided looking at me.

"No!" I pummeled his broad chest. "Don't go! We'll lock ourselves in. Call the neighbors, the priest. We'll protect you. Listen! I forbid you! For once in your life, do as I say." But the whine in my voice told it all. He had just begun to do my biding.

Sofia and friends paced around him, each one begging him to stay. She lifted a hand to touch him, hesitated. His eyes fixated on a spot way out past the terrace. Searching for a way to escape? Trinity covered her mouth, her eyes screaming with fear. They're gonna take him! My father. My chauffeur. My movie buddy—"Jaws".

He sensed our terror and shook his head, meaning no. "It's gonna be all right." Hollow words. He knew nothing good came from the regime. They were not like Chico, trained in the principle of Duty, Honor and Country. Brisk steps took him through the vestibule to unlock the iron gate.

"If I don't go, they'll come get me. I don't want them in my house."

"Stop him!" Tony said. "Sofia. *Señora*. Stop him. Don't let him go!"

"I have to do this. Alone." He relocked the gate while we stood stunned. The soldier in him never looked back. He quickly got into the car while we stood paralyzed unable to react fast enough to stop him.

"No!" Tony said. "I'm going with you. Wait Colonel. I'm coming."

The lawyer was too late. Chico backed the Audi out of the carport and left. We stared at the empty garage, hoping he'd change his mind and return. His women knew him; our warrior never shirked his duty. A hopeless situation made us feel useless. Tension turned explosive.

Our futility finally peaked, and we all spoke at once. "Call somebody. Yeah. Great idea. You're the lawyer, make that call." He looked excited momentarily and then said, "Your father's a Gringo. I can't help him. Call the US Ambassador." They all got excited again and Sofia reached for the phone. She handed it to me. I shook my head.

"Your Dad will get angry if I do."

Doom hung heavy in the living room. Silence gripped us and nobody dared look at each other. Grandmother clock bonged ten. An hour had passed since he left. Tony and Luis went to the terrace; the girls to the kitchen for juice and water but didn't drink either one. I asked Trinity to go to bed, school tomorrow. She balked; then stretched.

"OK. If you promise you'll wake me soon as he comes home."

The rest of us took turns pacing and glancing at the tall clock. It struck eleven. "He should be back by now," Tony said, pulling out his keys. "Come on Sofia, let's go find him." I decided best to stay, "In case he calls."

As the four of them drove away, I panicked. What if they lock up the kids? I ambled around the house and washed empty glasses. Sitting gave me the jitters. The only one who could save my husband was Chico. I washed my hair. Threw in a load of laundry. Hung it up to dry. Nothing calmed me. Grandmother clock bonged twelve, its sound no longer precious as my husband claimed. The phone rang.

I jumped, knocked off the black receiver, its cracking sound jolting.

"It's me, Mom. No trace of Dad. Immigration's closed. They must'a taken him somewhere else. No Audi either. We've been driving all over this area."

"OK. When are you coming home?"

"We have one more place to check."

Hanging up too quickly, I panicked. Where were they going? Hellquarters? I needed to keep busy. Found scissors. Trimmed my hair. Gave myself the quickest haircut ever and then switched to dusting tables. Swat here; Swat there. Put dishes away. Cleaned the refrigerator. Turned off all the lights and finally sat on the cold floor of the vestibule, peering through the bars of the iron gate. A pale ceiling light in the garage barely lit the carport. I leaned against the wall. Wished I could pray. No spark lit my thoughts. Not even to beg heaven for help.

A car pulled up. Chico? Voices in Spanish. Lots of them. Sofia's voice, tired, gave a sad, *"Buenas Noches."* She could not see me, but I detected in her footsteps exhaustion and devastation. No need to ask if she found him. I didn't move and she nearly stepped on me.

"Mom! Why are you sitting on the rocks? In the dark? Turn on the light."

She flicked the light on. Glare blinded me. She said, "We didn't find Dad or the car. We walked around immigration a bunch'a times, tried to find a guard. Nothing."

"Let's go to bed, dear." I walked over to hug her. She squealed and backed off.

"Ouch. What've you got there, Mom?" Scissors in my pocket, I'd forgotten.

"What were you doing?" She walked around me.

"Oh Mo-o-m, I can't believe what you've done. Look at your head. Bald spots all over. You look awful." I felt even worse. Guilty for Chico's plight. She hugged me.

"Come on, we've had enough. Dad'll be home soon. Let's go to bed."

Standing in the hallway, we heard another voice.

"Is Dad home yet?" Trinity, hair tangled, stood at the door to her bedroom. We walked over and hugged all together. Heard a bong. Half past one and nothing was well. Disheartened, they went to bed.

Too tired to mop, I gazed at our wedding photograph: a happy young couple under the arches of Sacred Heart Chapel in Ancon. He in his sharkskin white uniform, me in a wedding skirt wide as the arches, gazing at each other with love. I lay on the sofa hugging the photo, watched the front door and remembered the first time Chico went to Vietnam. Our friend, the other Chico Stone, went at the same time. The other Chico came from Texas, was blonde and sweeter than my Chico from California. Months after they left I overheard women talking in the Army commissary. "Chico Stone was killed last week." The Texas Chico was single and left no children behind.

Someone else's death cauterized me so I could deal with my own pain.

The clock struck three. The phone rang. I jumped. The picture crashed to the floor.

"Jenny? I'm in Miami. Gotta talk fast. Don't have much change. Panama immigration locked me up in a private home in Bella Vista on 42ⁿᵈ Street. Wouldn't let me call home. Then put me on Lloyd Boliviana Airlines. I arrived about an hour ago."

"Miami? Why?"

"Listen, it's important. Get the car quick. Before daylight. I parked near the Bella Vista Theater. Couple of streets away. Knew if I parked near immigration—we'd never see the car again. Send me some clothes. Call the US ambassador first thing in the morning. Tell him what's happened. Gotta go. Operator just cut in."

My husband was gone! Removed by his very own Panamanian colleagues. I slumped to the floor overcome by what I had done. But not really. God must have helped after I begged Him—on my knees—more than once. I asked God to remove Chico from Panama or take my life. And he chose to let me live. I thanked Him. "He's safe. They can't hurt him anymore."

Suddenly very sad for him, I turned off the lights. He lost what most Civil Crusaders still had: family, friends, a car, and a house. Our warrior was gone.

The problem was my girls. Our lives had nowhere to go but continue here in Panama, dangerous as it was.

26

NEW ERA

Chico's world collapsed. What could hurt more than deportation by your own colleagues in the Panama Defense Force? While he crumbled, I needed to muster strength—for our girls—tell them he's better off in the US and sound believable. Dawn approached, I had not slept and it was time to wake my daughters. I paused at the door of the bedroom Sofia and Trinity shared. Their breathing, slightly agitated, gave the impression their dreams were violent. I contemplated the difficult task ahead: tell them without sadness or fear that we will live in Panama without their father. After all, we met here. As I dickered, a pink ray of sun flashed first light. Its beam heated the perturbing question harassing me these past hours. Who lifts his daughter's spirits when their warrior-leader is torn from their side?

I softly shook Sofia's shoulder and pulled a pillow off Trinity's face. "Wake up. Your father called. He's in Miami and he's OK. Sofia, please hurry, I need your help to find the Audi," bitter words, worse than swallowing medicine.

Choked by the words I rushed out of their room. During all the bitterness of their arrest, burned car, and Volvo destroyed by the regime, none of us cried. Neither time nor desire permitted it. My job now demanded I take the helm and headed for the kitchen to see what we could eat. Within seconds Trinity stormed in, furious.

"What did you say?"

"Your father's in Miami. He's much safer there," words I'd repeat for months.

"How can you act like nothing terrible happened?"

A CLANG on our iron gate spared me from her wrath. Someone was ringing our cowbell. Who could be here so early? I tiptoed over to listen through the open transom above the door. Women's voices!

"How horrible! Poor Chico!"

How did they know? I opened the cedar door to find my neighbors crowded at the iron gate. Behind the black iron bars they looked like prisoners.

"Oh Jenny! Your poor husband! You poor women!"

"How'd you know?" I asked, rushing though the vestibule to the iron gate.

The four women wore bathrobes, slippers and one still sported curlers, a dress code never observed on our street. In happier times I would have laughed.

In unison the four answered: "*La República*. Chico's picture is on the front page."

"He looked so sad," said the one in a floral robe.

"With a beard!" added the one in a blue robe. "How long did they keep him in jail? He'd even grown a beard!"

Turning the key in the iron gate, I gestured for them to enter but they stood still, busy talking with flying-hands, motioning for effect.

"Yes, and *La República* accused your husband of being an advisor to the Civil Crusade," said the neighbor in a blue robe, "They said he grew a beard for camouflage. Nobody believes them. "Wasn't Noriega his friend? He sure treated him terribly."

Again, I motioned for them to enter. Talking all the way, they coaxed each other into the house, and I had what I needed: company.

"Jenny, what will you do? You can't leave Panama. He'll be back soon. We'll take care of you," the one in curlers sobbed. Her tears would have delighted Chico, even if his own wife shed none.

"All the media lies. They own it," huffed another neighbor. "I saw on TV when PRD legislator, Lucho

Gorilla, blamed Chico for Armando Morán's murder near Roosevelt Statue, the day of the Crusade march there. They're such trash!"

Already dressed in her blue-plaid Maria Inmaculada uniform, Trinity bumped into the neighbors and tactlessly scolded me. Not for the bald spots on my head, she didn't care about that. She blamed me for her father.

"M-o-o-m. Why didn't you wake me like I asked?"

Fact is she was wrong. She instructed me to wake her when he came home, but he never returned. Sofia burst from her room fully dressed for the bank. Trinity complained to her, "I told Mom to wake me."

Sofia sensed her pain and tried to console her, "This isn't Mom's fault, Kiddo. This assault was planned; nobody could stop it. Immigration was after him. Our Dad's a hero. Just like many Crusaders are daily. Miami is better for him. Nobody can touch him. Besides, now Noriega will forget about us."

The neighbor in the blue bathrobe butted in, "You stay here! We'll protect you!"

Sofia glanced at her watch, "Mom, get your purse. Let's go rescue the Audi."

The neighbors nodded at each other, hugged us and left.

Trinity came after us, "Mom, does Daniella know? Or is she gonna hear about this terrible thing after everybody else in Panama does? I gotta go, my bus will be here soon."

"Please tell her." I visualized Daniella and Lulu asleep downstairs, oblivious to the terrible news. How upset they would be. We hadn't eaten breakfast. The neighbors' visit interrupted. It was worth it.

Early sun warmed the air as Sofia's sleek sports car sped down desolate Tumba Muerto Highway. My empty stomach turned with the curves.

"Mom, didn't you think the neighbor's comment was a joke? Ridiculous, telling us to stay in Panama and they would protect us. With what? The curlers in their hair? Those contraptions might scare a baby."

But we couldn't enjoy the humor, and she accepted the severity of our situation.

"Oh Mom, poor Panama. Nobody knows we have nowhere to go in the US. From now on we must be alert every second." She slowed down as we drove past the boarded Bella Vista theatre and turned on the next street.

"I see the Audi! I wonder why Dad parked it here?"

"Look how strange life is. See that house in front of our car. It belonged to my grandmother. Your grandmother lived here as a kid, 45th Street. When your father called last night, he said immigration was closed. A guard there sent him to a private home in Bella Vista. He left the car here and walked to the street where the Bella Vista Theater is. The horror in all this is somebody else told me the regime runs a torture house near the theater, house #18, but I'm not certain what street. Someday we'll know."

We got out and inspected the Audi. It appeared fine. No smashed windows as they'd done to the deceased Volvo. We checked under the hood for torn wires. I jumped when Sofia slammed the hood.

Sofia sighed, "Why didn't they take it? Or tear it up?"

"I know why! I switched the license plates when I went to march at San Miguelito, the day Dignity Battalion goons assassinated Guzman Baúles and burned the Datsun. The Audi is wearing the Datsun plates issued in Arraijan. These criminals don't know whom this car belongs to. According to its license, the Audi lives in Arraijan. No Gringo prefix 26 license plate exists in your Dad's name anymore. They burned it in San Miguelito."

"Great tradeoff, Mom. Datsun for an Audi." But she wasn't happy or excited.

I reached out to open the door and get into the Audi and nearly succeeded when she stopped me. "Stop! No Mom! No! It could have a bomb!"

Not accustomed to bomb talk, I argued. "You've seen too many movies. No bombs in Panama. Too sophisticated."

"Who says?" She pulled me harder, and we bantered for a while. I kept disagreeing and didn't notice when she decided to switch tactics, using psychology. In short sentences she explained, as if to a child, "Mom, you and I. We. Together. We go to my Bank."

Her strange talk accompanied by mime may have convinced her I agreed with everything she suggested. Satisfied, she turned to walk to her car expecting I'd follow—childlike. She didn't look back.

I jumped in the Audi and turned the key. No explosion.

Shocked at my deceit, she charged back, grabbed the door, and found it locked. Waving at her and faking a smile through a closed window, I pressed the gas pedal and rolled downhill. Her face revealed the terrible suffering one of her parents put her through once more. In the rearview mirror I saw her hands cover her eyes as if expecting an explosion.

Halfway home I began to shake hard and pulled off the highway. Still early, bus traffic was nil. My heart beat faster than the pounding in my head. What if there had been a bomb? Sofia's mother blown to hell before her eyes. Agonizing thought. Cars and Red Devil busses raced past, honking as I edged the car back into traffic to head home.

Taped to the cedar door, Daniella had left a note. "How Horrible! Poor Dad."

I called the US ambassador first as Chico asked. The secretary called back with the ambassador's message, "Let us know when the suitcase with his clothing is ready." The US Ambassador never called personally to ask about Chico. My thirty-year veteran was discarded upon retirement.

My mother was the last one I called. She made a habit of speaking badly of her son-in-law, and he treated her kindly. When we lived in the US, he invited her to stay with us six months each year we were there. Her reaction surprised me. She cried a river over him.

Her son-in-law was right when he said, "Women only love the man after he's buried."

Fortunately, I felt no remorse. I nagged him, but strived to make him happy. Immersed in the memories, mid-morning a sweet voice interrupted, calling from out front. "Jenny, Jenny."

I recognized Flori's nasal voice and immediately unlocked the iron gate for my parish favorite. Her snowy hair crowned a much-deserved halo on her. I had treated her badly and now she came to console at my worst time. She said the wrong thing, "Blessed are those who suffer persecution in their pursuit of justice."

Biting my tongue, I wanted to say: No! No more suffering. Much as I admired her for all her success, I needed a miracle. Her words failed to strengthen me. I wanted her to tell God the Stone family and all Crusaders have suffered enough. But I understood she was right. If I had to face terror again for my country, I would do it. As so many other Crusaders would. Oh, but so much pain.

Flori sat on the sofa and her feet dangled above the floor. "God will help you."

Like a bolt from heaven, our cowbell out front clanged again, harder. It was Padre Durán. The two of them comprised the most dynamic pair I knew and now I had them in my living room. Pillars of strength. My great fortune.

Father Durán greeted us with a kiss on the cheek. "Count on me for anything,"

Even before he offered, I knew. He'd help anybody, even felons. Walking around the living room, he excused himself for not sitting, inspecting windows and doors to see if iron bars covered them. When satisfied, he reiterated his help making minor reference to the trouble heaped upon our family.

"Chico will be back soon."

I didn't believe it. According to scripture "Soon" can be centuries. Padre sensed my chagrin and repeated a popular expression. "No evil can last a hundred years." He remained standing and Flori took it as a signal and stood up. Moved by the gloom of the impasse, she patted my hand.

"Jenny, you're tough. All this will pass." They departed.

I thought of my mate alone in Miami, penniless. I had the girls. Trinity arrived first dragging her heavy book bag, heavy as the calamities burdening her inner peace. She rejected the cold papaya she usually ate while studying. Sofia arrived. Together they rehashed, "Dad's safer in Miami," over and over. Daniella and Lulu came upstairs to join our disgruntled clan. Lulu asked for her grandfather. Nobody told her the truth, only that he was away on a trip.

"I'm not leaving," said a sister and the others echoed. "Me neither."

Chico called in the evening. We had no way to call him; he was staying in military lodging near Miami. We listened on the two extensions. Trinity spoke up.

"Hey Dad, bring the Green Berets. Kick some ass here!"

Lacking her exuberance, her Dad rehashed his kidnapping: "I drove straight to immigration and found it closed. A guard told me to go to Calle 42, same street as the Bella Vista Theater. To house number 18. I parked two streets away, the street where your grandmother's house stood. I walked back to a Spanish style chalet with a center patio. Nobody interrogated me. Left with a guard, I could hear them on the phone. They'd ask somebody what they were supposed to do with the Gringo. They didn't allow me to call you or the US embassy. Three hours later a guy came in and said, 'You're being deported.' I didn't argue. At the airport, I had to pee real bad. They wouldn't let me use the toilet back at the pretty old house. I suspect they didn't want me to see something. I had to pee so bad, had to cross my legs to walk. In the bathroom at Tocumen Airport, I found a sales slip and scribbled a note to call my wife. Coming out of the men's room I snuck it to a woman carrying a baby. No luck. One of their spies saw my maneuver and four gorillas pounced on her. She nearly dropped the baby. It screeched. The mother screamed. What an ugly scene!"

He stopped talking. We waited. Finally, he sighed as though tired, profoundly beat.

"I'm going to Washington soon. Gabriel Lewis and Aurelio Barría are exiled there. Lewis is paying for my trip. He's got important contacts in Washington. He's arranging for me to testify before the Western Hemisphere Branch of the Senate Foreign Relations Committee. Jenny, send clothing. I don't have any cash."

Busy packing Chico's clothing, I didn't stop when Sofia came in. She objected, "Why's that Hawaiian shirt going, Mom? He never wears it." She lifted a pair of trousers. "Look at these pants! I gave them to him for Christmas before I went away to college. The tags are still on. He said they were rock star stuff. Why do you punish him?"

"I like this clothing. When he finishes there, he can trash them."

"You know he won't wear it, Mom. And look at this! You're sending his gold-plated golf tees? He never used them here. Never. The leather box is torn from old age. What's Dad gonna think when he sees all this garbage?"

"It's not garbage." I closed the suitcase. "How would it look if I discarded his things now that he's gone? Like he'd died. I'm saving his best clothing for when he returns.

"Poor Dad, all alone and badly dressed. Double punishment!"

Minutes later I heard her mumbling to Trinity.

196

"Mom's lost it. When Dad sees these threads, he'll know she's nuts."

"All right," I whispered, knowing they couldn't hear. The only things I'll discard are the big, black, army boots. Fetching them from his closet, I put them in the trash, securely covered so no Doberman could spot them and use them to kick Crusaders.

Sadly, I lost my daughter's sympathy while their father became their hero. Who could have believed it? He chose the scum of the earth, devil Doberman and in supporting them became an accomplice. In my zeal to do what was right for my country, I hurt my family. To prove my mettle I intended to protect our girls and his dream house until he returned.

27

RAVENS

Chico's mournful photograph in La República sold plenty of newspapers for the regime. Crusaders saw his gruesome gray beard for the first time. All opposition newspapers in the country had been destroyed by tyranny. Nor had Internet arrived in Panama. Cellphones were a dream of the future. But the Civil Crusade bulletin did exist and it deserved a prize for the perfect one-liner describing our warrior's woe.

"He who breeds ravens gets his eyes plucked out." Bitter lesson confirmed in our own back yard: ravens kill little birds by pecking their eyes out.

Birds. Who would feed his feathery friends now? Not I.

As usual, I turned to Holy Trinity Church for consolation, sat up front to catch all the blessings. Fellow parishioners commiserated, "You can't leave Panama. Chico will be back."

Our home became a catacomb. We whispered, carried on under candlelight and went to bed early. Supposedly, candles diffused light and made us unnoticeable. Any excuse sufficed to ward off fear. Togetherness made the intolerable bearable. Inches a day the wall separating Trinity and I crumbled. She never admitted it, but the iceberg had existed. She quit blaming me for her father's absence. To assure our survival, we needed unity.

Sofia made the biggest sacrifice; she stayed home with Trinity and me, ignoring her new sports car. Her friends were getting together at night and kept calling. After two weeks, she got fidgety and cut the cord.

"Look you guys, the regime has nothing against us. Just Dad. He witnessed so many of their crimes using equipment he provided. He didn't fit in Panama anymore."

Based on this announcement Sofia started going out at night, seeking the company of school friends-turned-Crusaders.

One morning, hours after my girls had left for school and work, I heard Crystal Voice. "Yoo-hoo," she called from her living room window, the one facing my bathroom window. I climbed onto the mosaic shower bench to enjoy her gossip.

"Jenny, you've become scandalous."

"What? How so? I don't go anywhere."

"Listen, before my husband interrupts us. A gorilla wife came to our social tea yesterday and said, '*Coronel* Stone was such a nice man. His wife is the bad one.' Can you believe that? She's so stupid she doesn't realize her insult flatters you. *"*

"What? I haven't seen a PDF wife since Dr. Spadafora was beheaded. What have they got against me?"

"The nasty woman said you're from Arraijan and those people are trash."

"Well, ever since the military ousted Arnulfo Arias, Arraijan residents detest all of them including their supporters. And it gripes them putting up with the terrible PRD legislator in their town."

"Forget the politics. You're free! No husband to boss you. Enjoy your vacation. I'd love it if my husband went somewhere for a while. Find yourself a lover. Don't wait. Do it while you're still young!"

Lover? I nearly fell off the tile bench. I already had Chico. I needed a savior and knew exactly where to find one.

Crystal's gossip gave me a stomachache. I climbed down from the shower bench, realizing, I hadn't fixed lunch and Trinity was due home any minute. No time for tea to calm me. The sound of the front gate crashing into the iron frame announced Trinity. She came in with spice on her tongue. While unlocking the gate she was already scolding me.

"Mom, I could hear your voice all the way to the curve in front of the tennis court. Who were you arguing with?"

"No argument. I was at the bathroom window talking to Crystal Voice."

Serving herself leftovers, she sat chomping a chicken leg with her eyes closed. Minutes later she phoned her favorite neighborhood friend, the Chinese girl. Her tone of voice switched to alarm.

"What? You're leaving town going to another school? Why Costa Rica?"

Terrible news. Her dear friend, two houses from ours, was leaving before the school term ended. Some schools were closing due to the crisis. If she had cried, some of the accumulated pain could leak out. No tears came nor did her cheer return.

Parties stopped all over town, even at our house. At sixteen her social life fizzled. She never complained. Nor did she comment if at school during lunch break, classmates still turned on a portable radio to dance while nuns hid from the whooping festivities and the chorus of "*Ay Lucy querida;* Oh Lucy my love."

A jarring ring broke the solemn silence. The telephone. Trinity jumped to answer.

"That's gotta be Dad." I took the bedroom extension. He greeted her with enthusiasm, his sorrow well hidden. When I spoke, his voice changed. It hardened.

"I won't wear the clothing you sent."

"We told Mom. But you know how she is."

"The senate hearing on Panama is coming up soon. Glad you sent my suit."

"You don't sound excited. Won't it benefit Panama? Will they come down here and straighten out this mess? We aren't guerillas. The US knows that. Noriega is their man. The right thing is for the US to pluck him out."

"I'm not so sure. My impression is the US Government still favors Noriega."

"Treacherous. You tell them how terrible things are here."

"It's a closed hearing. No press invited. Panama will hear only what's left after censors cut out sensitive material. Confidential stuff."

Trinity grew impatient hearing our talk. "Dad. Have you seen any good movies?"

"Haven't had a chance yet. How's school?"

"Same old thing. Flavio might come home soon."

"Wish I were coming home too."

Va-room, Sofia's car roared into the garage. She saw us on the phone located at the front door. Trinity gestured it was her father. She rushed in.

"Hi Dad. Did you get the newspaper clippings I mailed? You're on the front page."

"Yeah. I look terrible. Shaved the beard off soon as I saw the photograph."

Unhappy goodbyes from four sad voices without a plan for the future, we stood with eyes glued to the phone.

Trinity's effervescence fizzled, replaced by anger. "He sounded great at first. Till he talked to Mom. Sofia, you think Dad can convince the US Senate that Panamanians are Noriega's victims? At school that's all we talk about. We need the US to remove him. Do you think they'll pay any attention to Dad?"

"Every little bit counts," Sofia said. "That's what the Crusade's all about. Solidarity." She laughed. "Did you hear that? I just called Dad a Crusader. He'd be livid!"

28

ROBERTO PITTÍ

Seeking to unload my sorrows, I visited the hummingbird that frequented our back yard. He didn't argue and I could unload. "Colibrí, Panama's torn with troubles and you're oblivious. I wish I were like you, sucking *heliconia* flowers and able to fly away." Brushing the top of my head, hummingbird flew close enough to stress a natural law. I disturbed his kingdom.

One evening I accidentally heard Sofia speaking on the living room phone.

"No, Virginia, I won't leave. I can't. I don't trust my Mom. If I leave, who knows? She might be tempted to become a guerilla."

My daughter doesn't know me. I threw away my gun precisely for that reason. Guns don't solve anything.

The yard we planted ourselves suffered neglect and weeds took over. It turned into a cow pasture. Covered with dust, the Audi turned from silver to beige. My responsibility was to guard our house and daughters, and worrying about them, sleep evaded me. I took up prayer beads, fingering the rosary. Sofia showed up with a colorful one, just in case I lost one.

With our mortgage interest rate at 13%, I visited Chase Manhattan Bank monthly pleading they delay foreclosure plans on our house. I could not pay the entire sum. The bank treated me kindly.

"Lady, we cannot foreclose your house. We have 10,000 homeowners in your same situation. There is no market for so many houses. Don't worry."

The regime blamed President Reagan for Panama's economic crisis. Reagan withheld millions of dollars of canal revenue from the military regime. At first I agreed with the embargo: choke the military for lack of money and impose austerity on the populace, forcing Panamanians to overthrow Noriega. But in the long run the embargo hurt everyone. Paradoxically, with funds frozen, I could not pay my mortgage. Chico's deportation had split his pension funds between us, and it was paltry.

The following month I returned to Chase Manhattan Bank with the same question. Are you going to foreclose my house? Such was my existence. In that frame of mind I arrived at evening Mass. Padre Durán spoke of loss and addressed temperance and resignation. He referred to the liturgy, specifically the Old Testament and Book of JOB. "When a person loses all possessions, they're set free. Liberated from obligations and worries." I wished it were so simple.

Padre embraced the habit of reminding my daughters and me that we had a roof over our heads. I recalled when he took Chico and I to visit people living under tarps in San Miguelito. "The Roofless," he called them. The numbers had increased, and Chico had joined the roofless crowd. What irony.

Confiscated by Captain Pug, our Volvo had not reappeared. Chico insisted I visit Union Fire and Auto Insurance Company to inquire when they planned to pay. They refused saying a charred chassis is necessary for proof of loss. Leaving their office on Via España, I halted hearing a commotion ahead. Beneath two mahogany trees at the corner where I parked the Audi, people shouted. Drawing closer I saw an angry crowd, their piercing voices louder than the traffic roar to my right. The group blocked the path to my car. The main thoroughfare offered an escape route if I could bypass the angry people. But did I dare risk being hit by one of the infamous Red Devil buses menacing on the busy avenue on my right?

The shouts of the crowd intensified. Curious, I chose to move closer to the melee.

"Stop it! Leave him alone!"

A frenzied mob obscured my view. Edging closer I saw the backs of two Doberman, their arms flying up and down, pounding their heavy hoses on a man's anatomy. Must be a Crusader, judging by the ferocity of Doberman's hoses hitting him. Knowing the risk, I edged closer to peek through a space between two women hollering with fury at a gruesome image. A man clung to a lamppost while Doberman beat him with their hoses, probably filled with lead. The victim's body flinched like a rag doll with each blow. Attackers turned a deaf ear to protesters' shouts for mercy. People watching were too frightened to intervene. Instead, they kept yelling.

"Somebody stop them! They'll kill him. It's Roberto Pittí! Save him!"

Roberto? Was he the same young Crusader from Chiriquí who joined us at the first march on Via Argentina where Daniella, Sofia and I hid to escape attacking Doberman?

Impotence gripped everyone with the fear Doberman would turn on them using the guns hanging from their belts. Doberman kept pounding on the defenseless man.

The crowd groaned each time clubs hit the man tied to the post. Our crowd out-numbered Doberman twenty-to-one. But we backed away paralyzed with the fear that any moment a truck full of Doberman would zoom in and beat the daylights out of us.

Blood oozed from Roberto's head. He stood resisting the blows, but soon his body began to droop. What held him up? His hands, tied with a belt looped to the post, kept him standing. People's screams finally registered. Two men leaned out an open window on the second floor of the building rising next to us. They hollered they'd come down. Within seconds two lawyers in neckties charged past me. Both well known: Guillermo (Willy) Cochez, a Christian Democrat leader, and Freddy Garcia.

The two thrust themselves between the Doberman and Roberto, separating them. They raged, barking at the attackers.

"Don't touch this man! His rights are being violated! Get Away! Now!"

The lawyers continued yelling, quoting the constitution and its laws, confusing the Gorilla cops. The lawyers' courage inspired the crowd to react. Several bystanders stepped up to untie the belt holding Roberto's wrists.

The lawyers' aggressive attitude injected the crowd with courage. They surged forward and formed a wall between the Doberman and lawyers who lifted the bleeding Roberto Pitti. Overwhelmed by the crowd's solidarity the Doberman stood stunned; their vile hoses listless, unsure whether to stash them or swing them against the crowd. The angry crowd boxed them in. Doberman shriveled like worms and scurried away. Every so often they snuck a look behind. Nobody stopped them. A few hands grabbed rocks and pelted their vehicle as they drove away. The ping on metal proclaimed our victory. I considered myself part of the conquest.

"They're cowards when their gang isn't with them," said someone.

The lawyers half-carried a nearly unconscious Roberto. As they passed, women touched him tenderly, others wiped blood from his head. His voice, barely audible, youth favored him. Within minutes he regained strength as a result of the love shown by the crowd and the lawyers' rescue. Someone asked who had tied him to the post.

"That's my belt. Doberman followed me from the bus stop, planning to arrest me. I tied myself to the post knowing if they took me I was dead." He coughed blood.

"Smart move, risky but brilliant," said a lawyer as they placed him in a car. Cochez addressed the crowd, "You people best leave! Doberman will return in a rage over the humiliation we gave them. Spitting venom, like snakes minus their tails."

I ran to my car and drove home singing, "Love is in the Air." Events like ours occurred daily in different parts of the country. We heard about acts of valor and unity through the Crusade bulletins and word of mouth.

The lawyer's warning prompted me to stay home more than ever. On the contrary, my girls ventured out daily for school and work knowing they had nobody to rescue them. One evening Daniella came home fuming. She by nature is jovial, but we had all changed. It showed in her voice.

"Sofia, the regime plans to take our cars! 'Cause they're brand new. They'll ruin us!" She kept ranting and I had no idea why. Daniella calmed down and explained the exorbitant tax the regime slapped on new cars. I stated the law exonerated our cars. They corrected me. Without their father's presence the exoneration ended. The fact he paid $1,000 to immigration for his resident card to facilitate the exoneration ended when immigration confiscated his card at the airport.

"Yes, Mom, as of yesterday, the law changed. We can't get a license plate. We're driving with provisional plates from the agency. We must pay tons of money."

Sofia sat down with a calculator. "Between our two cars, the tax is more than ten thousand. Impossible to pay that."

Daniella, pacing the floor like a guard, suddenly perked up.

"Wait a minute, I've got an idea. My best friend's lawyer, Jaime, Crusader to the bone, offered to help if we had trouble."

The next few days were tense. Sofia refrained from playing the usual salsa music when arriving home from the bank . . . until one afternoon when Daniella came home exuberant.

"Great news! Remember I told you about Jaime, the lawyer. He took the case and verified our exoneration. It's valid! He's tight with the regime because his wife represents a famous champagne, the kind the regime likes. Now I have to sell him a Toyota at cost. Lose my commission. It's worth it."

Truth lay in small groups as prayer circles sprouted overnight, both Catholic and Charismatic. "Opium of the People," Trinity called it. Retired schoolteachers in our parish recited five rosaries daily; they prayed walking in circles in their living room.

Prayer power disturbed the G-2. The regime's intelligence group failed to crush silent resistance from the Civil Crusade. In private they accredited civilian prayers to Crusader staying power. Out of their minds with ire, they began enacting satanic black masses, the kind of trivia enjoyed by lowlife mentalities in third world countries. Afraid to be considered devil-worshipers, they added sacredness to their dark cult by stealing consecrated Hosts from Catholic Churches. Such 'divine comedy' delved deeper. Their plain-clothed henchmen wore amulets—black rosaries—around their necks. Someone in our prayer group saw the item. Instead of a crucifix depicting Christ on the cross as in the Catholic rosary, theirs hung a horned beast on their black-beaded rosary.

Accidentally, I confirmed it. A relative from Arraijan was diagnosed with cancer. I visited the young victim at the hospital next to Cristo Rey Church. The dying young woman's husband was a Noriega bodyguard. The husband was in her hospital room when I arrived. Seeing me he bristled, announcing he needed to leave. Perhaps the family had talked about whom my husband was. He walked over to kiss his wife goodbye, and bending down over the hospital bed to kiss her, a black amulet slithered out from under his shirt. The infamous black rosary and its horned beast. His lips on hers, the horned beast caressed her cheek.

She died several days later at age twenty-six. I never saw him again.

Next time Chico called I had plenty to tell. Nothing flustered him until I said my mother still cried over him. Pleased by the detail, he chuckled sarcastically.

"How do you like that? I'll never understand women. She never cared while I was there. Women adore men after they're gone. Jenny, you're not like that. Are you?"

Faking a laugh, I denied it.

Chico's deportation affected Trinity so negatively she quit swimming with me at our usual 5:30 p.m. plunge. To punish me for her pain. I also quit and filled my vacant swim time by attending 5:30 evening Mass. Crusaders packed pews every day—all over the country. Padre Durán lamented this fact.

"When there's no national crisis, the church is empty. It shouldn't be that way."

Before Mass I loitered at the entrance eavesdropping for political gossip.

Flori approached sweetly asking for a donation for altar flowers. She caught me at a bad time; distressed over Chico's ferns I had donated for the altar. Shriveled from thirst due to a janitor's neglect they drooped, bordering the altar.

"Jenny, it's only five dollars. Once a month. You can afford that."

I laughed in her face saying, "Some other day". I should have told the truth. I could not even pay my mortgage. She walked away, her plump, petite frame drooping from the weight of my sting. Inside I seethed resentment, not at her, at everything, primarily Chico's dying ferns. I grumbled. How could Flori ask for money for flowers? They die overnight in our excessive heat. Walking into the church, I took my usual place. Chico's lush ferns could have lasted years at the altar, but instead hung tortured from thirst.

Padre elevated the Host for communion saying: "May the Body of Christ give us peace the world cannot provide."

His words came too late to save Flori from my anger. I had crushed her, my favorite. I snuck a glance across the aisle where she always sat with her gray-haired pals in the first row. Raw horror invaded my eyesight! The three women looked like ghosts. My sick eyes beheld them naked to the waist. I rubbed my eyes, but no improvement. The old women resembled statues in a pornographic mausoleum. Their breasts, naked, in gargoyle gray, hung long and wrinkled; gouged deep as the crevices in a morbid sculpture. Flori. Ghoulish. Her breasts reminded me of those I saw at the Fort Bragg reception: the general's mature wife with gray-tinged, wrinkled tits. That same night seven years ago, Chico told Lieutenant Coy I was coming to Panama to kill Omar Torrijos. Why was I remembering that now? Because Chico's ferns were dying of thirst.

Padre Durán prepared to pass out Hosts. I could not move; my sweaty legs stuck to the folding metal chair. Padre in heavy vestments stood cool as a Popsicle. I did not deserve to receive the Host. Soon as Padre left the altar, I dashed out to the car to avoid Flori. I needed solitude to quit hallucinating over a bunch of dead ferns.

29

BURNING TIRES

Only twelve old automobile tires fit in the Audi. I needed to make a second trip to pick up the rest. Free of charge, the employees at the Albrook gas station never asked why I wanted them. Nor would I have told them. Leaving them in the car was out of the question. One at a time I carried them into the laundry area. Sofia and friends planned to block traffic on a busy street by setting up a burning tire barricade.

Her friends kept coming to visit. Young men visited Sofia often as if she were an oracle and they came for a prophecy. One of them laughed at his own jokes.

"Sofia, when I tell friends I'm coming here, they ask why I'm not afraid. Can you imagine that? They're convinced you women are kept under surveillance." Had he truly believed this, he'd have quit coming.

One evening I crossed the living room lit up with the sun's last shocking pink rays bursting through the terrace. A young man chatting with Sofia on the terrace jumped from his seat. He rushed over to air-kiss me. What if I'd been wearing my usual frayed housedress? Hastily the stranger explained the reason for his enthusiasm.

"My mother is afraid you'll leave."

I wanted to ask who his mother was, but the gentleman rambled on as if I should know. When he left, Sofia said his father was one of the Civil Crusade leaders. Since so many existed, the information carried little weight. What struck home was an imperative we all recognized. A silent bond held the Civil Crusade together. All were leaders, a strategy aimed at preventing anyone from becoming a martyr.

My own mother checked on us in a similar way. She bragged to relatives in Arraijan that I would never abandon her. But just in case, she visited often; shed a few tears for Chico, blamed me for his deportation, then hugged the girls tight as if restraining them from packing to leave town.

On one visit Sofia paid excessive attention to her Abuelita, met her at the door, helped her limp into the house. More interesting was Trinity's sudden and overt attention to her grandmother. She had avoided her Abuelita since childhood, claiming fear.

"Abuelita might kill me while I sleep." Her trauma derived from an incident when Abuelita deliberately stepped on the gas pedal attempting to run over pedestrians with Trinity sitting in the car.

"Abuelita did it lots, yelled at pedestrians, 'get off the road,' then lunged at them."

At sixteen, Trinity finally decided to become chummy with her for economic reasons. She had witnessed her sisters needle money out of Abuelita. Now Sofia worked on her, setting up their grandmother for a stickup. Piling huge scoops of soursop ice cream on a dish, Sofia sang Jose Feliciano's song, "Light my fire, Light my fire." Abuelita devoured every scoop.

Sofia asked to borrow her station wagon. Our Volvo station wagon ripped off by the PDF captain was still missing. Sofia had acquired everything necessary: the accomplices, twenty-four tires, gasoline and rags . . . all she needed was the station wagon. When Abuelita departed, Sofia came in juggling her grandmother's extra car keys.

Early in the planning stage for the fiery barricade, Trinity nagged Sofia. "Aren't you afraid of getting burned? Dad took me to 50th Street and those burning barricades were towering infernos. Hotter than hell. Frightening. Aren't you scared?"

Sofia responded, "We're the avengers."

"Avengers? Who? Us?"

"Yep. We're Beowulf's descendants."

"Aw, come on. Who's Beowulf?" She followed her sister around insisting, "If you're doing this for Dad, I don't think he'd like it. Not one bit."

Sofia laughed. "Dad's ancestors were warriors. Tough people, both sides of our family had a bunch of them." Trinity went on mumbling unintelligibly and worried.

Sofia and Trinity cleared dinner dishes from the table setting up for the final meeting. The first recruits arrived, a young medical internist, Eduardo Thomas, his friend Rambo, a college senior, and his sister. Five aspiring arsonists whose major pyromaniac training entailed burning dry leaves in their back yard. They sat down to check their plans. I was messenger and cohort. Trinity thumped her fingers loud on the rosewood table and shuffled her chair creating annoying scratchy sounds. Nervous, she preferred gatherings with music and silly talk.

I offered mango juice from our fruit tree but all recruits said they had recently dined.

Sofia tapped a pencil and pointed at the yellow pad, a map showed arrows and small vehicles. The scale drawing showed the route their vehicles would transit to the chosen street. She designated persons responsible for loading tires and gasoline onto cars and later placing them on the target.

"Two neighborhood women promised to participate. They already know their jobs. Interceptors. They will block traffic. Protect us in front and back when our cars park in the middle of the street. They'll drive back and forth perpendicular to the street. From one curb to the other, blocking oncoming traffic while we set up the barricade, start the fire and go. It's a narrow street but has lots of traffic. You all know these women, they're neighbors too." She pointed at a spot on her homemade road map. "The maneuver starts here. At Betty's Beauty Salon. Let's go over it again."

Six heads peered over the paperwork as Sofia's pencil pinpointed the process. Then she reviewed who carried gas cans and rags.

"Everybody agree? Then we're ready. Any questions?"

Everyone agreed except Rambo.

"Who carries the matches?" He brought laughter, the loudest from Trinity.

Sofia went on. "Does everybody understand? Time is the most important element. We have sixty seconds. One minute. Block the street, light the fire and disappear. Time is critical." Then her voice dropped. "We do have a problem; the two absent women are vital. Their job, blocking traffic, is critical. Shall we cancel everything?"

Rambo jumped up and threw a punch, "Never! We'll show those damned Doberman whose boss in Bethania! I'll find those dames!"

"OK! I'll repeat the plan . . . Starting next to where I put the first tire, we stack them three-deep straight across the street. Trinity stuffs rags inside the tires, and Mom pours gasoline." She closes the presentation by pointing at the internist. "We follow. Torching the rags soaked with gasoline."

Doc stretched. Rambo threw him a playful punch. His sister whispered to Sofia.

"What's my job?"

"Your job is to monitor the blocker's cars. Keep 'em moving—fast." Visibly piqued, Sofia checked her watch. "Wish those two ladies had come."

"Perfect!" They all jumped up, satisfied. Sofia closed with a warning.

"Don't talk about this on the phone. They're all tapped."

The two young men planted kisses on the girl's cheeks and left. Rambo once more pretended to punch the doctor's arm.

Crystal Voice had volunteered to block cars with her baby blue Chevrolet Impala. The other blocker had recently returned home from exile. Stripping away her citizen's rights, the regime exiled her for publishing abroad atrocities committed by the military here. She insisted on taking part to honor freedom of press. Sofia wanted to revenge her father. Trinity and I yearned action.

Next day, Trinity arrived from school raring to go, by-passing food and breathing fire. She called Sofia at the bank begging her to come home. Minutes later Sofia arrived. At four p.m. the rest of the fire brigade waltzed in—no air kissing—all whispers and serious business. Rambo and doc hustled back and forth carrying tires to the cars. Rambo broke the silence. "Matches?" Sofia tossed packs to everyone.

Screeching tires careened around the corner. We jumped out of oncoming danger, as a car sped straight at us. Crystal Voice! Behind came another auto. Beeping. Our exiled neighbor! Sofia showed them the drawing pointing to key locations and reviewed their responsibilities.

We hopped into cars and rolled downhill. Our caravan penetrated traffic at the corner of Betty's Beauty Salon. The interceptor cars stopped mid-road and started the crazy maneuver: speeding back and forth perpendicular to traffic and blocking oncoming cars. We parked in between the two cars, jumped out and started unloading.

Infuriated drivers honked, shouting obscenities. "Move that shit!"

"Get out of the way! Asshole!"

While they raged, Rambo and Doc stacked tires. Trinity stuffed rags. Twenty-four tires across the street blocked traffic. I poured gasoline. Ten gallons of gasoline. Unfortunately, I overdid it. Enough to burn the whole neighborhood. Sofia torched the soaked rags.

WHOOM! Fire leaped sky high! Saffron tongues licked heaven! Flames tickled utility lines!

"Let's Go!" Sofia yelled running to the car. "Sixty seconds! We did it! Success!"

Flames soared behind us.

Our car engines roared and we peeled rubber. Our escape paths sped in every direction. In two minutes we were home. Alone. Everyone else went to their homes. Sofia unlocked the iron gate at our house with me close behind. I smelled something distasteful, like burned meat. "Do you girls smell something awful. Like burned flesh?"

At that moment Sofia withdrew the key from the lock. Then I noticed her hand. Raw flesh. I grabbed her arm, questioning if it hurt terribly. Her answer encouraged me.

"It only hurts a little. Let's go in. I'll wash it off. I'll be fine."

Unaware of the calamity, Trinity pushed between us.

"Sofia, we did it! Just like you wanted! What's wrong Sofi? Why aren't you excited? Hey, did you see the doctor's pants catch fire?"

Sofia's silence spoke tons. Her hand. Burned. Pain must have been unbearable. Eyes semi-closed, shoulders pinched, she walk away slowly. Gone was her earlier bounce. She went straight to wash her hands and we followed, honoring her immense pain. Trinity realized the pain was far worse than her sister admitted. Water caused worse pain. Her knees buckled. No matter how she tried to hide it, pain consumed her.

I applied peroxide, not knowing its negative potential. She clenched her teeth. I thought of infection and insisted we go to a doctor.

"No. The others are coming over after dinner. It's nearly dark now."

We wrapped her hand with white gauze. When nearly finished, a shout from the terrace identified Daniella. With Lulu in tow she jabbered excitedly about something.

"Wait till you hear the latest. Great stuff! A friend called raving about a burning barricade. She says it's right

215

down our street. At the corner of Betty's Beauty Salon somebody lit a barricade. Fire! Burning right now! Crusaders here! Right near us!" She noticed the huge white bandage on Sofia's hand.

"Sofia! What happened? You look like a prize fighter!" Daniella laughed.

Not the slightest cheer touched Sofia's face. Daniella recognized something was wrong with her sister and her joy vanished. Lulu caressed the white mitt and Sofia cringed. We told Daniella what we'd done. And that Sofia was burned.

She exploded. "You did what? You could have all been killed! How dare you do something so dangerous? Trinity, you're too young for arson. Mom, you're too old for such danger. Damnit! You think arson's a game? I could have lost my whole family!"

Her scolding continued so long it bored Lulu. She wanted to play with Sofia's white mitt while the rest of us tried to distract her, singing the same song Sofia had sung for days, Jose Feliciano's: "Light my fire! Light my fire!" Pain kept her from singing. Lulu understood none of the English and was surprised to hear her women singing in a language unknown to her. She thought her grandfather was the only one who spoke that way. But she stuck close to Sofia's mitted, white hand.

We four held Sofia captive with no intention of leaving her for a second. I had no camera. Our portrait, the Stone women venerating the leader of the fiery barricade, was sublime. Wounded, the warrior's daughter lay prostrate while the smallest of the clan fixed her adoring, baby blue eyes on her heroic aunt.

In that historical moment we made a solemn pact of secrecy. Never tell Chico what we did. Not until he returned home. He'd get upset as Daniella did.

30

TELEPHONE TERROR

Sofia pretended all was well and tried to hide the violent pain of her burned hand from her family. For days she arrived home from the bank and announced, "I'm not hungry," skipping dinner. Her farce succeeded until she crawled into bed taking a fetus position facing the wall. There her facade crumbled.

Trinity went into the bedroom and saw, challenging her sister.

"You're always hungry! Who are you kidding? You spend half your time with your head in the 'frig searching for yummy treats. I don't know how you stay so thin. Look at you all shriveled into a ball. I know the pain is killing you."

Trinity gave me courage to call our neighbor who specialized in hand injuries. Sofia refused to see a doctor with a legitimate excuse. Reliable sources confirmed the presence of spies everywhere and she might become a target for reprisals. Our neighbor, the one who specialized in hand surgery and broken bones, came immediately when I called. She started by scolding Sofia with kindness.

"Sofia, do you plan to overthrow the regime with your bare hands? If so, next time consult with an expert. And you, Jenny, stop being an accessory. Gasoline is very explosive and the fumes are dangerous."

She checked Sofia's hand, cleaned it and reprimanded me for using peroxide.

"Soap and water are better and less damaging. Excuse me. I'll be right back."

She ran home to get an ointment and returned quickly with a tube. She proudly held up the tube and explained its properties.

"This is magic. It's called Silvadene. Sofia, tomorrow come to Gorgas Hospital. During my lunch hour I'll take care of your hand." She left.

Sofia sighed deeply as if releasing pain she had hidden from us for days. She truly thought herself capable of coping with the pain unattended by a professional. At twenty-two Gorgas Hospital was no longer at her disposal. She lost the privilege of utilizing US installations in Panama. At sixteen Trinity still held the privilege.

Prompted by pain, Sofia went to Gorgas as the neighbor recommended. For several weeks the specialist treated the hand and exercised it so the skin kept flexible as it healed. Over time the bandage became smaller. As the patch shrunk, music echoed once again in our home. One of those afternoons as the house vibrated with guitars, the phone rang. Not a word had we said to Chico, and Sofia answered eagerly, hoping it was her father. She no longer begrudged him for associating with the PDF.

Soon as she answered her voice changed, sounded cold and suspicious. The black phone in the grasp of her white mitt seemed symbolic. She signaled the call was for me.

"It's a guy. Wouldn't identify himself. Sounded weird."

Overly friendly, the caller said, "Hello, Jenny dear."

I interrupted him asking who he was. He ignored the question.

"I wanna see you. Caress you. Enjoy your body. I don't intend to hurt you. Just a   little. I'm large. What are you like? When can I see you?"

I gagged. Grabbed onto the first thing I found nearby, a chain suspending a glass lamp over the telephone. It came crashing down. Glass flew everywhere. Sofia rushed back.

"What happened? Is Dad hurt? What's wrong? Mom, are you cut?"

We stared at the black phone on the floor amidst shattered glass. Sofia picked it up returning it to the cradle, asking who called. I didn't know. Shocked, I said too much.

"That criminal wants to hurt me. Threatened to . . ."

Instantly I hushed, knew I must lie to them. Protect them from the telephone terrorist. I recovered and said, "The caller mistook me for someone else. Wrong number."

I was not cut. Sofia's burn was enough.

Trinity, sweeping the broken glass, paused to question, "I wonder who's the poor victim they're trying to torment." She was wise for her young age.

The phone rang again. Afraid it was the terrorist and one of the girls might answer, I dashed to grab it. Sofia beat me to it and chewed out the caller.

"You scum! Stop calling. Understand!"

"Sofia, let me handle this." I grabbed the phone not wanting the man's filth to reach my girls. Facing into the corner, I swallowed my medicine same as Chico did his last night here.

"Hello. What did you wish to tell me?"

Trinity came up close to me.

"Mom, don't let anybody scare you. Tell him to go to hell. Remember what you always said when I was a little kid and you were scolding me. You'd say: I eat nails. OK? One nail removes another nail. Tell him to stick a nail up his rear."

Unable to laugh, not with a criminal in my grip, I kept nodding repeatedly, letting Trinity know I was strong. Telling the pig, 'Yes. Yes', I covered the earphone making it impossible to hear a word he said. Let him spill his dirty guts. Then I hung up.

"Girls, please don't tell your father. He can't come back. Why make him worry?"

Trinity, sharp as a tack, caught on. "Yeah, he'd make us leave Panama. But I don't know where we'd go."

Within minutes the sisters relaxed, listening to Latin jazz and chatting about Sofia's new sports car. They lived the Panamanian paradox: youth can survive terror and at the same time retain a passion for life. It's their birthright. It runs in their veins.

At midnight, I was jolted upright. The phone rang next to me. Chico would never call late at night; it had to be the telephone terrorist. I broke out in a sweat. The phone sat inches from my head. If I let it ring, he'd wake the girls. I picked up and whispered, "Yes?" and waited. A male voice laughed.

"That's the way I like my women. Always willing with a yes. Any day now. Yes."

I smothered the phone into the pillow and let him vomit his filth.

Tossing, I struggled through a sleepless night and by morning felt drained as though dragged through a sewer. The girls left. Determined never to be a maudlin Mom, I cleaned the refrigerator, the stove, and was attacking the floor when a sweet female voice uttered, "Je-n-n-y." I peeked out the window and saw white hair. Flori! Visiting me? Such a sweetheart! And I treated her wretchedly for asking for a donation to buy fresh flowers for the altar. No wonder everyone loved her. I ran to the door but was ashamed to hug her. She walked in limping from recent knee surgery.

I brewed gunpowder tea. My favorite. She liked the name as well as the flavor.

"You don't look too bad, Jenny."

She rose to leave. I blurted out the telephone terrorist threat as though a hot potato burned my tongue. I asked she not repeat it.

"Jenny, don't let those guttersnipes ruin your life. I know you hope your husband can convince the US Congress to do something; take us out of our misery. Clean up the human garbage they left us. In the meantime Jenny, don't let these devils get you down. Let me tell you what they did to me. A PDF captain stole my house. Yes. Don't look so frightened, Jenny. My beach house in Farallon. I had no plans to sell it. My kids had stopped going there ever since Panama became so dangerous. The captain convinced me. Gave me a $5,000 down payment saying he'd pay the remainder in a week. A month went by and no money. I called him. He never returned the calls. I lost patience and went to PDF Headquarters. No sign of him. I was upset. Drove to the beach and the bastard had changed the doors, and of course the locks were different. He had posted a guard and I couldn't break into my own house through the window. My house! Panama belongs to them. Who can save us? I hope your husband can."

Rubbing her knee, she continued. "Sorry I unloaded on you, poor thing. Now you look scared. Things always get better. Remember what Padre Durán says, 'Sit in your doorway and watch your enemy's funeral caravan pass by.' Don't let material losses get you down."

The thought of losing my house was unbearable. As we parted, Trinity arrived from school and caught Flori on the sidewalk. They hugged. Flori's granddaughter was a classmate at Maria Inmaculada.

Trinity came in cheerfully talking of something that reminded me what she said twenty-four hours before. "You're made of iron, Mom." Flori suggested something similar. These two women had no idea I spent my life faking it, pretending I was tough. Neither imagined I already had a funeral procession marching through my insides.

31

RETREAT

Sofia's hand was nearly healed. Trinity came next. Her jaw cracked loud and painfully each time she chewed or opened and closed her mouth. A yawn hurt her, and while sleeping she ground her teeth. "TMJ," the specialist called it and put a retainer in her mouth. As the annoying and painful crack-crack continued, she acquired a frown.

Two weeks into her misery she tossed the retainer aside, dressed in a floral mini skirt and went to a discotheque with friends. They ignored the curfew imposed by the regime that used any excuse to arrest people on the street. Trinity's friends believed if they chose discotheques owned by civilian associates of the dictatorship they were immune to arrest and barbaric treatment.

Our antique grandmother clock chimed twelve strokes and no Trinity, I worried Doberman had arrested her again. She had no Dad to save her this time plus it was nighttime. Anxious, I sat on the cold rocks in the vestibule to wait and watch the street. The rocks punished my bones. Clock bonged once announcing how late it was. The rock seat was unbearable, a painful reminder of when I hit her unjustly in Coronado because I was miserable with worry. Conditions had not improved; on the contrary, danger had increased.

I rose from the rocks at the moment a car approached. Darkness obscured it until it stopped in front. Was it her?

Her sweet voice lilted, "Goodnight," and a door slammed.

In the dark her shoes tic-tac on the concrete sped to our iron gate. Darkness covered my presence. I held the garden hose and turned it on. The blast of water soaked Trinity. She shuddered aloud. Someone behind her jumped away to avoid the spray. Poor girl, her great pain in the darkest night. No one heard the silent howl dying inside her. She walked past me in silence, dripping water all the way.

Speechless for days, she studied constantly. Friends called, invited her to swim, to party; she refused. Her body reacted to her sorrow by developing a sinus infection. A doctor prescribed antibiotics. Again, her sister Sofia stayed home evenings to cheer her up.

A week remained before the annual senior retreat for two parochial schools, Maria Inmaculada and La Salle. Just in time Flavio returned from Japan. Trinity's classmates planned to celebrate before the retreat at Javier Academy. Trinity and Flori's granddaughter went to MAGIC discotheque with Flavio. She was in good hands with two responsible friends: Flavio a giant and the girl friend a stellar student and sharp. I did not bother to get up when she came home. She went straight to bed.

Very late, I woke to the sound of a tiny voice.

"Mom, help me."

Was I dreaming? The voice repeated.

"Mom, I'm dying."

I ran. It was Trinity moaning, "I can't move my legs. I don't know why. I can't feel my legs."

We drove to Gorgas US Army Hospital Emergency Room. A tall doctor in olive green scrubs examined her legs and feet. He found nothing wrong with them. Then he checked her throat, bones in her neck and took her blood pressure. He asked her whereabouts that evening as though he'd smelled liquor on her breath. She responded, "MAGIC."

He put her chart down on the metal table and crossed his arms.

"Your chart shows that last week a doctor from Gorgas prescribed antibiotics for a sinus infection. Are you still taking them?"

She said, "Yes" and the doctor continued.

"The medication contains codeine, tylenol and other substances. Did you know?"

She nodded.

"What did you drink at MAGIC?"

"Tequila."

He leaned back on the metal table observing her, and then spoke in a cold voice.

"Are you suicidal?"

Head down, she stared at the hole on the knee of her bluejeans. She pulled on a hanging thread. Her voice barely audible, "I don't care anymore."

My heart jumped. Trinity didn't care if she died! Who did this to her? The answer could wilt a flower. Who lives with her? Who mistreats her? And her father, her buddy, was deported.

As the doctor spoke, I rejected every word he said. Denied the truth; twisted the facts. In my mind I invented a lie saying the doctor blamed MAGIC and suggested a waiter slipped a drug into my daughter's Tequila. Lie after lie. The doctor never diagnosed such a thing. I refused to take the blame for Trinity's emotional distress.

The doctor said Trinity had an allergic reaction to the codeine in her medication when it mixed with alcohol. Tequila or any alcohol is dangerous when mixed with medicine.

At four a.m. we finally returned to bed. At seven a.m. a loud CLANG on our cowbell at the front gate jolted us out of bed. The hand causing the ruckus was Flavio and Flori's curly-haired granddaughter from last night's MAGIC madness. The two yelled for Trinity to hurry so they wouldn't be late for the retreat at Javier Academy. Too sick to eat, she slipped on last night's blue jeans, the ones with a tear on the knee, and a clean shirt and left, yawning.

Sunset brought Trinity and friends smiling into the house. Jubilant, they danced through the vestibule. Curly-haired friend chattered, "*Señora*, Trinity was a star! See how her face shines!"

Trinity said nothing; she glowed. Flavio couldn't stop raving over the mysterious marvels they experienced because of Trinity. Curly, ecstatic, could not stop talking.

"Trinity is blessed! She stole the show! Let me tell you, *Señora,* how it happened. We were late. The only vacant seats in the auditorium were in the front row. The choir sang, animating the crowd. Students acted bad, reading comic books holding them down low so *Monseñor* Vazquez Pinto couldn't see them. The priest just stared at them. He started off reading the Bible, then expanded on the subject. Kids yawned and stretched, bored with everything he said. He cut for refreshment break. Trinity was already asleep, leaning on my shoulder. Flavio and I had a soda and chips while Trinity stayed in her seat, drinking water and pulling on the threads in the hole in her blue jeans." She stopped talking to point at the knee. "Right there."

"Pleeezz, you guys. Let me tell the story," said Trinity. "It was so hot. Kids were passing notes, showed no respect for the priest. I was sleepy, hungry and had a huge headache. Somebody threw a wad of paper and it hit my ear. Felt like my ear exploded. I wanted to lie down. Guitars played for us to sing. I couldn't keep my head up.

"Then *Monseñor* called for a volunteer to come up on stage. I ducked, but it didn't work. We were sitting up front three feet from stage. Nobody volunteered and *Monseñor* didn't wait. He pointed at me. 'You. Blondie. In the front row. You with the hole in your blue jeans. Come up here! Don't be shy.' Kids cracked up laughing. Torn jeans aren't cool in Panama. There was no place to hide. I had no intention of going on stage. I turned away, hoping he'd call on someone else." She turned to the girl friend saying, "Ok, Curly, you tell the rest of the story."

"Flavio and I dragged and pushed and practically lifted Trinity on stage. *Monseñor* loved it. He smiled big-time. He told Trinity to stand next to him while he read from the Bible. She did. When he stopped reading, he paused a minute then reached out to touch Trinity's shoulder. Wham! She slid down and lay on the stage floor, stretched out flat. Looked like she was asleep. The weirdest part was her smile, like pasted on. Huge change on her from the last few days. Frowning all the time. But that wasn't the only thing spectacular. Two hundred loudmouth kids hushed. And there lay Trinity. Like dead. Priest said nothing. Not a sound anywhere. Priest seemed delighted to have her sprawled on the stage floor. It was eerie. A divine silence. Imagine, that huge auditorium full of kids and all of them quiet. It seemed like a long time. *Monseñor* stood silent and smiling, holding onto the podium, looking straight ahead and ignoring Trinity. He acted like: 'Who cares if there's a girl passed out at my feet? Happens all the time.' But students didn't know that. Finally, kids got antsy, shuffled in their metal seats. All this time Trinity's still passed out on the stage floor. Just then some idiot behind us yelled, 'She's bewitched.' Everybody jumped all over him, called him an idiot. Stupid."

Curly paused to breathe then continued.

"Finally, *Monseñor* spoke, 'Blondie, your friends want to hear from you. Get up.'

"Then like a zombie... no, better than that, like a puppet, only without strings or cords. She lifted like a bird's feather, something that floats."

Flavio interrupted adding, "Trinity looked beautiful; her face was shiny like varnished."

"Luminous," corrected Curly. "Her face was luminous.

"But lemme continue. Trinity got up wearing this precious smile and stood watching us. *Monseñor* asked, 'Blondie, is there anything you'd like to say?' She started talking as if rehearsed, quoting from the same scripture

Monseñor Vazquez Pinto read before she collapsed on stage. Her voice sounded like an echo, like it came from far away. A message directly for Panamanians.

> 'The Queen of the south will rise and she will
> condemn them. At the judgment day the
> people of Nineveh and Panama will arise
> with this generation and condemn evil acts'

"Trinity hushed. Just stood there smiling, like expecting a response.

"*Señora* Jenny, you should have heard the screams! Aieee! Two hundred kids jumped up and howled! They whistled, banged chairs, clapped, screaming, '*Viva Panamá.* Down with dictators!' *Monseñor* just kept smiling; his expression confirmed what he said earlier. 'God speaks today as he does everyday.' He raised the Bible he uses."

Flavio interrupted, "Trinity was the queen. Our queen."

Curly cut him off.

"*Monseñor* called it the repose in the Holy Spirit of God. He took her hands. Anointed them with oil blessed by him. Drew a cross on her palms. And when she climbed off stage, the kids crowded around wanting to see what he put on her hands. She just kept smiling. Like nothing bothered her anymore. They touched her hands, checked them out. Kids asked who told her the message for Panama."

"What message?" Trinity asked, her face perplexed. "I said that? I can't remember. Tell me what I said and I'll try to remember."

"But we couldn't either 'cause we don't read the Bible like my grandmother Flori always says. Then a few guys went to the priest asking him to give them some Knockout Spirit to take home. He touched them but it didn't work on them. Not one dropped to the floor."

Her two companions said goodbye.

"Mom, my jaw stopped hurting. Headache's gone. I feel good."

I was thrilled, overjoyed and curious. "I need to meet that priest."

"Parents are invited to come the last day for Mass. Come, Mom."

I went, and during snack break I chatted with the *Monseñor*. I thanked him for saving Trinity and admitted I'd treated her terribly, caused her great anguish because of my anger at the regime. He seemed amused, smiling.

"Listen, the military's dirty politics have poisoned your capacity to love. One time I got fired up against Omar Torrijos' government when the young priest, Hector Gallegos, was murdered. I was his superior. Got furious. Besides, that administration accused nobody nor arrested suspects. I went to Chiriquí. Those country folk are very brave and I knew I could trust them. I needed to let off steam around that specific group. They were still angry at the military for ousting President Arnulfo Arias. That's when Chiriqui hill people rebelled and the military murdered many. Archbishop McGrath got wind of where I was and sent for me. I guess he was afraid I'd start something. McGrath ordered me back to the city and put me in charge of a new movement, one as old as the apostles. It's called Spiritual Renewal; locally called Charismatic Movement. McGrath did the right thing. Nothing is solved with guns. But at the time I was like you, full of passion to correct evil and determined to get revenge for Gallegos's murder, no matter how."

Trinity walked up and started to chat with the *Monseñor*. He asked how she was doing in school. She smiled constantly; the two shined like gold. I envied their gift: both full of grace achieved through suffering. Why not me? Unable to fathom I lacked humility, I wanted their gift of the Holy Spirit, but I wanted it on my terms. Now.

228

32

US SENATE

God works His magic in strange ways. He chose an activist-for-justice, maverick priest, *Monseñor* Vazquez Pinto, to salvage Trinity from depression. Hundreds witnessed spellbound as he lifted her from abysmal sadness and led her through a mysterious conversion. Entranced, students watched the priest lift her to a spiritually sublime state. Miracles are contagious and we Stone women thought ourselves safe from military repression. We believed nobody spied on us.

Chico called, excited that his day to testify before a US Senate hearing drew near. We jumped for joy thinking the US would rectify Panama's dreadful situation. Our joyful attitude dulled our wits. We missed catching the severity of his statement.

"Jenny, I can't go back to Panama while Noriega's in power. Abandon the house. Come up here. Bring all the girls, Lulu included."

For once my standard reply received no rebuttal. "Where will the six of us live? And besides, we still have to pay mortgage here."

He sounded sad and embarrassed for having nothing to offer.

But I stuck to the problem. "US politics towards dictators are strange. No congressman requested your testimony. It took a Panamanian, Gabriel Lewis, to force the issue. Never again will I complain he was a Torrijos man. I forgive him. His efforts are instrumental to inform the US public what's going on here; that's why your testimony is so important. Who are the senators interviewing you?"

"Jesse Helms, Edward Kennedy and Christopher Dodd. Jenny, don't expect the US to save Panama. The US needs to settle bigger problems in Central America first."

I felt my temperature rise. "Meanwhile, Panama burns. But it's not your fault. Will the press be invited to the hearing?"

"It's a closed hearing, confidential. I'll send you a tape."

Sofia and Trinity arrived after he hung up and missed talking to him. Saddened, they asked a thousand questions. Crystal Voice came over, curious as the girls.

"Chico testifies today, doesn't he? Aren't you scared, Jenny?" She placed both hands on her hips as if waiting for me to react dramatically.

"Why worry? He's safe, right near the Pentagon. Nobody can hurt him."

She smiled, clapped her hands and did a little jig.

"A wise man once said innocence is a form of insanity. Watch the US fart on your husband's testimony. I was married to a New Yorker once. I know them." She waltzed out having rained on my parade.

As the day wore on, each breath of air felt lethal and I blamed my neighbor's pesticide spray. After my daughters went out, the cowbell clanged. I heard a masculine voice, "*Señora* Stone." I peeked. Roberto Pitti. Surprised, I rushed out to open the door for him.

"How did you know where we live?"

He smiled. Weeks earlier I witnessed Doberman beat him, nearly to death. Facial scars had aged the young man. I forced a feeble smile but he noticed my distress at seeing him so. He claimed feeling fine and then inquired about the colonel. Did he know Chico was scheduled to testify today at the senate hearing? And how did he know my address? Did regime cronies know also? The analysis failed to frighten me.

Roberto walked in and headed straight for the terrace. Attracted by the panoramic view of our beleaguered city, it magnetized him, as everyone visiting for the first time.

"How are your daughters?"

"Fine, thank you." I offered him cold juice.

"I'd love it after I do something important. Have any black paint? A brush?"

I had both leftover from painting Padre Durán's white church wall. We traipsed downstairs to fetch paint. Three floors down. He carried the items back up. I asked where he was going and what he planned to paint. He signaled me to follow.

On the street in front of our house he squatted and quickly painted: NORIEGA GET OUT! On the street. I surmised Roberto enjoyed flirting with death. I didn't think much about it. On the contrary, I figured he couldn't think clearly since the Doberman beat him on the head. In a flash he was gone without having cold juice. I guess something big drew him. And, he forgot to take the paint and the brush. Did he come to paint my street only?

Hungry, Trinity walked in from school without noticing the black paint. Over dinner we brainstormed the senate hearing, hoping her father's testimony would spurn the US to send the green berets. Energized by great expectations, I couldn't sleep. Very late I heard the girls talking in the bathroom. They no longer shared a bedroom. Sofia had switched to the front room facing the street when her hand burned while incinerating the old tires barricade. They chatted in the hallway where I could hear them.

"What time is it in Washington, Sofia?"

"Don't know."

I picked up the rosary beads Sofia had recently given me. Designed by Mother Teresa of Calcutta in five colors. I dozed with the rosary coiled on my chest. I'll never understand how I slept through the chaos happening outside our front door, and the rosary stuck to my chest. Nailed, a fanatic might have described it.

While we women slept, Doberman arrived. Three truckloads of soldiers. They stomped, painted and stayed so long they probably urinated in our front yard according to our neighbors. Worse still, Sofia slept up front and usually kept the windows open. But since the burned hand kept her awake, she ran the air conditioner. Closed windows spared her one hellish night. Outside her window boots kicked paint cans, and Doberman talked loud, disturbing the neighbors. Desperate to warn us, yet positive they couldn't save us, neighbors phoned us all night.

Trinity's room was in between Sofia's and mine. Downstairs in the separate apartment, Daniella and Lulu slept. None of them heard anything, nor did I. Extraordinary considering the slightest breeze wakes me. Perhaps our exhaustion of recent months culminating with Chico's deportation left us fatigued to the point of zero resistance. Only one sound did I hear that night, the telephone, loud and constant, located inches from my pillow. I ignored the ringing nuisance; certain Chico would not call so late. Wiped out, I refused to raise my hand and answer. Might be telephone terrorist.

Sofia would comment for months, "I'll never understand how."

What if we had known forty Doberman took over our garage? Stomped around painting everything black. What could we have done? Cry? Call for help? Call whom? Had we opened the door, what would they have done to us?

I don't want to know. Nor imagine.

At sunrise I started to rise when something cold and slippery slithered from my chest. My rosary. Then I heard noises out front. Voices. Before opening the wood door leading to the iron gate, I identified many voices. Women. I opened. Four neighbors stared at me. Open-mouthed. Shocked. Dawn patrol checking on me again? Why this time? Now they came fully dressed. No bathrobes. I rushed out. Alarmed.

All four spoke at once, chattering with emotion.

"Jenny, are you all right? Were you here last night? Are you sure you didn't go out? Where are your girls? How did you manage all those Doberman? You couldn't have been here. Three truckloads, the huge kind, full of Doberman. Forty bastards doing as they pleased. Painting and chatting like they owned the place. I thought they had taken you. Look at the cigarette butts everywhere. Your entrance looks terrible. See the black paint everywhere? I called you twenty times."

All four chimed in. Another neighbor said, "I called you too. Lots of times. Where were you? Where were your daughters?"

Behind them everything was painted black except the grass. The garage floor, the posts, sidewalk—all black. But they didn't paint Sofia's new car or our silver Audi. Which meant their orders came with damage-control limits. They intended to terrorize us sufficiently to make us leave, my daughters and I. Immediately.

The stench of paint intoxicated. A few times one of the neighbors touched me softly checking to see if I was real or about to disintegrate. Disbelieving what they saw, they couldn't handle last night either. The proof was everywhere, black. I had forgotten until then the regime recently painted the Chamber of Commerce building black. Then it registered: the seriousness of the warning.

Their grim talk gave me jitters. My voice quit. This was no dream. A nightmare. Speechless, I gestured for the neighbors to follow me into the house. We sat down and within seconds firm footsteps came up the vestibule. Another female voice asked.

"Jenny? Are you here, Jenny?"

Altogether the neighbors answered.

"Yes. Come in. She's here. We're all here."

Trinity and Sofia came out of their rooms asking what happened. "Why are the neighbors here?" The neighbors spoke at once and took the girls outside to show them. Trinity, in her bright orange and yellow striped nightgown, contrasted with the harsh blackened environs. Sofia inspected her new sports car, touching it. Two neighbors stood with her, talking.

"There were forty Doberman. I counted them. Look at the floor."

Trinity asked loud, "Why didn't they break in and take us women?"

The neighbors threw a fit and vetoed the idea. "Dear God, no. How horrible. Don't even think such a thing, child."

"Where's your other daughter? The one with a little girl?"

Nervous and shaking her hand as if swatting the air, Trinity said, "That little one is getting big. Soon she'll beat me at cards," then ran off to get Daniella from downstairs.

Still stunned, I pursued Sofia leaving the neighbors talking in the living room. Trinity came back with Daniella towing Lulu. Crystal Voice arrived exuding her usual boldness, eager to relate a message from her husband.

"My husband is European; his family lived through all these horrors. He thinks their next step could be kill you women."

The four neighbor women jumped all over her, pulling her outside, scolding.

"Tell your husband not to be such a despot."

The four neighbors surrounded us, watching our every move and eager to do whatever we desired. One glanced at my ragged nightgown, my favorite for its softness, and she sweetly asked I go change. I did and hurried back out, hoping neighbors had not left. The four women flirted with Lulu, fussing over her curly golden hair and asking if she could sing *Los Pollitos dicen,* the little chicky song.

Unaware of the terror at our door, she turned looking for something.

"I'm hungry, Mami." Daniella peeled a banana.

The neighbors grew uneasy, apparently needing to go home but wanting to stay and guard us. A man's voice spoke out front causing the neighbors to flinch visibly. When the voice bellowed, "HOLA!" the four women recognized our priest's Castilian voice. They rushed out to bring him in, telling him how wonderful that he'd arrived. I asked how he knew so quickly.

"Your neighbor called me," he pointed towards Crystal Voice's house. She had presaged our death minutes earlier.

Padre kissed every lady's cheek, all eight of us. Neighbors thanked him for coming. He told a noble truth. "Jenny you're in God's hands now."

Intrigued, Padre admired Sofia's white-patched mitt. She blushed and withheld confessing to having ignited a fiery barricade. She mumbled something exotic only the two of them understood. Or pretended they did. With his usual calm, Padre pronounced our destiny.

"Stone ladies, you must leave. Not Panama. Move out of this house. For a while. Until things improve. Trinity, you go live with the nuns on Justo Arosemena Avenue at their convent-school. I'll call Mother Superior and arrange it. Collect your belongings, everything you need for moving over there right now."

He turned to the older girls intending to secure their habitat and somehow subdue their nightlife. They hastened to impede his orders. Sofia revealed her friends had already invited her to stay with their families. "They offered the day after Noriega deported Dad."

Daniella announced something similar and edged over to console Trinity.

"Sorry dear, maybe living in the convent won't be so bad."

Lulu held Trinity's hand, released it to face her and dictate orders of her own. "Take me to your school. I wanna play with your big friends. And Barbie."

Padre walked over to me. "You cannot stay in one place. Each night you'll sleep in a different house. See me after Mass this evening. By then I'll have a family arranged, perhaps a parishioner's house."

He said goodbye and exited through the same vestibule as Chico had. One dark night. It seemed so long ago. The same height, the same type of man; both dedicated to protecting mankind. One with weapons and the other with faith and spiritual work. But the priest better understood the machinations of dirty politics.

The regime taught their followers: "Divide and you shall conquer." They divided us in a cruel way. We had wrongly believed the regime would leave us alone after deporting Chico. Our strength derived from us women staying together. They tore our family apart. I snuck a look at my girls, standing rigid, military daughters, immersed in shock and very aware of our vulnerability with the removal of their father-warrior-protector. Our turn had come to taste their father's bitter cup. He was alone. And now each of us-alone.

Fortunately, none of us questioned how long this isolation might last.

Lulu broke the painful impasse. She tugged at Trinity's blue plaid uniform skirt.

"Trini, let's go. Take my toys to your school."

The sound of shoes scraping cement headed for our door. "Let me come in!"

A familiar and loving voice, Sofia's hand therapist stood behind the iron bars of the gate. Sofia rushed to unlock. Her therapist smiled, silently hugged each of us tight enough to feel the sad beat of our hearts. She lifted Sofia's white, gauzed hand. This time she neither scolded nor joked. "See you tomorrow. Not today. I called the office. Told my boss I won't be in today. The hospital will survive. I'm sticking to your mother all day."

Altogether we left the house. Our exodus. Nobody cried; we were strong as stone but sad. Therapist became my rock for more than one day. She replaced the missing Stone the criminals removed. She spoke softly and continuously; aware I was dazed.

"They want us to leave." I finally acknowledged.

"Lots of Crusaders are living the same hell. We need you to stay in Panama and support our movement."

Trinity was not alone, merely confined to more intense studying. She would learn the marvel of nuns' dedication and willingness to sacrifice themselves for others. Mother Superior, unfettered, accepted her new charge. She, more than any Panamanian nun, understood her vulnerability. She was a foreigner. Peruvian.

A refugee in my own country, I felt I would drown without my girls. Long ago I should have learned how to breathe under water . . . to survive terror.

33

CONVENT

Two years went by and none of us Stone women shed a tear. Living in danger allows no time for self-pity. Our background saved us: my daughters, warrior offspring and me the disciple. Wearing masks of serenity, our farce of inner peace served to strengthen others. Luckily, nobody photographed us during the period. Photos don't lie; they expose facades and reveal the inner life of people like x-rays. They unveil true sorrow hidden deep in the eyes, the window to one's soul. Had we seen ourselves, we may have crumbled.

Chico had no idea we took refuge in strangers' homes. Telling him would add to his anguish. Now a fugitive, the status destroyed my legitimate excuse for staying in Panama to protect our home. A travesty. In the case of Daniella and Sofia, hiding among friends offered fun. For Trinity the convent became prison. For me changing beds every night was a cross I grew to detest. Daily, I drove past our house, spying to see if someone confiscated it as they did to Flori's beach house. Plus I hoped to catch Lulu and Daniella picking up some toy they left behind.

I found solace reading at Fort Clayton Library and swimming at their pool, reminiscing the times Trinity splashed past me to show off she swam better than I. Trips to Arraijan stopped. I feared the drive alone on the desolate road. My Mother seldom came; her granddaughters and Lulu no longer lived at home.

Evening Mass at Padre Durán's church provided directions for my next bed. With it began my nocturnal odyssey: dreaded nights in strange houses. My days varied little. I seldom cooked, ate less and looked scrawny.

Sundays I picked up Trinity to go home and collect essentials for convent life. She groused, "Look at me. I'm Chunky Chicken. The younger nuns stuff me with cookies and milk while I study, and the cook piles my plate like it's for a construction worker. Then she gets sad when I leave food on the plate. Imagine what she'd say if I toss out food. Oh! How I miss swimming after school."

Wow! Mouth shut, I celebrated she finally realized swimming is a treat.

"My sisters should have gone to the convent with me. They'd have stuck those nuns in their pocket in a flash. But where would Lulu go? What a problem. The saddest part is I'm not allowed to sit and eat with the nuns. I eat alone either in my room or in the kitchen. The cook is sorry for me so she piles food on my plate. Eating far from the nuns isn't the worst part, it's walking upstairs at dusk. Bats own the place at night. They fly close practically brushing my hair. They hang in the center patio sleeping all day. All kinds of bird life fly in and out. They like it up there near the open roof in the center. With me. Ah, but the heavenly voices before breakfast. Nuns sing like angels. And me all by myself. Another problem: the bus. I no longer ride in the bus Mother Superior drives. She put me on the big yellow bus that drops off girls in Bella Vista. Classmates keep asking why I ride their bus. They all know Noriega deported Dad. Everybody does. But they ask anyway. Dummies."

Our getting together on Sundays at home consisted of complaints and little joy, but seeing her made my heart sing. On occasions when I took her a clean shirt or underwear to the convent-school, I'd run into Flavio. Wearing a La Salle school uniform, he paced around the building and gazed up at her window, calling for her to come down. Losing patience, he tossed pebbles at her window. Finally, he'd yell, "Hey Trinity! Come down!" She appeared.

Flavio's gifts of plantain chips, a science book or a red rose stirred no excitement until he cracked a joke about the rose. "Trinity, don't put the rose near your nose. Bugs inside the rose might get'cha." Making fun of her Stone nose made her laugh.

I liked Flavio, but his visits interfered and I felt jealous.

My strange nightlife continued. A lawyer friend, member of the Civil Crusade, offered to assist the priest in finding families willing to hide me for the night. Few people wished to hide a Crusader in their house. Some members of the PRD party took me in. In other instances their relatives did. Most people feared my presence but risked putting me up, perhaps as a favor to the lawyer or the priest. I am eternally grateful to those who took the risk and sheltered me. Brave souls. Their homes were safer for me than Crusader's homes. The regime trusted their kind.

The lawyer's mother gave me refuge. Fearless, she kept me several nights and I grew fond of her. She enjoyed a dry sense of humor saying, "Three people can keep a secret if two of them are dead."

Night searches for my next bed grew tedious. Driving in poorly lit neighborhoods where trees and foliage obscure street signs took a toll on my patience. In the beginning I sipped *Anis del Mono* brandy to sleep but got a headache. Anger set in and I raged like the dogs in uniform that attack Crusaders. I concluded anger combined with loneliness turns explosive. I sought Padre Durán's confessional to unload my criminal soul.

"Padre, I have killer's cravings. With my own hands I want to stick a knife into Noriega. He's destroying me and many Panamanians." I awaited my penance. His calm response shocked me.

"God loves Noriega as much as he loves you and others. For penance I want you to offer your communion for him."

Never! Nor would I tell Padre of my decision. I charged out of church promising myself never to return. Offer my communion for a criminal and torturer? Never. Emotionally adrift, I stayed away from Mass several days. Padre had no idea where I was or how to contact me. Worried, he showed up at my mother's in Arraijan. He figured if he went to Trinity at Maria Inmaculada High School, a scandal would explode over news of my disappearance.

Padre Durán knew where my mother lived. He'd accompanied me recently going to Arraijan to visit my mother. The priest liked going there to visit Lucas Bárcenas, a judge and also my Mom's cousin and neighbor. Lucas, physically handicapped, turned his life into a success story by studying. Padre and Lucas were fellow Lion's Club members and long-time friends.

I missed going to daily Mass and swallowed my pride, accepting the bitter penance, and took communion—for Noriega's soul. For several days I managed to stomach the sacrifice. Being a daily communicant, over time it began to feel less punishing and a marvelous feeling set in. Inner peace replaced my anger. By placing my anger on God's altar I received a gift. No fury can survive in the presence of Jesus's sweet love.

Trinity faded like a flower needing water. On Sundays when I picked her up to go home, she let off steam. "I miss watching soap operas while eating lunch, watching the wild antics of those Venezuelan cowpokes. Pretty women cry over everything. Then handsome men play guitars to their women. Classmates talk about soaps fulltime. But never about homework. At the convent I haven't seen a TV set. Young nuns, novitiates, aren't allowed to circulate in the convent. I am. Novitiates only come upstairs if they carry something for me to eat. Tons of cookies. Look at how fat I'm getting! What can I do with so many cookies? Mother Superior brings them too, with milk after dinner. I can't hide cookies in my room. Somebody might find them while cleaning. I've started throwing them out the window. How sad. Dad loved cookies more than anything."

For me trauma began at night. Finding a strange house in the dark was pure hell. Streets run in all directions, like cow paths, no urban planning. Especially in Bethania. One night I awoke thirsty in a strange house. To find the kitchen I followed the scent of fried food and the rumble of the refrigerator. Light switches are always near the doorjamb. I pawed around and flicked one. Horrors. Thousands of cockroaches scampered in all directions. I skipped the drink of water.

My consolation came from daily Mass and Communion. I decided more consecrated Hosts would bring more strength. I added another Mass. Mornings I attended Mass at *Monseñor* Vasquez Pinto at 7:00 a.m. and Padre Durán's at 5:30 p.m. Two Hosts daily; a divine solution. My anxiety disappeared. I walked on air. Fortunately, I had no idea I broke ecclesiastic rules. Host is limited unless for a special reason. In my case the reason was ignorance.

Flori noticed something odd and mentioned it. "What's new, Jenny? For some reason you seem less uptight. Pretty." She stifled a laugh.

I kept my divine solution a secret while Trinity faded noticeably. Sad, she no longer cared about Flavio's overtures from the sidewalk, paying homage to the girl in the tower. He caught on and joked about the buzzards circling above paying more attention to him than Trinity.

"Ugly as they are, buzzards care. They watch me like I'm a tasty morsel. Probably hope I'll fall in dog poo so they can pounce on me."

Trinity glossed it over.

Sofia noticed Trinity's gloomy disposition and proposed an outing for all of us. Pizza at Romanacchio's on Tumba Muerto near our house. We entered the aroma of toasted cheese, tomato and olive oil. A mouth-watering atmosphere.

Menus on the table, Trinity noticed Sofia's naked hand. "Your scar is awful. Does it bother you to write? It hurts me to look at it."

Someone else said it resembled a tattoo of the Isthmus of Panama. Artsy. As we chatted, Sofia's friends arrived and studied the scar as though seeking to read the future on the reverse side of her palm. The waiter brought our pizzas just as two hoodlums walked in. PRD brutes: a legislator from Arraijan and his son. Dizzy with power, they strutted through the restaurant with pistols bulging under their clothing. Mothers grabbed their children.

The legislator's son mouthed off. "Look, Crusader weirdos sitting over there. Conspiring." He pointed at Sofia's friends.

Many present recognized the legislator from his recent appearance on a US TV news program. Someone next to us called him a clown for repeating the same phrase over and over again in broken English while ignoring the question the TV host had asked about Panama's grave crisis.

A customer at the next table repeated out loud the worn-out phrase and laughed. The legislator's son heard and got furious assuming the remark came from Sofia's friends. He reacted with threats.

"Hey, wise guy, let's go outside. I'll show you who's got the balls here," and he grabbed his crotch. His father touched the weapon under his shirt.

Mothers shielded their children's eyes. A kid screamed. Panic broke out and parents clutched their children. A waiter came out of the kitchen carrying a tray loaded with hot pizzas. Unaware of the pandemonium inside the restaurant two waiters met head-on at the swinging doors. They crashed into each other barreling back into the kitchen. Pizzas flew like frisbees; glasses of water crashed to the floor and soiled table utensils everywhere. Customers thought the explosion came from a fired gun and ducked under tables. Others ran for the exit. In the end, the only victim was the restaurant. Romanacchio's on Tumba Muerto Avenue, for whatever reason, closed shortly after.

The fracas continued outside. PRD devils waited for us. "You Crusader freaks!"

Nobody replied to their insults. We jumped in our cars and left, me driving. Sofia yelled, "Don't go home! They'll follow!"

We escaped again and refused to lose hope our situation would improve soon.

Unquestionably my days posed no demand or stressful moments. Nobody chased me. But come nighttime, constant bed hopping eroded my stamina. One evening, after Mass, I brazenly asked Flori permission to sleep at her house to be near my own home. She was jubilant. I made the grave mistake of parking the Audi in the carport under her house and repeated it for two nights. Her son-in-law, worried about my car, pulled in behind to conceal my car. Big mistake. New at the game of hide and seek at the criminal level, I never suspected the effectiveness of regime spies.

Flori's three-story house was already full. Her grown son and daughter still lived with her. So I slept with her in the king-size bed she once shared with her deceased husband. Happy to be a half-a-block from my house, for once I didn't care where I slept.

A loud sound woke me, sounded like a broom swatting the wall. Again and again. Flori was not in the bed. Her shouts nearby spoke alarm. "You die! How dare you come into my house?"

Die? I scrambled towards the sound. Nobody else got up. I figured her offspring weren't home and found her wielding a golf club. Blood dripped from the clubface in Flori's hand.

"Glad you're up, Jenny. Help me get rid of this dead possum. He's the third one I've nailed. Their mother leaves these critters outside the window and they crawl in."

Flori proudly held the bloody club pointing it at the mangled victim of her fury. I held the plastic bag open while she stuffed the possum and secured the bag. Nearly dawn, we sat over tea and toast and I related Trinity's sadness. She insisted I held the solution.

"Tell people everywhere you divorced Chico. The regime will hear and quit persecuting you. You don't frighten them. Not you! Your husband worries them. Didn't you tell me he's making speeches informing the public of the criminal treatment we get from the regime? Chico's message compromises you. Start now. Tell everyone you divorced Chico. Take my advice. Those horrible men will leave you alone."

She rose and went to the sink to wash blood off the golf club face.

"I can't Flori. Padre Durán always says; 'Homicide perhaps; divorce never.'"

"He's stopped saying that. He realized it was dangerous advice. The husbands are committing the homicides. Not the women. You need to practice. Right now. Repeat after me. I'm divorced. Divorced."

We laughed, oblivious to what turned out to be a great mistake. My Audi, parked in her carport, stirred up more fur than the dead possum.

A few days after I moved out, Flori's granddaughter told Trinity of the robbery.

"My father's car was stolen. From the carport."

Same spot I parked the Audi two nights in a row. Poor man, he parked his car behind mine to protect it and his disappeared. Neither new nor expensive, the car was essential to him. He took leave from work to search and found it a week later, in San Miguelito, where Dignity Battalion burned ours. The damage included slashed tires and ripped seats. Regime punished him to hurt me. Flori's son-in-law feigned gratitude; the engine was intact. He never blamed me for staying two nights. The regime destroyed his car to let me know all my moves were tabulated.

A new worry for me. Did they discover the Audi wore a fictitious license plate? The one issued in Arraijan for Daniella's burned Datsun. My mother lived in Arraijan. Was she in danger?

Trinity told of spies watching her at night through her window at the convent. After lights out, a circle of light hit her walls. To spare the nuns she kept it secret, but told Flavio. After dark he stalked the area and confirmed the light beam nearby came from a higher level. He suspected photographers.

"Mom, my anxiety must show 'cause yesterday Mother Superior asked why I looked so glum. I lied. Said physics class was getting tough. I thought she believed me. Then last night I turned off the lights early so the novitiates wouldn't bring me cookies. You won't believe this. Mother Superior brought the cookies and milk. She walked in, flipped on the light and . . . Wham! I flung myself on the floor. What if somebody was watching and took photographs of us two? Together. You should'a seen what she did. Mother Superior dropped to the floor next to me, soiling her starched white habit. Then, she asks why we're down on the floor."

"What did you lose, Trinity? Something important?"

"Can you imagine, Mom? It was funny and terrible at the same time. I lied, saying I dropped my retainer. I wear it every night. Stops me from grinding my teeth."

The nun got up saying, "OK, I'll help you find it. Let's look over here."

"I panicked but stayed on the floor. Worried she'd insist I get up too, I clutched my stomach and groaned, my belly aches. I hoped she would leave. She dropped to her knees and tried to hoist me up and help me get in bed. I rose and lunged at the bed and told her the light bothers me. She switched it off then headed for the door saying exactly what I didn't want to hear."

"Trinity, I'll call a doctor. Maybe you have an appendicitis. I'll be right back."

"I lied again. It was awful, fibbing to her. I told her I was having menstrual cramps. Mother Superior left and that was the last time I saw her. She wasn't in school this morning. I asked around. Nobody's seen her today. I worry about her."

34

GOING HOME

Mother Superior had not shown up. But I thanked heaven for small favors in that my sleepless safari rendered a triumph, my telephone torturer lost track of me and quit harassing. While in hiding we consoled ourselves believing our warrior-father was achieving great things for Panama. It backfired. His testimony before the US Senate put our lives in jeopardy. Foolishly, we thought ourselves hidden, but dictator goons knew where we were, particularly me. Given the choice, I'd rather have slept on the moon.

We awaited the audio-tape recording of Chico's testimony at the US Senate hearing. Due to arrive any moment, the intriguing tape Chico labeled confidential divulged dictator secrets. Nobody had access to the hearing. So what could have gone wrong?

The tape arrived. Trinity happened to be with me. In the car she opened the package, her fake giggle more like a puppy panting. I turned on the Audi air conditioner, closed the windows and plugged in the tape expecting to relish the PDF's death sentence.

Censored! Somebody in DC purposely sabotaged my tape! A heartless censurer erased Chico's testimony about Noriega and his accomplices from my tape and perhaps on the Congressional Record. What kind of lackey destroys a family's sacrifices? Our terrible suffering was in vain. No wonder Chico was sad when he called the night before the hearing to say the US Senate at the last minute invited Juan B. Sosa, Panama's Ambassador to Washington, to his "private" hearing. Sosa knew everything and I knew nothing. Whose side was the US on? Sosa blabbed to the regime on the phone immediately and that night three truckloads of Doberman painted the front of my house black. The same night. Our neighbors watched, fearing they were next. Why did the US betray the Civil Crusade and our family? It wasn't the first time.

Senators Jesse Helms, Edward Kennedy and Christopher Dodd were on the panel questioning Chico while Ambassador Sosa listened. He was more important to the US than the Civil Crusade effort and the safety of Chico's five women.

Resentment was a sentiment I could not dwell on. Trinity grumbled as we drove to her dentist. Everywhere busted traffic lights hung, grotesque skeletons of our country's chaos and sinister symbols of our national crisis. Trinity labeled the busted skeletons of traffic lights hangman nooses. But traffic no longer jammed streets; people stayed home, short of cash for gas. We endured years with destroyed lights. The military left lights broken on purpose to cause us more misery. A few exceptional Civil Crusaders stepped out of their autos and waved traffic during peek hours. Only Crusaders did, never PDF cops. No longer did Crusade bulletins appear. Panama's economy was in shambles. Scarcity of basic necessities prevailed and talk was Panama would be another Cuba if the US didn't step in and remove the dictator.

The opposite applied to the regime. Hellquarters received money in large suitcases. So much money they set up a bank called Banco Patria inside Hellquarters.

Trinity continued to worry about Mother Superior. In private classmates referred to MS by her chosen name, Elsa Maria. When the nun took refuge in the Papal Nuncio's residence, students sang aloud a tune they previously sung in private, a popular song they adapted to her. Their choice of words proved their admiration and gratitude, especially for her teaching them self-confidence.

"*Elsa María me quiere gobernar, y yo le sigo le sigo la corriente.*

Yo no quiero que diga la gente que Elsa María me puede dominar."

"Elsa María tries to order me around, and I go along, tag along with her game.

I don't want people to say Elsa María can tell me what to do."

But sadness crushed their joy to dance to the nun's song as they once had.

Each night I edged closer to home and finally slept next door to ours at Crystal Voice's house. Content and sleeping soundly, I woke startled. A warm body had pounced on me. Too dark to see, the object shook then nuzzled me. Crystal's cocker spaniel. That was it! No more sleeping in the doghouse!

On tiptoes I made it to their front door and discovered it was a double door. A wood door first and an iron door behind it. No way to escape. It was four a.m. and my jail stood three yards from my house. I dared turn on a light. Crystal's house is so big any noise I made would never be heard in their bedrooms. I searched the kitchen and failed to find a key stashed anywhere. Left no choice, I returned to the dog's bed.

Next night, I deceived two men: the priest and Civil Crusade lawyer. I took asylum at home. Disgusted with the vagabond life, I left the task of hiding in strangers' homes to other victims of repression and risked hiding in my own home.

The Audi I parked three streets away, each night in a different place. Thrilled beyond control, I restrained from laughing. Sidling through my own house in the dark and stroking familiar haunts, I walked barefoot on slick floors gorging on the forbidden. The telephone held its tone; I had paid all utilities while hiding so Chico could call us on Sundays. We had no place to call him. A week living in a pitch-dark home and sitting on the terrace appraising my mournful city under the gun, I tasted joy, even without music.

Daytime I stayed away and knew nothing of who came and went. The unexpected happened one night. A car engine roared driving into the carport. The Audi was hiding down the street. Panic gripped me when a car door slammed. My first thought: wished I hadn't thrown my gun in the garbage bin.

A feminine voice hummed, growing louder as it came closer. "*Mirala como baila, pegadita de los hombres*; See how she dances, snuggled close to men."

Sofia! The music lover, coming in singing!

"Aiiieee!" She shrieked hearing me laugh while opening the door.

She begged to move back home. I agreed. It seemed a year since we stopped sleeping here. Chatting while sitting on the terrace in the dark, the city appeared abandoned and mournful as though a dark blanket of tears covered it.

Sofia suggested a system for her to call home. "Something they won't bother to track. For our safety. First I call. You let it ring and I hang up. Then I call again. Don't answer. The third time, you answer. OK?"

Days later, the phone rang. I followed the code. No answer till she called three times. Must be Sofia. I picked up.

"Sorry to frighten you Mom. Trinity called from school. She says Mother Superior isn't allowed to leave the Papal Nuncio's residence. PDF's after her. To deport her. She's Peruvian, remember? Trinity's classmates are hysterical. But what can they do?"

I took off for her school. The phenomenon of no traffic in the desolate city was eerie but pleasant. I reached Maria Inmaculada in minutes and asked one of the secretaries to call Trinity on the intercom. Sullen, the secretary's grim face confirmed trouble. Mother Superior was their human beacon, admired for her steadfast love. Guilt forced me to go outside the office to wait.

Seeking a pleasant distraction, I admired the simplicity of campus: classroom buildings fanned around an enormous open patio utilized for sports and performances. Tropical plants at a minimum. Mother Superior and other nuns sacrificed to make this construction a reality. They devoted their lives so Panamanian girls could benefit from this institute. Our three daughters loved their school.

Trinity stomped my way, her blue plaid skirt swishing angrily left to right.

"Mom, it's my fault! She's not coming back! Wait till you hear this rumor. Some girl said the nun's getting deported 'cause she failed a girl. The girl's mother's sister is the dictator's mistress."

"Don't dispute the story, Trinity. If he wants to deceive Panamanians with his lie, so be it. Let it go. Thank God Mother Superior wasn't murdered like the nuns in Salvador."

The horror of those words shocked me.

Trinity visibly trembled and asked if I thought they intended to murder the nun. "No!" I said, withholding facts I heard from the nun's lips. The incident frightened the nun, and she believes it caused her trouble with the regime. It happened shortly before Trinity sought refuge in the convent. A discussion took place in the nun's presence when a Crusader spoke rudely to friends of Noriega. The nun hushed. She suspects her silence marked her as accomplice. A Cuban couple had showed up at the school seeking baptism for two girls. By coincidence the Crusader was there and heard the request. She butts in saying, "Why do you want to baptize them? You're communists." Mother Superior was shocked but didn't intervene when she saw the intensity of the woman's fury. Probably the nun was unaware why she angered. The woman, a dynamic presence in marches, was raped and tortured by the regime in Carcel

252

Modelo Prison. They forced her to sit, hands up, while they beat her on the kidneys. She suffered kidney failure the rest of her shortened life.

Trinity kept talking, "I can't go back to the convent. Mother Superior is gone. There's nothing there for me. Sad part is now I'm sorry I didn't appreciate it. Mother Superior must have known the danger to her and what could happen. She knew about the black car with two men sitting in front of the school day and night. Flavio saw them, scrutinizing everyone who goes in and out. Now I see how wonderful the nun was."

"She still is." I said.

Trinity didn't cry. None of us did; suffering had hardened us like rocks. Trinity learned early crying debilitates, and we couldn't afford to crumble.

"Mom, I don't want to ride the bus home. Please wait for me; class is nearly over."

I sat in the car recalling Flori's words, "Jenny, tell people you divorced Chico."

Daniella and Lulu moved back into our house. The nest full, all of us together again, filled the void left by Chico.

While we enjoyed our togetherness, the PDF prepared the scenario leading to a major blunder. They caused death to their own troops by bringing Cuban military instructors to train a special Panamanian unit. For graduation they planned a spectacle using live ammunition and explosives. Normally blanks are used to protect lives. Their mission was to blow up US petroleum fields near Howard Air Force Base. Nobody can confirm whether it was a miscalculation. The US got wind of this deadly assault and sent Special Forces to block the event with an ambush. Many Cubans and Panamanians died. The regime faced the problem of covering up the tragedy and failed. International news had a field day reporting the crime.

Chico began calling on Saturdays instead of Sundays. He had surprising news. He was leaving Washington. His stay there to testify before the US Senate was financed by Gabriel Lewis and the Civil Crusade. It caused his family to hide like mice. For nothing.

Excited he was going west; the girls did most of the talking. He sounded less excited than his daughters and soon I understood why.

"Jenny, has anyone from the US Ambassador's office called to offer assistance." The girls answered no. I asked if any of his West Point classmates had contacted him. He said no.

"Chico, has the Department of the Army called you?"

He answered no and it griped me. "Where's all this fraternity baloney when an officer is in trouble and needs his colleagues?"

He pretended it didn't hurt, but we knew silence covers pain. We were experts.

"I'm moving to LA and live with my sister. Out west I'll speak to civic groups and businessmen. Ask constituents to pressure their congressmen to change US government policy towards dictators."

"Good. I want Trinity to stay with you for a while. Her school may close early. Is that OK?"

He agreed.

On the other line, Trinity balked, "After all these months of waiting for Flavio to return, and now I'm leaving Panama?"

"Jenny, you come too. Abandon the house."

Never, I thought, but refused to argue. I reminded him, "Dear, we've talked about this before."

Chico dropped a bomb, "My Dad says wives are obligated to follow their husbands. If you won't come here," he paused, took a deep breath to soften the bitterness, "Dad says I should divorce you."

35

DIVORCE?

How ironic. So many times Flori insisted, "Spread the word you divorced Chico." I refused. And now General Stone has the audacity to tell his son to discard me. Maybe he lost his marbles. How out-of-place coming from him of all people. A general who spent five years fighting in Asia during WWII. In China and India away from his wife and children the entire time. A three-star general, he went the extra mile for his troops; he chose to risk death flying on raids with the Flying Tigers. His 14th Air Force flew B-24 bombers over Burma Road.

His criticism was absurd. I met his son here in my country and the general went around the planet to fight. Maybe the man had lost his fighting spirit. It hurt and I reminded his son, "Panama needs you, dear. You're the best man qualified to inform constituents to convince their congressmen to stop supporting devil dictators. Especially now that Reagan left office."

"Jenny, stop dreaming. Your people, those Crusade leaders, are astute. They'll forget all their promises after Noriega leaves. They'll grab power for themselves and forget the poor. It happens everywhere. Power corrupts. It's in the Bible."

In some cases he was correct, but I still had my head in the clouds and argued.

"We must trust our Creator. Do it for Panama, sweetie."

"You drive God crazy," he said. "But I'll do it for you."

We prepared for Trinity's departure; schools closed ahead of schedule. With the country in crisis, her marching baton retired after so many years performing.

All the way to the airport she ranted, "I don't wanna go," and as we drew closer her disdain diminished. "Well, it'll be great to see Dad."

Trinity's departure left me sad. Driving home I turned on the radio hoping for salsa music, but I got Babylon, mayor of San Miguelito, threatening Crusaders.

The holidays found Trinity in Arizona with her father and his family eating Thanksgiving turkey at a desert picnic ground. Later they moved to LA where Trinity turned seventeen and dated a rock-star-wannabe. I saw his handsome face in photos and imagined him sweet. On one of their outings eating pizza, his fans recognized the blond, long-haired singer. He signed a few autographs, smiled and waved at admirers as he departed. Getting up to leave the rock star left a quarter tip. A grave error. The waitress, a Mexican, spilled water on the star while clearing the table, probably on purpose.

The singer turned ugly and said, "You wetback Latina." He started saying something worse but Trinity objected, apologized to the waitress and pulled him outside. He began mouthing off again at Trinity. "What's with you? You're just another wetback Latina. Same shit!"

Trinity recoiled and drew back her fist. When he looked back, he saw a tight fist coming at his face. She landed one punch—squarely—on his nose. Knocked him to the pavement, unconscious. The impact broke his nose. Chico paid plenty for his surgery. The blond rock star never sang again.

Sofia and Daniella whooped with delight upon hearing the story. Proud of Trinity and astounded that she, who never took karate and wasn't a black belt like them, calmly flattened a guy with one punch—hands of stone.

After years of oppression by the military, I fell apart and cried for the first time.

My grief and Daniella and Sofia's euphoria ended quickly. A relative from Arraijan called saying my mother was taken at gunpoint from her home. Seen limping while two Dignity Battalion conscripts prodded her with their guns, neighbors sounded the alarm, but refrained from interfering. I sped off to Arraijan. There, frightened neighbors apologized for not saving her. "They had guns. What could we do?"

The Attorney General, Carlos Vampire, ordered my mother's arrest. Her companion, a coward, ran off leaving her alone. Crippled and old, she never meddled in politics. It was May 10, 1989, three days after presidential elections had revealed the landslide winners: Endara, Ford and Arias Calderon. The dictator exploded. His own followers voted against his candidate; the tally proved it. The regime punished everyone in its path. Caught in their vicious sweep, my mother was arrested for renting a small house to a Civil Crusader.

Mom looked okay considering what she'd been through but when she started telling me the details, I sensed a change in her.

My Mother tells her story

Yes, Jenny, the worst part was climbing that steep hill, practically crawled my way up. Tripped with my lame foot more than once. I'll start from the beginning. The gunmen showed up here, banging on my iron gate. Two of them, with rifles. Rude. They pushed me out of my house. I was so scared I didn't ask why or where we were going until one gunman told me the Attorney General was waiting for me. Me. Imagine that? I climbed the tall hill to Napoleon Franco's house. I couldn't understand why they were taking me there. I seldom go there; Napoleon and his wife always come to my house. The Attorney General was handsome, told me to sit down. I needed it. Then he ruined everything. Called me an Old woman. I detest being called Old Woman.

"What did he want, Mom? Why did he arrest you?"

He asked me if I knew whose house we were in. I said yes, but he repeated the question as if he was deaf or I were dumb. I told him it belonged to Napoleon Franco. My friend. Then he accused Napoleon of being a Civil Crusader. I kept my mouth shut. Napoleon is a grown man, can do whatever he wants. Then the general told me to look at a pool of blood on the floor. I hadn't noticed it when I came in, gasping for breath. He asked me whose blood I thought it was. I shook my head. The blood didn't scare me. I figured somebody killed a chicken. He got impatient, said I couldn't go home until I said whose blood it was. I told him it was an unlucky chicken that ran out of the kitchen after the maid killed it, or botched up the killing. I've seen it happen more than once. We kill chickens at home all the time.

"Was Napoleon there, Mom?"

That's the confusing part in all this. Napoleon Franco hadn't come out to say hello to me. Nor his wife, which seemed odd. Attorney General kept pointing at the puddle of blood on the floor and insisting I quit calling it chicken blood. He pointed at a painting on the wall of Napoleon Franco, accused him of being a Civil Crusader and said that all Crusaders need punishment. And that's why Napoleon's blood was on the floor. Not some chicken's blood.

Jenny, I kept hoping he'd say go home. Instead he walked around the room, looking at a small notebook and then came back and stood in front of me. Never smiled. Then I worried, told him he was wearing a nice shirt and that somebody at home really loved him. Pressed those pleats down the front of his shirt with love.

"You said that, Mom?"

Such a handsome man. And a general. But what's strange is he wasn't wearing a uniform. Do you think he's really a general? I decided to keep my mouth shut. Then he quit telling me to look at the puddle of blood. Then he called me an Old Woman again. Accused me, said he was perturbed at what I was doing. Renting a house to some Crusaders. Said Crusaders are trouble. I told him I needed the money 'cause I was an Old Woman. He said so himself. Over and over.

Apparently the Attorney General disliked my mother's answer 'cause he sent her home alone. Nobody helped her climb down the steep hill.

Hours after her arrest she kept mentioning the nicely pressed shirt on the handsome Attorney General but never referred to the puddle of blood or that it belonged to her good friend, Napoleon Franco, famous swimmer, sportsman and diplomat. Nor did she recall that neither Napoleon nor his wife came out to say hello, in their own home. She carried on about the general's shirt. The incident affected her permanently.

Trinity had not returned from visiting her father in California. After my mother's arrest, I often risked driving to Arraijan to check on her, knowing regime devils called *Macho de Monte* controlled Arraijan and had set up a torture house there.

On the road I listened to radio and regime news. No other radio stations existed. Only those belonging to the regime. The station played a recording of a horrible phrase by Babylon, the mayor of San Miguelito. She ranted, *"Civilista visto, Civilista muerto;* Crusader seen, Crusader killed." Terrible message. I switched it off.

After Mass at Santísima Trinidad, I invited parishioners to accompany me to Arraijan. None acquiesced until I invited Padre Durán. He agreed to go with me to my mother's home out of town. Padre liked going so he could visit his friend Lucas Bárcenas. They were friends from the Lions' Club. Lucas, a retired judge and Mom's cousin, lived next door and like her was crippled. Worse off than Mom, he was born with two clubfeet. Tall and distinguished, Lucas overcame his physical defect by studying and acquiring great knowledge. My mother bore the stigma of polio. She made efforts to conceal the limp by adding a cute bounce to her limp. Lucas admired her perseverance in trying to look good and raved over her piano playing.

Padre chatted with my mother and offered to hear her confession. She refused with a laugh. Padre took the hint to go next door to visit Lucas for serious talk.

As a writer, Lucas collected great books. His writings portrayed images of Arraijan's founders and romanticized them by utilizing witches' lore. To this day his writings are treasured. Before a library existed in Arraijan, he loaned his precious collection to young students. He finally has a library named after him.

My Mother disliked books but loved her Steinway piano. She played like a virtuoso. Lucas played guitar. As a clubfoot, he honed a keen sense of humor and called her affectionately, "Diancha." She rolled her eyes with anger each time he said the name Diancha, a name given locally to the devil's wife. For this reason she resented Lucas. He ignored her disdain, knew her since childhood and her appetite for hurting others.

I bought TIME magazine. Bloody-faced Billy Ford graced the cover, the vice-president elected by us on May 7, 1989. Dignity Battalion thugs had attacked him. Since Election Day the winning threesome, Guillermo Endara, Billy Ford and Ricardo Arias Calderon, avoided going home, sleeping wherever they found shelter. The day the picture was taken for the cover of TIME, the three had driven down a main street waving at constituents, smiling while aware repression lurked at every corner. They got out to walk and regime goons caught them. Wielding iron bars, Dingbat goons beat Billy Ford and murdered his bodyguard. Barehanded, Ford fought back. He took on the would-be assassin pictured in the bloody photo on the cover of TIME magazine. The photo traveled worldwide.

Panamanians knew who led the Dignity Battalion plainclothes goons, Benjamin Crocodile. Thanksgiving passed and Advent brought Trinity home from the US, changed for the better. The pounds she gained living with the nuns she increased in LA eating burritos. She still called herself Chunky Chicken. Happier, she expressed it well. "My new love is pretty shoes. All kinds. It's a shame I didn't have money to buy any." The sweetest part was she stopped being angry with me for her father's deportation.

"LA's too crowded. And people are rude." Then as though she hadn't looked me over well enough, she blurted, "You're too thin, Mom."

"I feel fine. Tell me about the handsome guy you clobbered."

No answer. The morsel would have to wait until she described LA women—all gorgeous according to her.

"My Aunt was nice, Dad's older sister. She has lots of girl friends and those two party all the time. Here's the cool part. They drink. They aren't boring like you."

She moved closer to study my face.

"Yeah Mom, you need makeup. 'Specially round the eyes. This friend of my aunt's has eyes the same swamp green color as yours. But she paints them terrific. Eyeliner makes her eyes look really 'wow'. You need eyeliner."

I didn't inquire why she wanted me pretty, or the slippery tidbit about her father. The knowledge might hurt. Living in such perilous times left no time for vanities. My responsibility was to protect our family and the house. But her comments left their mark. When a year had passed since Noriega deported Chico, I went to visit him. He had learned to type with two fingers and was proud. I never asked what else he learned.

36

ELECTROCUTION

Home at last, all four Stone women under the same roof. Precious Lulu counted for two. Our clandestine life brought on by forty Doberman painting our front entrance black provided benefits and losses. Telephone Torturer gave up on me completely. Trinity's LA trip to visit her father established her prowess at knocking-out an aspiring rock star. Sofia chose enlightenment and added the ecclesiastic to her musical repertoire.

Trinity disliked it.

"How contradicting, Sofia! You play church music but can't stand going to Mass. What's the difference?"

"It's your fault. You said Gregorian chant sung by the nuns was the only wonderful part of the convent. I'm celebrating Mother Superior with Gregorian music. Our brave nun."

"Don't be difficult. The guys on your tape sound like they're gargling. Our nuns sang great!"

"You win. What do you want to hear?"

"Celia Cruz. Let me show you. Here it is, *Abusó.*"

Thus ended our short appreciation of enlightenment in Renaissance Period music.

Four-year-old Lulu fell victim to tyranny the night her father drove them home from family dinner with his parents. Osvaldo slowed down at an intersection aware all traffic lights were destroyed. Busted traffic light skeletons continued to hang everywhere, another tactic of regime repression. Osvaldo was about to proceed when a whistle blew. In the dark he saw nobody and proceeded, stepping on the gas. A dark figure jumped in front of his car. He slammed on the brakes. His headlights illuminated a Doberman approaching, gun in hand. He rammed the gun inside the open window within inches of Osvaldo's head. Lulu saw the gun and her father's shocked expression. She heard the attacker's fierce voice threatening him and she screeched. "*Papi! Papi!*"

Fearing for both of them Osvaldo controlled his hot temper and sweetly told Lulu the pistol was fake and all a game. Without moving he softly asked Doberman to take his wallet. In that instant Doberman noticed Osvaldo's white shirt and went berserk.

"Don't you Crusader idiots respect anything? There's a curfew! What the hell are you doing on the street at night?"

Osvaldo faked a weak chuckle to calm Lulu. She whimpered each time the gun moved in front her father. In a soothing voice he said, "It's OK sweetheart. Don't be frightened, Lulu, he's not gonna hurt me."

Doberman flipped the gun left and right, from Osvaldo to Lulu.

She screamed again, "*Papi! Papi!*"

The soldier pointed the gun at Lulu and hollered, "Shut up! Damned kid!"

Lulu screamed again. Her hollering enraged Doberman. She crawled out of her flimsy baby seat and lunged at her father to hug and cover him. Sitting in Osvaldo's lap, she reached for Doberman's weapon.

Osvaldo pleaded, "Lulu. Please go back to your car seat. Don't be afraid."

He turned to the Doberman begging, "Please, put the gun away. Take my wallet."

Lulu began to cry. Again Doberman flipped the gun left and right between father and child. Undecided, he barked, "Beat that kid. Make her shut up. Do as I say!"

"Lulu please, honey, the man wants you to sit down. Go back to your seat. Do it for *Papi.*" Tremors in Osvaldo's voice alarmed Lulu. Her screams dwindled to a whine. Osvaldo repeated his plea to Doberman.

"Please. Let me reach my wallet. You can have it. Take the car too. It's yours. But please put down your gun so I can reach my wallet."

Doberman backed away and lowered the gun. Osvaldo retrieved his wallet and handed it over. Doberman grabbed it and hurried away.

That night back home with her mother, Daniella, Lulu slept fitfully, sobbing often and calling for, "*Papi, Papi.*"

Lulu learned terror at the hands of a Doberman. Days passed before Osvaldo was able to comment on the incident. "Lulu saved our lives," his nervous laugh unconvincing.

Not fully recovered from my grandchild's near-death encounter, one day I opened the front door and saw two white envelopes wedged into the gate. I crossed the vestibule to retrieve two electricity bills from IRHE. One for the upstairs residence and the other for Daniella's apartment downstairs. Both bills were in my name. Her bill totaled $3,042.00 for one month! Outrageous!

Fuming, I drove to IRHE, the electrical company run by the regime, as was everything else including our lives. The attendant checked the records and confirmed.

"Yes. There's no mistake. Your bill is correct. You owe that amount."

I wanted to argue but instead agreed with her I should request their electrician come check the meter or whatever was wrong. "Somebody will call you," she said. Nobody called or came to check.

That evening when Daniella came home, I showed her the bill. She lost control.

"That's absurd! Nobody consumes three thousand dollars of electricity in one month! Nor in a year!" Her shrill voice matched the absurdity of the bill.

When she finished venting, I recommended she visit IRHE to arrange payment options. She never did. Time passed without payments and sure enough, IRHE cut off the downstairs electricity. Her apartment was an inferno without air conditioning. Solid plate glass windows framed a marvelous view of the city but also cut off any slight breeze. Much as I begged her not to, Daniella and Lulu moved to a small house on my mother's property in Arraijan, making her grandmother very happy. Trinity, Sofia and I grieved over their departure until the day I came home to find my electricity cut off . . . upstairs. Come night we'd be totally dark, too. Both accounts were in my name making me liable. Immediately I drove back to IRHE; fortunately, it was nearby. I asked the attendant to review my bill. She said, "Pay a portion while our inspector checks both meters." Electricity was reinstated temporarily. A month later it was cut off again. I returned to the company. An inspector came and removed my meter leaving us without current. As he walked away lugging my meter, I stopped him.

"You can't leave us without current," and offered him money. He accepted, fussed with the wires a bit and our refrigerator started humming.

A month went by and we still had electricity. I had started paying the minimal monthly amount to cover the downstairs bill from my little angel's apartment.

Thirty days later my electricity was cut off again. Driving back to IRHE, I wondered why I wasn't screaming with anger. Then I remembered; psychological torture keeps people subdued. The attendant said my meter was irreparable and I should buy a new one. I paid for the new one. They installed it. Four weeks later, without warning, IRHE cut off my electricity.

Enough. I quit messing with IRHE. Trinity needed to study and candles were inadequate. Behind Padre Durán's back, I sought out his electrician working at our church and offered him a fee to come to my house. Electrician arrived.

"Teach me to how steal electricity. I know other people who do. I'll pay you."

He nodded, went to his truck and returned with wires he called "copper bridges." Covered with plastic, the two heavy copper wires he had cut the same length. Long as miniature bananas. With a knife he peeled both ends. It looked easy. He climbed on a stepstool and told me to get another chair to observe what he did. I climbed up and watched him install the wires. Two wires he set parallel. The wires touched the live terminals left exposed when the meter was removed. Our refrigerator started humming.

"Looks easy, like flossing teeth," I commented, less frightened.

"Be careful, lady. This current kills." He shattered my notion of simplicity.

"Let me demonstrate again." He removed the "copper cables" as he called the innocuous-looking wires, pocketed the money for the lesson and left.

As if Doberman weren't enough, I now faced a new threat: juggling high voltage larceny. Removing the cables was simple but installing them grew agonizing. Within a few days the task began to suck energy from me. Each day, my exhaustion intensified. Fear of mishandling the "copper cables" while my hands trembled, I resorted to chewing gum to avoid biting my tongue, but bit anyway. Constant thirst grew unbearable. In the process of installing the killer "cables" twice a day, I often forgot to apply deodorant and smelled like a dead dog. Two realities haunted me: Trinity not being able to study and failing in school; and the other worry, my body, electrocuted, twisting and writhing while foaming at the mouth.

Trinity never knew the trauma of stealing electricity. Nor did I comment when she'd say, "How nice not to study by candlelight anymore. It burned my eyes."

I stuck close to home when "copper cables" were in their proper place, feeding us electricity. The stolen kind. Obsessed, I began carrying a spare pair of copper wires in my purse. Sometimes I dreamed of being arrested.

One night instead of the jail dream, the stench of smoke woke me. I jumped out of bed coughing at the smell flooding the narrow hallway connecting our three bedrooms. I ran in the direction of the smoke. Never did I steal electricity at night. Too risky. Rushing past the bathroom, smoke engulfed me. There, on the counter, a candle flickered. The culprit. I blew it out. Damage was done; I'd see it tomorrow.

Daylight revealed a badly burned counter. Damaged completely. The previous night Trinity had brushed her teeth by candlelight. The loss meant nothing. Formica counter was ugly regardless of how new the house.

Trinity's sad face stared at the counter. I consoled.

"Don't fret, Trinity. When this crisis passes, we'll install a pretty marble counter."

One afternoon I climbed on the stool to install copper cables to steal electricity and nothing happened. I tried again. No hum from the refrigerator. The hookup failed. I drove down the hill to church to fetch the electrician. Accepting I'm a thief, I felt no shame. Why shouldn't I steal a few kilowatts from the regime? Hell, I stole much greater things. I stole Hosts. The Body of Christ I took twice daily at morning and evening Mass. He gave me strength. My daughters knew I stole electricity, and agreed our Lord didn't give a hoot if I stole both. Under pleasant circumstances the enormous significance of my thievery would have thrilled me. Instead, military repression squelched all joy.

Electrician said, "Go home and check the electrical post on the curb in front of your house. Look for a thick black wire that crosses your yard from high on the post to your house. If the black wire's still up there, there's hope. If the black wire is gone, it means IRHE cut it. No wire; no electricity."

I rushed home, looked up and saw no black wire. IRHE removed it and Trinity's finals were coming. I went back to IRHE and paid the price.

We ate ice cream again, soursop flavor Trinity liked so well. I nearly giggled with delight for not having to steal electricity anymore. Nor did I hint to her the torment.

Our water was cut off. Not just ours, everybody's water on our street was cut. The cut-off lasted four months. Water arrived on our hill only at night at twelve. No water in the daytime, only at midnight. I took all my paid water bills to IDAAN, the water company, to prove my payments were up-to-date. Although my neighbors were waterless, none dared go there to complain personally. They called on the phone.

IDAAN building, the main office for the water company, has a creek running through the middle, man made, with fancy little bridges like Disneyland. There, an employee said, "Set up an appointment for an inspector to check for a leaky pipe." I put my name on the list and a grumpy employee added, "Somebody will come out in a few days." I nearly made it to the exit when a dark hand reached from behind pushing the door open for me. "*Gracias.*" I thanked.

The face came forward. Him! Leader of the Dignity Battalion killers who burned our car at the Civil Crusade march in San Miguelito. Never forgot him! He saved my life that day. He still wore the gray side-burns and fancy moustache curled at the tips.

"*Señora*, when may I come to your house and inspect your pipes?"

And now as a water company employee he plans to come into my house and resolve my water problem? Never.

I ran down the steps and finally understood why my neighbors never came to IDAAN. Near the car I heard his loud, "Let me know, sweetheart."

Surely the killer recognized me. I recognized him, proud of his career and flirting with his victims. They owned the country and our lives.

To hell with running water! I'd carry buckets of water if necessary and wash toilets at night. It was June and rains had started. My neighbors were in the same boat—waterless. I stopped complaining. Outside it rained rivers; puddles everywhere while on our hill twenty homes ran dry.

37

ARRAIJAN

Cradle of my ancestors, I spent all my vacations and weekends throughout childhood and adolescence in Arraijan, riding runt horses and playing softball. Arraijan flavored my taste for Good Friday with the meal that breaks the fast during Lent. *Locoro*. The dish relished once a year is loved by children and adults. First step: soak dried codfish in water all night to withdraw the salt. Some cooks substitute canned sardines for dried cod. Prepare a sauce with sautéed onions, garlic, cilantro and tomato and add the soaked cod. Dribble the sauce on top of a puree made of boiled and mashed yucca, otoe, and other tubulars. The red sauce crowns the dish. Lemon squeezed over this delightful plate cinches the taste. *Locoro* appeared faithfully every Good Friday at house #3397 on Juan Demostenes Arosemena Street. My mother's home. Today my relatives in Arraijan have forgotten the superb recipe. I recall every detail.

On Good Fridays in Arraijan my cousin, Juan Bautista Bárcenas, portrayed the living Jesus. He carried Jesus's cross to Calvary in the procession starting at the church. Dark-skinned, thin and bearded, he was my favorite in the role. I baptized him when he was twenty-five years old. For years he lived a clean life, his only vice cigarettes and pinball machines. With maturity he changed. One afternoon someone saw him running out of the neighbor's house with his trousers in his hand and his bare ass naked.

Picturesque as Arraijan was, the townsfolk took politics seriously. The majority were followers of Arnulfo Arias, coffee grower in Chiriqui and three times President of Panama. When the military ousted him in a coupe, my townsfolk established themselves as staunch opposition.

Unarmed always, my kin paid the austere price of government neglect. No water system was ever installed by the government, schools suffered, no emergency medical center existed and sewage trickled down main street after heavy rains. For decades political loyalties made conditions grim without government aid.

During the 1989 elections, my Bárcenas relatives hung a candidate's photograph on a mango tree behind their house. The photograph of presidential candidate, Guillermo Endara, caught the eye of a member of the regime's party, PRD, who quickly notified Hellquarters. Assassins were removed from prison and sent to erase the Bárcenas boys. They barely escaped. Running barefoot miles through the jungle, feet bleeding, they reached the US Howard Air Force Base. The US military verified the teenagers had relatives living at Fort Bragg, North Carolina. The US gave them asylum and flew them to safety to North Carolina to join their relatives.

During Panama's crisis, the Dignity Battalion, (all of them undignified) left painful footprints in Arraijan. Precisely during this crude period, Daniella took little Lulu to live in Arraijan when IRHE cut off electricity in her apartment. My daughter made great efforts to stay in the city near her job, university, and family. She even went to Panama's Housing Ministry and applied for a duplex to rent in the reverted area, formerly the Canal Zone under US jurisdiction. Several days after submitting her application she returned to inquire its status. A civil servant outlined the procedure.

"Take the application to PDF Headquarters in Chorrillo, to the commander's secretary. There you will get authorization."

She charged out and tossed the application in the first garbage can. Everybody in town knew going to Hellquarters meant suicide. Any woman entering the PDF lair seeking favors was doomed. The military labeled women fair play and considered the "favor" an open door to violence.

PDF Hellquarters. Same place where Doberman dragged Sofia and Trinity two years earlier for waving a white flag. Same hellhole their father rescued them from. Now they invited my oldest daughter to voluntarily waltz into Hellquarters and be subjugated to their abuse. Audacity has no limits.

Preparing for her move to Arraijan, poor Daniella had me chewing her ear.

"Dear, it's dangerous. And so far away. Water is always scarce." An endless number of difficult situations I portrayed for her if she went to live in Arraijan.

Daniella ranted for a while and unloaded woes. Finally she calmed enough to blurt out an unforgiveable treason committed by her Abuelita, my mother.

"In Arraijan I won't need to pay for electricity. Abuelita would do anything for me. When I was fourteen, she smoked marihuana with me. That's really love."

How could my daughter believe giving marihuana to a minor is love? Didn't Daniella understand the crime committed by her grandmother? Perhaps she was blinded by money. My mother gave her money often, a limited resource for a pensioned widow. Poor Lulu.

Children always suffer the consequences of uprooting. Lulu needed to leave at dawn daily so her mother could attend the university while the little one went to preschool. They would return home at night. Poor little Lulu wore dark circles under her eyes. We never spent time together. My only grandchild.

Months after the exodus of my loved ones to Arraijan, my mother called asking for Daniella. She surprised me with a litany of complaints.

"I hate that man. Drunkard."

"What man?"

I thought she referred to her companion. The same man who abandoned her when Attorney General Carlos Vampire arrested her. Two Dingbat gunmen marched her down the street prodding her with rifles. Her companion habitually binged for days. Then my cousins, the Bárcenas boys, stepped in to keep her company. Especially Tito. He slept at her home to stop her from getting up at midnight to seek her companion. Often she was seen limping up the street in the dark headed for the bar. There she sorted through a pile of drunken bodies lying on the floor of the cantina, mice crawling over them.

She continued complaining, "Daniella is sleeping with that man again."

"Which man, Mom?"

"Osvaldo! Who else?" Her excessive ire made me happy.

Overjoyed, I tasted the delight of Daniella trying to reconcile with Osvaldo. I pictured a happy grandchild and played it dumb.

"But Mom! They're still married. Don't you understand? Married!"

"I don't care. The divorce is final soon. I know. I paid for it!"

I felt the urge to remind her she also paid for the judge who married them. Right there in Arraiján. Lucas Bárcenas. And I didn't learn about it until much later.

"Don't be selfish, Mom. For the little girl's sake, let them get back together."

"He's worthless."

She preferred having Daniella divorced and the two living a few yards from Abuelita's kitchen. Finally satisfied, she hung up.

Days later my mother showed up early at my front door playing the victim role. She never arrived before 8 a.m. And there she stood. Months had gone by since her last visit. Precisely when my two angels moved to Arraiján because IRHE cut off their electricity. What brought my mother to my door? Frisky about something, she forgot to fake the cute skip and bounce to conceal her limp. Her wrinkled hand held firmly to a woman, her human cane who appeared only when Mom's regular companion was drunk.

Mom's effervescence conflicted with her battle cry on the phone a few days earlier. Her delight presaged something sinister. Who could be the target of her deadly selfishness? Poor victim. I never dreamed the victim could be a family member. Her attacks were inconsistent. I thought I had nothing left to lose. Several loved ones were gone: husband, a daughter, and only grandchild. Gullible me refused to accept everything Mom did ultimately affected me.

Anxious to know what current cruelty she concocted, I moved closer. She delayed spilling the beans and asked for ice cream. For breakfast? Sofia piled a dish full. Her noisy "mmm . . ." over the ice cream confirmed a celebration. Trinity sat next to Abuelita, no longer afraid of her. Daniella and Sofia had taught her Abuelita's weak points— sweets. I put the ice cream back in the freezer and straightened the kitchen. My mother's companion sidled up to me. I knew her well as a passive person, but today her forehead frowned in acute preoccupation. Raising her index finger to her lips, she gestured for me to hush, pulling me outside under the clothesline.

"Don't repeat this to your mother. She'll punish me. Not pay me today."

She looked behind her making sure nobody else heard.

"We came here directly from Osvaldo's house. I've never seen anything so shameful. Your mother and daughter. Punched each other like trashy women do."

Shocked, I recalled my mother's recent words, "She's sleeping with Osvaldo." I asked where Osvaldo was during all this.

"Must'a left for the bank. I didn't see him in their apartment. I'm sorry Jenny."

My poor mother. Could her terrible antics be a result of the horror the Attorney General subjected her to? Who witnesses their friends' blood on the floor and stays sane? Now Mom acted crazy.

I did something similar bringing my daughters to live in Panama. Thought I'd offer them a better life than in the US. I did it mainly for my mother who complained constantly of not having any family nearby. I sought justice where none existed. Neither in our homes nor the streets of Panama. Two dictatorships. That's why Padre Durán repeated often, "Aside from our duty to evangelize, the most sublime task is politics."

38

BANKS

Water and electricity are luxuries my people take for granted. Except in the 1980's. Panamanians lacked water for showers, but we Stone women had a roof over our heads. Poor Chico living in high-rent Los Angeles, CA, owned nothing. We women intended to hang on to our house until the regime fell.

One disaster outdid the other. In March of 1988 the regime closed all banks, not one or two, the whole banking center—130 banks. For three weeks the poorest people of Panama anguished especially those who made a habit of purchasing food weekly on credit at small stores in their barrios. Hunger threatened a large portion of the population.

My check bounced at the US military Post Exchange. With Chase Bank closed my money was cut off. I couldn't buy food nor solve the problem. Credit cards were a novel item and not commonly used. Broke, Trinity and I depended entirely on Sofia to eat. She worked for Citibank in Panama City and they paid in cash. We continued eating during the entire bank-closure fiasco. But not Panama's poor people.

A miracle performed by one human kept thousands of Panama's poorest from starvation. The ability and tenacity of one person made it possible. Padre Laureano Crestar Durán.

He spent twenty years working with the poor as National Director of CARITAS, the Latin American equivalent to US Catholic Relief Service. His success with CARITAS established him as best qualified to lead the poor out of famine. Panama's tyrants for years took advantage of Durán's humility and sent all welfare seekers to him. The priest never rejected anyone. He quickly mobilized to alleviate disasters, be it floods, fires and/or health problems. He called on merchants requesting donations of mattresses, clothing and whatever necessary to rescue citizens, Catholics or otherwise. Padre Durán won the trust and admiration of everyone.

When banks closed, supermarket owners and other businesses went to Padre Durán and offered food, labor and whatever inventory he needed. Only Durán, in the entire country, did they trust. Within hours contributions and volunteers flooded Santísima Trinidad Church. The parking lot jammed with contributions. Refrigerator trucks hummed, full of perishable food. Utensils and dry goods of all kind packed every corner. Intense activity of cars and people coming and going obstructed traffic flow in front of the church. Doctors, students, nuns and members of other religions and sects showed up eager to volunteer. Trinity carried bags of onions, rice, bread and every kind of commodity to help pack trucks for delivery to the schools. In a matter of hours donated trucks loaded with fresh food dispatched to outlying communities, mainly San Miguelito. Padre Durán and assistant Esther distributed food to schoolyards as the best place to cook and feed 75,000 persons per day. One square meal daily, complete and nutritious, kept the great majority of hungry people from starvation. A formidable task in a country with a population of two million and torn by political crisis.

While this small miracle took place, the regime media silenced all news covering Padre Durán's accomplishments. The supernatural work directed by CARITAS and its many volunteers was never made public.

Trinity's volunteer work with CARITAS was tougher than schoolwork, but she didn't complain. While snooping in a schoolyard she heard cooks say they needed bigger pots. The two of us went to Fort Clayton, to US Army Salvage. They had ten-gallon cooking pots with lids. The attendant refused to issue them saying they'd be auctioned someday. We went to see General Bernard Loeffke, the US Army commander and a West Point classmate of Chico. I explained what was happening at our church and he gave us the pots. For CARITAS. Unannounced, the next day Loeffke and his wife showed up at CARITAS. They came to meet the priest who fed 75,000 people daily and their friendship crystalized.

"Bernardo, your presence fills my heart," the priest would say when the general arrived often dressed in civvies.

General Loeffke, born and raised in Colombia, spoke Spanish perfectly. He and Padre walked around the busy parking lot jammed with volunteers and vehicles. They chatted like old chums, both experienced at conquering adversity.

Trinity continued carrying bags at CARITAS and often came home parched with thirst. She'd turn on the faucet. Nothing. Without complaint, she'd help me carry water from the lowest street in Bethania. Her reward: she lost all the weight gained while living in the convent and later the pounds she added when visiting her Dad in Los Angeles.

Banks reopened in April and Padre Durán laid out guidelines for programs to reduce poverty. "Don't give them the fish, hand them a fishing rod."

Born under his guidance, schoolyard vegetable gardens sprouted in key places.

As a true disciple caring for and feeding the poor, Padre Durán lost twenty-five pounds. His forty-day-fast serving the Lord rendered him a prize: a headful of new ideas. He convinced MIDA, the Ministry of Agriculture, to participate in a program with CARITAS to teach rural poor to cultivate rice and fish in the same pond. MIDA's job: excavate a small pond with a bulldozer on rural farmland, fill the pond with water and throw in rice seed and small fish to grow a balanced nutrition.

While the feeding miracle took place, Trinity worried about our lack of money. Daily she interrogated Sofia when she came home from the bank. "Why did the banks close?" Sofia provided a simple answer to a problem way above our understanding of economics.

"It's a logical strategy to stop funds from leaving banks. President Reagan's embargo on the military government forced a money crisis, one that's grown out of proportion. People began emptying their bank accounts. So Noriega closed the banks to stop the middle class and the wealthy from withdrawing their funds. That's why we use these ratty bills, dirty and torn. The US cut off Panama's dollar supply. But you don't have to worry, you've got me to bring home the money."

But Trinity did worry; schools hadn't opened on time and it was her last year at Maria Inmaculada.

Another good resulted from the ordeal. The gift of joy. Trinity and I had lost hope for Panama. Throwing all our energy into helping feed and save the poor from starvation gave us something money can't buy. Inner peace. Padre Durán in his quest to save lives reaped a whole lot of happy souls along the way.

39

EXECUTIONS

Our jubilation derived from feeding the poor waned in October 1989. Chico had been deported two years earlier and could not return. I stopped winding his antique Grandmother clock. It no longer chimed, but the PDF didn't waste one minute eliminating good people. The former head of Cárcel Modelo Prison, Coronel Leonidas Macias, had orchestrated the first coupe against his former boss in March of 1988, after banks reopened. He failed and was tortured in the same prison in front of his troops to further humiliate him. His attempt to overthrow the tyrant mirrored most citizens' desire for his success. The population suffered in silence when his coupe attempt failed. Not only for our fallen hero, we mourned for ourselves knowing the tyrant still existed.

My grievance for Macias was personal. I carried guilt for insulting him the day he called after Doberman dragged my girls to jail for waving a white flag. I knew him, cooked for him and his wife. That horrendous day on the phone he meant well. But I was insane with pain. Never did I imagine he would be the first to rise up against tyranny. He knew well the consequences. Failure meant torture or death. He dared and suffered torture but planted the seed for the next coup attempt.

Every Panamanian dreamed of a second coup. We knew the tyrant would fall only at gunpoint. Yet Crusaders had no intention of ever taking up arms. Noriega no longer trusted his own soldiers and lashed out at everyone like a snake that's been whacked headless by a machete. No loyalty means loss of power.

On the morning of Oct. 3, 1989, mouth-to-mouth rumors flew. There was a leak. Something big was afoot.

Expectation and desire made one dizzy; imagining the earth's rotation slowed. Via the coconut grapevine we heard great news. A second coup. As the event unfolded people's spirits expanded and contracted. First exhilaration, then suspense. We heard junior officers had taken Noriega prisoner. When too much time lapsed between messages, desperation seized Panama's citizens. We sensed death and suspected the wrong men were dying. Panama's saddest day. Before the news confirmed, we grieved suspecting noble soldiers had been summarily executed.

Murdered that day at the hands of their fellow soldiers were Major Moisés Giróldi and Captains León Tejada González, Eric Murillo Echevers, Nicasio Lorenzo, Juan José Arza, Edgardo Sandoval, and Lieutenants: Jorge Bonilla Arboleda, Fransisco Concepción, Feliciano Muñoz, Ismael Ortega Caravallo, and Deóclides Julio.

Arraijan, my small opposition town, suffered its own hell inside and outside a torture house belonging to a civilian member of the PRD. My godson, Juan Bautista Bárcenas, the dark, bearded Christ actor for Lenten season, worked construction as a master craftsman. In repairing the torture house he told me of visible signs of atrocities perpetrated on his fellow man. He recognized criminal equipment in the house during his remodeling, instruments used for torture.

40

WOMAN AT THE DOOR

"Shot in the face! A priest! How horrible!" Terrified, my neighbor covered her face with her hands as if to protect herself. Horror increased with each new detail of the Catholic Priest Nicholas Van Kleef's murder in the rural town of David. The priest had been driving around town announcing on a megaphone his plan to celebrate Sunday Mass on presidential Election Day, May 7, 1989. A soldier was dispatched to investigate the noise on the streets and he ended up inside the priest's vehicle. While the priest drove them to headquarters, the PDF soldier shot Father Van Kleef in the face with his AK-47 and later reported the shooting as accidental.

The PDF added another notch of atrocities committed on unarmed civilians. The terrible image was agonized over so many times it left an indelible mark. The priest's assassination marked a revelation, a turning point. Civilians began to show apathy, insensitivity to the suffering of fellow humans. Sages among us diagnosed the attitude as a psychosis explaining; "terror maintains the populace in a state of depression and shock." They said our former joy, the festive light-heartedness common among Panamanians in the past, had served to soothe our everyday tribulations. The new murder exposed a shift in personality. Nobody acknowledged publicly his or her inner feelings. Yet, in silence, we gave thanks our own faces were spared and not blasted apart by a bullet. Privately we made the sign of the cross and beatified the priest in our hearts: one more Civil Crusader Saint.

Crusader pots and pans banged louder than ever. My daughters and I retreated from our terrace railing to bang skillets with a hammer far from the edge of the balcony.

Already a stray bullet penetrated a cement wall near our terrace. Down the hill from us in modest rent buildings, PDF soldiers charged into apartments to attack civilians for banging pots in their homes.

A chance to lighten-up came. Our parish priest, Padre Durán, who fed 75,000 starving citizens, had a birthday coming. We pressed Trinity's long, white and lacy linen *pollera*, a gown embroidered in blue. She intended to surprise Padre Durán by dancing inside the church as done in the days of King David. She and Agustin Caceres rehearsed with drummer and accordion *tamborito* music and polished their dance steps for the occasion.

The day to dance arrived. Mass ended and our priest, still wearing vestments, sat on a folding chair at the lower level of the altar. At the church entrance a loud drum roll rose to the rafters followed by a joyous howl of "OOOPA!" Trinity and Agustin danced toward the altar. Swaying to the music of drums and accordions, Trinity pirouetted in her fancy, and lacey voluminous skirt she held high and stretched out alongside her. A fine lace petticoat peeked from beneath the garment. Agustin's feet tapped fast as they danced towards the priest, Trinity swishing the gossamer-thin linen skirt. The closer they got, the tighter Padre Durán's expression became. Dancing inside the church? The congregation, exhilarated beyond measure, joined in singing loud and clapping, undoubtedly releasing pent-up tension brought on by regime abuse.

Trinity's skirt waved dancing past parishioners, causing awe with her *pollera*. Women reached out to caress the fine garment. At the altar the couple twirled and curtsied to Padre Durán. His feeble *gracias* and weak smile confirmed the priest's relief the dance and program had finally ended. The congregation sighed with gratitude for the delightful moments.

Several days after the church-party fever ended, a stranger came to our front door.

Sofia skipped the courtesy of inviting her in and came to me.

"There's a woman at the door. A stranger. Something weird about her. Should I ask her in?" Before I could respond, she said in a muffled voice, "I think not."

I scurried out to the woman dressed in black and invited her in. Near my age, she fanned herself, an oddity that caused Sofia's suspicion. Nobody in our generation carried fans. The woman mentioned her name as she fumbled to store the fan in her purse.

"I'm in a hurry, but I came for advice. Where do you buy fish? Fresh that is."

I confessed not knowing.

She turned to leave then paused as if forgetting something.

"Incidentally, is this house for sale?"

Startled, I asked why she asked.

"I personally think every woman wants to live with her hubby."

She dug out the fan and pointed it at me, studying my reaction. Satisfied she'd thrown ice water on me, she turned and left.

"I'm not leaving," I retorted loud as she climbed into a black car.

Chico called. I refused to tell him a woman came to torment me to sell our house. No doubt he'd love to know somebody besides him was pressuring me to leave. His exuberant tone of voice pertained to a job offer. Job?

"My title is Vice-President for the region. Daily Mass made it happen, and the prayers. Now I won't have time to make any more political talks. There's no money in that."

I quit listening, resented the news and wanted him to return soon. The job was a bad idea; it meant he'd stay in the US.

Conversing on the phone was risky; anything I said was monitored. Most Crusaders had the same problem. But I risked it anyway. Told him what a woman in our rosary group said about the house in Bella Vista, the one immigration took him to the night the regime deported him. She once lived in the same house. The regime used the house for torture. He asked me to repeat it.

"It's a fact. House number 18. The Laffargue sisters lived next door to the torture house. The sisters heard horrible screams coming from that specific house at night. In the penumbra they often saw men come out the back door carrying a wrapped bulk resembling the length and width of a human body. They'd dump it in the car and drive away. My prayer pal says one of the sisters suffered so much from hearing the agonizing screams she cried herself to death."

He tried to cut in but I stopped him. "Wait. I wonder who the priest was who heard those women's confessions? The Laffargue sisters were active volunteers in their parish, friends of Archbishop McGrath. I betcha' the Archbishop made lots of trouble for the regime. McGrath took horrible stories to the grave with him. That's probably why the regime gassed his house."

November brought torrential rains. My daughters and I were drawn to sit on the terrace watching rain sweep in from the ocean over our wounded city. Gray sheets, a massive curtain cleansed dust in its path. We romanticized the rain, nature's way of caressing oppressed people.

The strange woman returned and banged the cowbell at our iron door. Again, she refused to come in. No fan this time, she went straight to the point.

"Are you interested in selling your house?"

"No," I said without fear. She pretended not hearing and turned left observing our large, leafy ficus trees growing in splendor in front of our house.

"The roots on that type of tree break pipes. Did you know that? Whoever buys this house will need to cut them down." She walked away.

Sofia must have been listening behind me. She stomped up bristling.

"I heard her. So smug 'cause she prob'ly knows we're vulnerable without Dad. Pay no attention to her, Mom. If she comes again, we'll send the priest after her."

Her sarcastic laugh, intended to be funny, flopped. She hurried me to come eat. From the kitchen wafted heavenly smells: garlic baked in olive oil, oregano and tomato. Pizza! She pulled two large pizzas from the oven. Stacked high with cheese and broccoli we sat on the terrace to devour it. The cowbell banged at our iron gate.

"Yoo-hoo!" Sung from our front door. Crystal Voice!

We agreed not to tell her about the House Nabber. Crystal waltzed in, a million times more fun than house-nabbing woman. Crystal turned down a slice of pizza.

"I don't care for broccoli. That pizza's loaded with it. You're vegetarians!"

She made a painful smirk and sat down to review the country's dire conditions. Eyeing the pizza she concluded, "I'd serve wine with that, Jenny. But that's not why I came. I want to offer you a hiding place. Again. Don't look so frightened. It's my house in El Valle. It's yours, whenever you want. You're not the only one they're after anymore. The whole country is gonna explode any minute. So get ready. I know 'cause my sister is a nurse at Gorgas Hospital. She says the hospital is getting tons of medical stuff daily. Like the Big Bang is coming. Be warned, Jenny."

Frightened, I drove to my mother's in Arraijan; told her companion to get my father's old 12-gauge shotgun ready in case we must leave town in a hurry. "If so, you need to stay in our house and guard it". As I related the bad news, my mother didn't blink. I expected her usual outcry. She acted empty, as if not comprehending the horror of what I said. Apparently, the DA's arrest and psychological terror damaged her plenty.

Returning home, I saw a woman at our door; the same one in black garb. House Nabber. I parked and stepped out slowly, head down, singing softly, "Come, Come, Holy Spirit, come, come . . ." Then I smiled. How I managed, I'll never know. Her dour face cracked no smile. No mistake, the woman had evil intentions. I invited her in.

"No thank you. I'm in a hurry, but wanted to mention I have a friend who likes this street. She wants to live here. Have you decided to sell?"

We had recently identified the woman. Her husband has close ties to the regime. So I played dumb, pointed out a plant near our feet, agronema with a heart-shaped green leaf. She barely glanced at the variegated texture. Instead she left, as though miffed.

In Trinity's second year at the Panama Canal Junior College she applied to UCLA. Part of the required information was to list her mother's vocation. She classified me as farmer. The opening sentence in her essay stated: "I was arrested at sixteen for waving a white flag. Three months later the dictator deported my father for witnessing a political assassination."

A few weeks later I stood chopping carrots at the kitchen counter. Trinity came in bouncing happily about something. The description, happy, had not applied to her for a long time. She grabbed a carrot before unloading happy news.

"I'm accepted! Me! UCLA accepted me! Look! Here's a letter from them!"

Sadness engulfed me. I felt none of her enthusiasm. Excited and jumping, she nearly crashed into the refrigerator. "I'll be fine in LA. I'll be living with Dad."

Stunned speechless I kept chopping carrots. She asked if the carrots were for salad and came closer to check. Then she gasped, "What happened, Mom? There's blood all over the carrots." Quite possibly my heart was bleeding.

"Don't be sad, Mom. Wash your hands. I'll come home for Christmas, you'll see. I won't stay in Los Angeles with Dad."

The wounded hand had nearly healed by the time the strange woman, dubbed House Nabber, came over to practice her worn-out pitch. Again, refusing to come in, we talked standing at the iron gate.

"My friend, the one who wants to live on this hill, is eager to make an offer."

I gazed at the bandage on my hand thinking how amazing such a small cut bled so profusely revealing my hidden pain. This stranger haunting my door neither stabbed nor cut me yet inflicted deeper pain, intending to take away the only possession we had left, our home. Cut the very heart out of our family. The woman kept talking. Her mouth moved but I heard nothing. How wonderful. My mind closed down. She couldn't scare me anymore. My distraction did nothing to stop her tongue. She stiffened saying, "Oh, I left my car running." Turning away, she shouted, "You better wake up and sell."

Those words I definitely heard.

I confided in Padre Durán, told him about the woman, expecting him to repeat his usual: "Don't leave, nothing will happen to you here." Not this time. He reacted drastically. Could his change of mind be the result of the priest's murder?

"Yes, Jenny. Go! For a while. It's time for you and your daughters to take a vacation. Go to Chico. When you return to Panama, all our problems will be solved."

Equatorial heat demands relief and nothing soothes better than swimming. En route to the pool few cars moved on the street. Approaching the entrance to the US Army Post at Fort Clayton, the array of heavy fortifications installed there overnight alarmed and pleased me.

Midway through laps, the splash from a huge fish in the shape of a woman wearing a white cap swam past me. The small whale swam past several times. She stopped at the edge, removed her cap and coughed, gasping for breath. Her eyes still closed, she jabbered impatiently to herself in English. Why hadn't she noticed me?

"Whoa! I've had it! Never got so winded back in the States. Must be this awful humidity making me breathless."

She was so talkative it seemed an enticement to ask if she arrived recently. She continued talking, looking everywhere else except at me.

I persisted. "Where are you from? Are you staying long in Panama?"

She responded by talking to the water, "I came to Panama to bring computers. They're needed to test new equipment for air traffic control."

Computers! How modern we'd become. Still breathless and looking at the water she continued talking. So similar to men who talk to the mirror while shaving and then wonder why they cut themselves. The woman said something sounding foreign, lost on me. Above my head. Could she have mistaken me for someone else?

So strange someone would come to Panama during its worse crisis, especially dangerous for US personnel living downtown. They were catching hell from the PDF along with Crusaders.

Intrigued by the woman's talk about her team bringing computer equipment to run computers in Panama, I rushed home. Searching for a pamphlet that arrived at our US military mailbox, my excitement grew. Mail for Chico I had not yet forwarded to him. I located it, the information dealt with new technology for developing a cutting-edge airplane, none yet released. Was the ground being prepared for the arrival of a new phantom airplane in Panama? What if?

A clear warning. The time had come for us to leave. Chico would be thrilled. Days before Christmas.

TAXI

Union Fire and Auto Insurance exhumed our Volvo. Two years had gone by, ample time to strip our auto of every factory installed engine part. They switched Volvo parts for grass-cutter and washing machine parts to make the Volvo engine appear full. Pure junk. On top of stealing all original parts the regime fined me $426.00, accusing the car of seditious activity.

The insurance company forbid me to dump the car on the spot. Instead I paid a tow truck to remove it. How could it ever run loaded with interplanetary metal waste? The insurance paid for the Volvo repair using universal replacement parts. Perhaps the company decided the cost was too high for original parts manufactured in Sweden. Volvo never ran properly. I ended up selling it cheap to the garage that worked on it. The strange part is, considering our country is so small, I never saw it on the street again.

My husband's long absence prompted me to analyze his resemblance to our priest, Padre Durán. Both good men. Different careers and uniforms concealed idealist hearts. Chico risked everything to change Noriega and Padre Durán once said, "Upon taking my vows, my goal was to change the world. Make a better place for the poor." Both very difficult tasks. Did they succeed? Only God knows.

Medical doctors in Panama deserve a similar analysis for their adherence to the Hippocratic oath. Some are marvelous. Certain others are cut with a different scalpel. Dr. Hugo Spadafora was a hero. By himself he attempted doing what Dr. Mauro Zuñiga, leader of the first medical association, accomplished with his group.

The medical association, AMOACS, rejected all military activity in Panama, and for this Dr. Zuñiga was kidnapped and tortured. His captors used a razor to carve the symbols F-8 on the physician's back. Unstoppable, Zuñiga continued to resist regime action and push for democracy. Not all doctors have integrity. Certain regime doctors were rotten to the bone. They proved it by medically treating injured Crusaders in Cárcel Modelo Prison to later betray them. Still strapped to gurneys, when Crusaders revived, prison doctors had them wheeled back for more torture.

Prophetic signs of a US buildup in Panama sprouted everywhere. Civilian employees in US Army posts were agitated by the appearance of new equipment like camouflaged Hummers. These reinforced the notion something big was coming. I continued entering US bases thanks to the decal on the windshield of the car, issued to Chico for the purpose of entering posts. Heavy cement barriers forced cars to weave through a labyrinth to slow traffic. At Fort Amador causeway, running parallel to the Panama Canal, I saw frogmen swimming in plain view. Could they have been US Navy Seals checking for mines or explosives in canal water? Invasion fever grew significantly while the dictator soldiers seemed oblivious, lost in a sea of non-leadership. Neighbors said local soldiers acted drugged.

Osvaldo joined the list of those suspecting our country headed for something big. He encouraged Daniella to take Lulu out of the country.

I bought airline tickets. Ready and packed, Lulu and her mother brought their luggage upstairs, the child hugging her doll. I requested a large taxi for five women. My mental inventory of things left behind was short. My wedding ring lost in Padre Durán's chapel while planting foliage for Daniella's wedding ceremony. Also missing was the white, embroidered dress I purchased to wear for my burial.

Lulu knew exactly what she was missing.

"Is *Papi* coming with us?"

Five years old, Lulu learned early the value of loving the important things. Her question went unanswered. Forlorn, she wandered around climbing over suitcases.

In the dark Sofia walked in an out of our house, checking for the taxi's arrival. Trinity hissed orders. "Mom, did you pack Panama coffee for Dad?" Sofia warned, "Keep your voices down. Pleeezz . . ."

Trinity spoke louder. "I still have my passport from when I visited Dad."

Lulu stuck to her. "Trinity, do you like airplanes?" Trinity hugged her saying, "I like swimming better. Someday I'll teach you how to swim. Your Mama taught me."

The two sat commiserating, and Lulu enthralled with the attention until Sofia came in and scolded us again, "Keep your voices down; I hear a car, might be the taxi."

"Is *Papi* coming too?" Lulu asked and again nobody answered.

Back then taxi drivers were heroes. Nobody trusted men in uniform. Many times the job of rescuing Crusaders fell to taxi drivers. Some taxi drivers lost their lives rescuing opposition members. Soon as we boarded the taxi, the driver told of a checkpoint he'd passed through and feared another blockade en route to the airport. He said, "Panama's military stopped a US car. The soldier was out of uniform. PDF soldiers abused his wife in front of him. Terrible things are happening."

The taxi zigzagged to miss potholes in the road. The crevices resembled bomb craters. We made it; ahead glared the airport mustard-colored lights. Lines of citizens crowded the terminal entrance hoping to escape. Lulu asked again if her *Papi* was coming. Her mother succumbed. "We'll come back soon so you can hug him plenty."

In Los Angeles sleepy Lulu failed to recognize her grandfather. In broken Spanish, worsened by his years in the US without us, he fed her breakfast. They talked about Baby Jesus, mostly Lulu asking about Him. Christmas tree lights mirrored in her eyes, the smell of freshly cut pine tree tickled her nose. Unaware of how far we were from home, she said, "Baby Jesus is coming to Panama."

Few presents appeared under the tree. Lulu asked Trinity if Santa Claus had forgotten her because she couldn't speak English. "No, No," Trinity said and searched for a Christmas story on television. She found one in Spanish on the Mexican channel.

Trinity attempted to animate the child with reverse psychology as Sofia had done years ago with her.

"You're lucky, Lulu. Your Grandmother Jenny won't have time to make fruitcake this year. Cooked fruit. Yuk! Can you imagine that? Here, have some Spanish nougat I brought from Panama. Yummy. Melts in your mouth. "

Lulu and I constructed the Holy Family out of papier maché. For the first time in years, we played together despite living in the same country. We had to run away from Panama to enjoy each other, grandmother and child.

Dawn of December 20th the phone rang in Chico's dark apartment. Located in downtown Los Angeles, in the Metropolitan Building, the phone never quit ringing. Three television channels asked to interview Chico about Noriega's disappearance. His former associate had become a criminal at large.

Each television station sent a limousine to pick up Chico. His three daughters went along. I stayed home playing with Lulu. Her aunts complained of the odors in the stretch limousines, Hollywood star's favorite transport.

"They try to camouflage the bad odors with perfume spray which ends up stinking of dirty sneakers. Or wet cat," said the other sister.

Before Chico's interview, newscasters asked him a few questions. Trinity would later comment she was confused, her understanding of Dad's job distorted.

"Were you a member of the CIA, Colonel Stone? Your job in Panama was to protect Noriega at whatever cost. Wasn't it?"

His emphatic "No" awakened smiles on newscasters.

Did the newsmen mistrust their own government? Perhaps, since politicians have a habit of saying one thing and doing another. They interviewed Chico assuming he knew better than anyone the machinations of Panama's military.

Chico answered other questions directly on camera.

"Colonel, you knew Noriega well, do you think he had a plan to save himself? Will his troops support him? What will he do now?"

"Noriega will never allow himself to be captured. He'll commit suicide first."

My husband proved wrong again. History shows nobody knew the dictator. Chico worked with him five years and learned little. Panamanians still wonder about Noriega since his return to Panama following twenty-years in a Miami jail plus two years in a French prison as a high-profile criminal. Today, his followers request house arrest for him.

The famous Catholic mystic and priest, Thomas Merton, once said and it seemed he wrote directly to us in Panama, "Those who suffer risking their lives to achieve social justice must never attach themselves to the final result. To do so will break their heart."

Exactly what happened to our family and so many Panamanians—that long night we walked towards the light in our dreams.

The author was born in Gorgas Hospital in the former Panama Canal Zone and grew up in Arraijan among her cousins in the Bárcenas family. She holds a degree from Panama Canal College and continued studies in Accounting and Business Administration at Panama University for two years. She took creative writing at Harvard University Extension for two years. Her secondary focus has been reforestation in Panama as a contribution to nature. Married for fifty-two years to the co-protagonist of this historical book, Charles B. Stone, US Army Colonel (R), they live in Bethania, Panama City, Republic of Panama.

Made in the USA
Middletown, DE
18 November 2015